CW00420947

Elusive Settlement
England's Revolutionary Years
1637–1701

BARRY WILLIAMS

Nelson

Thomas Nelson and Sons Ltd
Nelson House Mayfield Road
Walton-on-Thames Surrey KT12 5PL

51 York Place
Edinburgh EH1 3JD

P.O. Box 18123
Nairobi Kenya

Yi Xiu Factory Building
Unit 05–06 5th Floor
65 Sims Avenue Singapore 1438

Thomas Nelson (Hong Kong) Ltd
Toppan Building 10/F
22A Westlands Road
Quarry Bay Hong Kong

Thomas Nelson (Nigeria) Ltd
8 Ilupeju Bypass
PMB 21303 Ikeja Lagos

First published by Thomas Nelson and Sons Ltd 1984

IBSN 0-17-445157-1

NCN 240-3255-0

Printed in Hong Kong

Contents

CONTENTS

Acknowledgements

The author and publishers are grateful for permission to draw on material
from the following book and to reproduce pictures from the collections listed
below.

C.D. Chandaman *English Public Revenue 1660–88*, Oxford University Press,
1975.
National Portrait Gallery pp. 21, 38, 39, 105, 167;
Mansell Collection pp. 21, 90, 104
Cover illustration. Cavaliers and Roundheads from 'A Parley between Prince
Rupert's Dog Puddle and Tobie's Dog Pepper', 1642 (Hulton Picture Library).

Series Preface

This is a new venture designed, first, to take account of some of the fresh ideas which have been canvassed over the past decade among teachers of history in schools, colleges and universities, and, secondly, to meet the needs of students preparing for advanced examinations, which in future will contain a greater emphasis on primary sources than hitherto. Each book will have a theme. Lord Acton's century-old advice, 'Study problems not periods' remains sound. Within a rough fifty or hundred year compass a particular argument will be explored, and sharp focus brought to bear on particular issues. In this way the series is intended to complement rather than supplement existing methods of work, and to provide teachers with evidence and lines of argument for seminar work or class discussion.

The series has two special features. History is about change and continuity, and the student will be required to set a premium on understanding, to think about what has happened and why, and to see connections. One of the GCE Boards offers succinct advice to its Advanced Level candidates: 'Analyse, argue, judge.' It is the series' intention to promote these qualities, and exorcise that bane of a student's life – dictated notes, one text and minimum discussion, a feeling that history is 'just one damn'd thing after another'. Textbooks have their reference uses, but for the student they suffer from one serious defect: a problem is solved at the outset. They are *too* complete, with insufficient consideration being given to the process of arriving at a conclusion; the student becomes the passive recipient of someone else's work. This series will offer a blend of narrative, analysis and, at a variety of points, studies to be undertaken. Some of these will be open-ended, some will require sifting of information or problem-solving; each author will make a few observations – not model answers, rather comments to the student on how a question might be approached.

The second feature is the extensive use made of source material woven into the main narrative. Students coming fresh to a period have often found original documentation difficult to obtain or handle – tucked away as it so often is in appendices or in separate, expensive volumes, with little guidance on a mass of detail. This series hopes that by constantly seeing edited portions of documents as integral parts of their work, students will treat primary evidence as a normal component of their study furniture, something though to be handled with care, showing proper concern for the pitfalls of bias, motivation and accuracy. Quotations have also been included from historians past and present, to give some flavour of rival authorities in interpretation of evidence, and to show how new research has modified traditional received opinion. The trust is that by including both primary and secondary sources students will be encouraged to seek out the full document or historical authority. A bibliographical note will feature in each book, with major text references identified, brief comments made by the author on reading matter, and some clearly directed further reading given, which a student should regard as obligatory.

B.W. January 1983

Series Editor:
Barry Williams. Head of the History Side and University Adviser, Sherborne School for Girls, Dorset. Sometime Schoolmaster Fellow, Pembroke College, Oxford.

Titles in the series:
Elusive Settlement by Barry Williams
Nationmaking in Nineteenth-century Europe by W.G. Shreeves, Gillingham Comprehensive School, Dorset

Forthcoming titles:
Parliaments, Puritans and Papists: England 1558–1630 by Brigid Davies
Left and Right in France 1815–1914 by David Pearse

Author's Preface

This book covers the period of England's revolutionary years from the late 1630s to the 1690s. It concerns people making decisions, arguing, even fighting in pursuance of an acceptable settlement of political, constitutional and religious issues arising from the collapse of a century-old framework of government in 1640. Radical, and at two stages even revolutionary, solutions were promulgated. The period was one of high principle, much prejudice and not a little deviousness.

The thesis for study is that the Tudor polity – essentially government by the monarch with the counsel of his or her chosen advisers on the Privy Council, and a significant but limited role accorded to Parliament – was under strain, but in no serious danger until 1637. Then three events, one of them an explosive miscalculation, were to lead to a collapse of conciliar government in 1640 in the face of a taxpayers' strike and a Scots invasion.

From the 1640 crisis emerged five issues, the settlement of which proved so elusive: first, the regularity of session and the amount of say the representatives of the people in Parliament should have; secondly, the control of appointments and the accountability of the King's ministers and the King's generals; thirdly, taxpayer–Treasury agreement on the probity of getting and spending in the nation's housekeeping; fourthly, who should control matters of conformity and diversity in religious worship, a question which evoked much partisan feeling; and finally, the chronic tension between the King's Privy Council aiming at a more centralised, efficient rule, and the county communities with their urban counterparts who in the name of English liberties paraded their resentment of executive interference.

During the half-century after 1640 the quest for a settlement of these five issues took a variety of paths: moderate reform disputed the route with radical policies, and occasionally with the extreme by-ways of civil war, religious fanaticism, and the execution of one king and the exile of another. Partial or *ad hoc* solutions were found to some questions, but never a total settlement – until the 1690s, when the peculiar circumstances of William III's reign, with its 'rage of parties' and a long war with Louis XIV, produced enough piecemeal answers for the phrase, 'The Revolution Settlement' to be deservedly applied, although one issue still awaited a pragmatic solution during the eighteenth century.

This is not a textbook, for there is no intention to provide comprehensive treatment of all aspects of the period. Rather it is the book's purpose to provide a line of argument, relevant, detailed narrative and analysis and selected documentary evidence – all punctuated with suggested study material and observations on how this may be tackled.

It is important to the development of a student's understanding that the 'Study' sections be tackled *before* the author's 'Observations' are considered. Rarely in the study of history is there a 'right' or a 'wrong' answer, and the observations are meant as comment on a problem, which will counterpoint the student's own considered thoughts and suggest possible further avenues of exploration. The studies vary in the tasks set: the full essay, the sifting of a mass of information, and the obligatory reading of particular specialist works offer different kinds of private study; whereas group work in seminars or full classes can benefit from considering the analysis of a document, the discussion of a historical issue, and the evaluation of a person's policy.

Significant quotations, from contemporary writings and from historians, are referenced by book number and page to the select bibliography at the end of the book. A note on sources and the Whig interpretation of history may be found on p. 219, and an important study section on the biographical approach to history on p. 214.

I should like to record my thanks: to Professor Gerald Aylmer, Master of St Peter's College, Oxford, for reading the first draft of the chapters on the 1640s; to Dr Gillian Lewis of St Anne's College, Oxford, for her suggestions and encouragement after she had read the typescript of the whole book; to Mr Cliff Davies, Dr Toby Barnard and Dr Menna Prestwich who offered valuable advice as I developed the theme of the book in the early stages; especially to the Master and Fellows of Pembroke College, Oxford, for electing me to a Fellowship in the Trinity Term 1980 – without such facilities for research (to say nothing of their fine hospitality) my task would have been all the more difficult; and, finally, to my wife, Ann, for her patient, ever-honest efforts to remove infelicities of style in the first draft of the manuscript.

The business of the historian is to make sense of the past. That is his primary task, but it is far from simple, for the complexities of historical forces are very intricate and their elucidation never easy.

J.H. Plumb,
The Death of the Past, 1969

Dedication

As always
UXORI DILECTISSIMAE
but also to
TINA HIPPISLEY, SARAH McMAHON
AND MY CLASS OF '81
(who had much of the argument of
this book tried out on them)

CHAPTER 1

The Early Seventeenth Century: A Background Sketch

Seventeenth-century England (encompassing Wales and Ireland in its governmental control, but not Scotland, which had different laws) was a land of about four-and-a-half million people. Its prosperity is difficult to assess, as evidence of economic and social living standards is hard to come by. Words like 'poor' or 'backward' are meaningless, because modern post-industrial revolution comparisons are implicitly made and give a distorted perspective. England was not a subsistence economy, for there is much evidence of production for the market – there were some 800 small market towns, with a third of them specialising in a particular product. Nor was it a static economy: new patterns of trade were taking English products, grain, cattle and dairy foods, iron and craft materials as well as the staple, wool, to places further afield than Antwerp and the Baltic, which had so dominated merchant enterprise in previous centuries. But the English economy was chronically unstable, plague and wet summers creating serious short-term crises. In the opening forty years of the century 16 per cent of harvests were very bad and another 25 per cent poor. The economy also failed to expand at a rate which would bring reasonable prosperity to its steadily expanding population: overseas markets were limited, agricultural yield low and the government regularly milked the economy by taxing merchant ventures with little regard for the national interest.

London was the capital and largest town: 50,000 inhabitants in 1500 had risen to 200,000 by 1650. It was more than twenty times bigger than any provincial town (only Bristol and Norwich had 10,000 or more), and it was the biggest urban area in the whole of western Europe. Massive migration from the provinces had been going on for years; apprenticeships were sought by the poor, trading outlets by merchants, and political advancement at Court by the wealthy.

The people of London and the provinces may be divided into a series of loose social groupings. (The term 'class', with its more rigid divisions based on industrial occupations, is best avoided.) Seventeenth-century social structure was based on status. For instance, among the many landowners there was much variation in wealth, income and standing. The greater gentry families of every county community exercised considerable power locally, especially through offices like Deputy-Lieutenant, Justice of the Peace, Sheriff and as elected Member of Parliament; they could own land of some thousands of acres. All gentry insisted on the title 'gentleman', which gave them the coveted right to bear coats of arms. Of a very different status were the parochial or minor gentry who might have only 200 acres. These lesser gentry blurred into the richer yeomen, many of whom claimed a greater status than neighbours might accord them. A yeoman's eighty or so acres contrasted with a husbandman's twenty or thirty. Some labourers had a little land, one or two acres only, but the vast mass of ordinary people, certainly three-quarters of the population, had none, apart from some rights to graze a cow on the village common land. Towns too had only a handful of rich merchant families with two-thirds of town folk around the poverty line. Evidence of incomes is thin: the best estimates put the aristocracy, a mere hundred or so nobles, at £3,500-plus per annum, around 500 knights at £1,500, and 'gentlemen' (16,000 of them) at £500; yeomen would rarely reach £100, and labourers earning a shilling a day would thus have an annual income of, say £15.

Real control was exercised by only a handful of the richer families in town and country, though those who could influence or claim a voice in national or local affairs, the political nation, might number 200,000 or so – a mere fraction of the total population. (15, chs. 1, 2 and 6)

Politics

For nearly a century Englishmen had been used to a framework of authority called conciliar government. Contemporaries referred with some reverence to its ideal features as 'the ancient constitution', though by the 1630s it was under some strain. The government was the monarch meeting with his personally-chosen ministers. These comprised the Privy Council of twenty to thirty members, which was both an advisory and judicial body, and had offshoots in the Council of the North (at York) and Council for the Marches (Ludlow), and in the prerogative courts of the Star Chamber and the Court of High Commission. Theoretically it was the central decision-making institution, but in practice real power often drifted out of the Council, either to an *ad hoc*, semi-official committee of a few ministers the monarch chose to consult, or to the Court where ministers vied with any influential courtier who might have the royal favour at a particular moment – perhaps even the Queen, a foreign ambassador as well as some favoured gentry. There were no political parties in the modern sense; 'faction' would be a better description, and political in-fighting and manoeuvring in Council or Court spilled over into both Houses of Parliament when they were in session.

The King meeting with his Parliament was the essence of 'the ancient constitution', and co-operation between monarch and representatives of the county and borough communities was a sign that the body politic was in a healthy condition. The monarch's powers were very wide. His 'prerogative' enabled him to choose his own ministers and frame the country's domestic and foreign policy; to summon, prorogue and dissolve Parliament, in which he chose the Speaker; to initiate legislation and veto any bills which had been drastically altered or were private members' bills of which he disapproved. The navy was the Royal Navy and, although there was no standing army, soldiers could be raised by a royal command called a commission of array sent to Lords-Lieutenants and their deputies in the counties, the senior officers in both services being royal appointments. The King was Head of the Church of England, whose forms of worship were the only ones allowed by law. He could regulate the economy by varying rates for customs duties, by the minting of money and also by issuing monopolies – though there had been much abuse of all three by past monarchs. Finally, he possessed the ultimate right of sovereignty, enabling him to act as he saw fit in an emergency for the good of the nation.

These extensive 'executive' powers of the government had been vainly challenged in Parliament and in the law courts on occasions in the recent past; but it was conventional to accept only three serious limits to a royal despotism. First, the Tudors had avoided the heavy cost of a standing army by relying on a small local militia force officered by the gentry for trouble at home, and for war a 'contract' army to go abroad which would be raised by extra-ordinary taxation, parliamentary grants called subsidies. Secondly, the ordinary income of the Crown was restricted to the traditional sources of crown lands rents, customs duties, profits of justice and some medieval feudal dues like wardship – known as 'living of the Kings's own'. These sources gave a variable income of around £750,000 rising to perhaps £1,000,000 when trade was good. It was only marginally adequate, even for a Crown which husbanded its resources with care; it certainly would not permit Court extravagance or adventurous, unpopular policies. Thirdly, the Crown greatly depended on the active co-operation out in the provinces of gentry and merchants, who as JPs (virtually unpaid) were the mainstay of local govern-ment, preserving law and order and enforcing Privy Council instructions. To most of these men the county was their 'country', their power-base: parochialism, with its limited mental horizons and concern for local vested interests was persistent and deep-rooted in seventeenth-century England. The co-operation of such men was vital to political stability because the Crown had no large centralised bureaucracy to depend upon for the execution of its policies. Interference by any Crown 'agency' – the Privy Council, Council of the North, Star Chamber, Church law-courts – in order to centralise authority would be much resented, and tendencies in this direction in the

1630s produced fear and alienation. Co-operation of Crown and JPs in a vaguely perceived national interest had worked, though with signs of strain until 1637; after this Crown over-confidence and misjudgement produced confrontation rather than co-operation. The 'body politic' suffered a seizure, then collapsed in 1640; efforts to revive the patient by a succession of 'doctors' of varying talent using a variety of remedies, some quack, some more purposeful, form the story of this book.

Parliament was not in session in 1637; it had not been summoned for eight years, though there was nothing abnormal or illegal about this. Bringing together the two houses of Lords and Commons was an occasional though important event with distinct functions. Parliamentary legislation might be needed: statute law, that is bills passing through both houses, then receiving the royal assent to become acts, was the most respected law in the country, superior to either royal proclamations or judicial decisions known as common law. Also, for taxation beyond the Crown ordinary income, Parliamentary 'extraordinary' supply was needed, mainly in the form of subsidies of around £80,000 each, though inefficient collection, petty thieving and dishonest declarations by the richer gentry meant that rarely more than 60 per cent arrived at the Treasury. Important to both King and the political nation was the third function, the settling of grievances. The King saw the House of Commons in session as establishing a useful point of contact when policies could be explained and current opinion of the provinces noted; members themselves came armed with petitions from their counties on some outstanding grievance to be presented to the Privy Council and hopefully remedied in statute law. If a really serious grievance concerned a King's minister, there was an old medieval procedure, revived in the 1620s, called impeachment. The House of Commons would draw up a list of charges (i.e. grievances) and the House of Lords, acting as a court, would try the accused minister. Of course the King, to save some favoured minister, could dissolve Parliament to prevent impeachment, but the grievances would still rankle until the next election.

There were around 130 lay nobles and bishops in the Lords, and 500 MPs in the Commons, the latter elected on variable borough or forty-shilling county franchises, a medieval figure which Tudor inflation had so altered in value that 300,000 or nearly a third of the adult male population could vote in elections. The dominant membership of the Commons was nevertheless that of the greater gentry; these men had often in the past found themselves in the ambivalent position of being, as MPs, critics of unpopular Crown policies while, as JPs, they were key agents of the central government in the maintenance of law and order. Also, when sitting in the Commons they rarely revealed themselves as a united body. About 130 were office-holders under the Crown, though their loyalty to the king was not totally assured; another fifty or so could be outspoken critics – 'some few vipers', Charles I called them.

The majority, best labelled independent country gentlemen, were there to co-operate with the King on sensible policies, but could on occasions be swayed by impassioned speeches of criticism to support the fiery spirits of the House. Attendance was usually around 200 (17, ch.1).

Religion

The spiritual arm of the state was as much under strain as the secular one. The Anglican Church was the product of the Elizabethan settlement of 1559. Its hierarchical authority was traditional, with bishops and parish clergy who accepted the King rather than the Pope as Head; its doctrine, based on Biblical reference in St Paul (Ephesians ii,8), was Protestant in that salvation was to be sought through faith rather than good works – though some bishops called Arminians had recently favoured a reversal of this priority; its ritual was built around a series of set services laid down in the Book of Common Prayer, conducted in a decorated church by clergy dressed in ceremonial vestments such as the surplice. This style of worship, organised throughout England and Wales in about 9000 parishes each with its own church, was meant to be exclusive of all others. It was imposed by statute law, the Act of Uniformity of 1559, which laid down financial penalties for refusing to conform. All Anglicans were convinced that theirs was the true Church, *Roman* Catholicism was such a distortion of the original teachings of Christ that the Pope was actually Antichrist: the Prayer Book still retained the word 'Catholic'. A fraction of people, some 60,000, including some influential county landed gentlemen, objected strongly to compulsory attendance; these 'recusants' still preferred the old Roman form of worship with its Mass, belief in transubstantiation, confession and priestly 'mediation' between man and God. The richer ones paid their recusancy fine of around £200 a year, reluctantly accepting it as an extra tax burden! There were also some separatists who refused to conform, and these 'sects', as they were called, met in 'gathered congregations' away from the parish church; but they were regarded as far too extreme by most people and were much harassed. Until 1640 their number was very few.

   Inside the Church of England there were also critics of the original Elizabethan Church; for three generations they had campaigned for 'purification' – the removal of 'the dregs of Rome' from its style of worship. These puritans were so variable in what they wanted that only a very general contemporary phrase, 'the hotter sort of protestants', will suffice as a definition. Some moderates merely wanted more sermons and less formal services, with an emphasis on Bible teaching and the black 'Genevan' gown rather than vestments; others had in Elizabeth's time sought to seize control of the Church from within and to impose their own Calvinist authority, which would mean substituting lay (often gentry) elders elected by local congregations for the more distant control of a bishop, and getting rid of the Prayer Book in favour of a Book of Discipline. These Presbyterian Puritans had failed in their ambitions, though they were to revive their efforts later on; meanwhile all moderate Puritans had enjoyed a relatively light control from the centre (i.e, Canterbury and York) in the two generations since the 1590s. They had grown used to a wider range in styles of worship than was technically permitted, and they became more militant again in the 1630s, resenting the campaign by the new Archbishop of Canterbury, William Laud, to restore uniformity, with its exaggerated clerical authority and persecution of puritan deviation. Many Puritans saw in the Laudian High Church a threatened return to Rome; they had always been worried about popish plots being hatched abroad or in 'the dark corners' of the remote countryside, but a new spectre terrified them – papists in high places in Church and State (20, pp. 57–122)

Politics and religion cannot be separated in seventeenth-century England. By the late 1630s the alienation of the gentry of the provincial communities from Charles I's Court and his government's ambitions of centralised authority had reached a serious level. We shall see that vigorously expressed resentments over issues like money, ships and soldiers, over 'evil councillors' like William Laud and Thomas Wentworth (Charles' powerful Lord Lieutenant in Ireland), and over the problem of limits to the King's power received a massive injection of high emotion and provocation from Laud's religious policies. As the historian, Barry Coward, concludes, Laudianism was 'the greatest potential threat to constitutional harmony in the early seventeenth century' (1, p. 98).

Two Trials and an Order of Religious Service

On 14 June 1637 three men, a lawyer, William Prynne, a doctor, John Bastwick and a preacher, Henry Burton, stood in the dock of the Star Chamber Court at Westminster condemned of a malicious castigation of the Church of England hierarchy in general and of bishops in particular. Bastwick had proclaimed, 'From plague, pestilence and famine – from bishops, priests and deacons – Good Lord deliver us!' On 6 October in the same year a rich landowner from Buckinghamshire, John Hampden, also stood on trial, this time in the Court of the Exchequer, for refusing to pay the trifling sum of twenty shillings, being the Ship Money assessment on his estate at Stoke Mandeville. To Hampden this was a matter of principle; previously an occasional levy, Ship Money seemed likely to become a permanent tax. A young lawyer in his twenties named Edward Hyde scribbled in his notes that this money promised 'an everlasting supply of all occasions' for the Crown; such a prospect horrified the gentry of England who viewed any increase in royal power with alarm. Between these two trials and five hundred miles to the north, on Sunday 23 July, the Dean of St Giles' Cathedral, Edinburgh, Dr Hannah, was reading from a handsomely bound, brand new service book based on the English Book of Common Prayer, when one of the congregation, Jenny Geddes, hurled a stool at his head. Uproar ensued, other women screaming, 'The Mass is come amongst us.'

Seen in historical perspective, 1637 was a significant year in the reign of Charles I. It was as if a zoom lens had focused his subjects' attention sharply on some vital issues of moment concerning authority in Church and state. Two men bore the responsibility for starting the chain of events which led to the court cases and the Scottish shambles: the King of England and his Archbishop of Canterbury, William Laud.

Charles, now thirty-seven, had been king for twelve years. As a young boy he had been noted by visitors to his father's Court as 'not of a strong constitution'. He overcame years of ill-health to take an active role as monarch. He enjoyed some sport, and showed ability in dancing and music; he read a great deal, especially works of religion and history, and had some mathematical knowledge; he understood Latin and Greek, and was fluent in three languages, French, Italian and Spanish. These attainments were marred by other features of his personality which were well-known at Court but only dimly perceived as yet in the distant counties of England and Wales and in Scotland which he rarely visited. It worried even his close advisers that he carried his enjoyment of Court masques into real life: he seemed always to be acting a part. His aloofness may be partly explained by a persistent stammer, but his many hesitations and indecisions at Council meetings were notorious and irritating. When he did make up his mind he declared he would not yield, and he meant it. His mother had noted his obstinacy as a child; it was a trait he carried with him to his death. His response to the news of the Edinburgh riot was, 'I mean to be obeyed' (16, p. 288). Whether he had the authority and power to secure obedience never entered his mind. The historian, Veronica Wedgwood, had written of Charles:

> He was of the intractable stuff of which martyrs are made – not the swift, ecstatic martyrs who run upon death in a high, impulsive fervour, but the sad, thoughtful martyrs who follow over long, patient years some logical sequence of thought and action which always may, and sometimes must, bring them to disaster. (62, pp. 91–2)

To his few friends William Laud was meticulous and a believer in order; to his numerous enemies, he was fussy and meddlesome, an upsetter of the forms of worship which had become ingrained over two generations. Laud had one ambition – and such was his driving energy it seemed exclusive of all others – to fashion a Church of England in such a way that a uniform doctrine and ritual was offered to the parish congregations for the salvation of their souls. Such uniformity would be buttressed by a powerful, wealthy, able and dedicated authority, the clergy, who in turn would be sustained by the state and its laws. Apart from uniformity, his own personal crusade was for 'beauty of holiness' as he called it. He favoured elaborate ritual and ceremonial, which would impress and develop respect in all believers.

Laud knew his task was of Herculean proportions. Investigations in the mid-1630s revealed much decay in parish church fabric; a lack of respect, with altars used as hatstands, and talking and arguing during services; and a neglect of proper vestments by some clergy. He had little sympathy with Puritans whose preferences led to a recourse to the Bible, not to the priest, for advice on the 'good life', and a fancy for *extempore* prayer rather than the state-imposed order of service in the Book of Common Prayer. This issue was perhaps Laud's, and Charles', gravest error. Neither was a Roman Catholic, but their open encouragement of candles, priestly bowings, music, clerical vestments and altars railed off at the east end of the church made them seem so. To a Puritan, both monarch and archbishop were potential revolutionaries, guilty of popish innovation which would be a prelude to a return to Rome.

A Test Case

The trial of the three Puritans, Prynne, Burton and Bastwick, attracted much attention. They were not the first to suffer the wrath of the Church, and Prynne, a fanatical, often exasperating man, was already in prison for an implied libel on Charles' Catholic Queen, Henrietta Maria, and her love of Court plays and dancing: actresses, said Prynne, were 'notorious whores' and those who enjoyed plays were 'devils incarnate'. Even from the Tower of London he managed to pen violent attacks on the Church and its bishops, so with Burton and Bastwick he faced new charges in 1637. Bastwick's *Litany* spoke of:

- the Egyptian darkness of Popery and error ... the servile bondage of the Beast (the Pope).
- bishops were 'those little toes of Antichrist'.
- the clergy were 'a generation of vipers, proud, ungrateful, idle, wicked and illiterate asses'.
- the Church Court officials were 'filthy locusts that came out of a bottomless pit' (40, p. 93).

Such vitriolic writing might have been passed over as eccentric, bordering on the deranged fringe of Protestantism, but Laud was aware that in London especially Puritan preachers were gathering large congregations for their lurid denunciation of bishops. So the three men in the Star Chamber in 1637 were a test case. They were found guilty, fined, whipped, mutilated by having their ears cut off, and imprisoned for life in areas remote from London. Laud himself delivered the final condemnation speech in the Star Chamber on 14 June:

> I have done nothing as a prelate but with the sincere intention for the good of the government and honour of the Church and the maintenance of the orthodox truth.
>
> For my care of this Church, the reducing of it into order, are the causes of this malicious storm. 'Tis apparent that the intention of these men was to raise a sedition, being as great incendiaries in the State as they have ever been in Church. Our main crime is that we are bishops. I say further that from the Apostles' times the Church of Christ was governed by bishops, and lay elders never heard of till Calvin's new-fangled device at Geneva. And here in England bishops are confirmed by Act of Parliament. No man can libel against our calling be it in the pulpit or in print but he libels against the King and the State by whose laws we were established (6, pp. 164–6)

Uniformity and order meant central direction. Here Laud and Charles were treading on the delicate toes of the gentry of the county communities. This great show trial of a lawyer, a preacher and a doctor, was bound to offend lay gentlemen. Throughout the drawing rooms of the great houses of rural England a question was muttered: when last did a cleric lop off a gentleman's ears? Moreover, provincial loyalties were strong and too much interference and control in any guise from London was anathema. John Hampden felt this too.

The Ship Money Case

Rex *versus* Hampden: the Ship Money Case ranks as one of the most famous and significant trials in English legal and constitutional history. Hampden's twenty shillings was merely a peg on which to display key questions of efficiency and the division of power and responsibility in the government of England.

Ship Money was not new; occasional contributions to provide auxiliary ships to support the King's navy had been required from coastal counties several times before in times of war. When demanded in 1634 from some maritime towns it provoked little comment, but when a fresh Ship Money writ was issued a year later to the twenty inland counties as well as the thirty coastal shires of England and Wales concern was expressed about its legality. Parliament was not in session, and there seemed little likelihood of its being called in the near future; Crown power seemed on the increase. Over the past two generations nervousness could have been detected among gentry taxpayers about the possible spread to England of continental-style absolutism – that is, concentrations of power in the hands of kings and princes. Charles and his advisers on the Privy Council, however, saw nothing sinister about Ship Money: they were showing a proper concern for the defence of the nation. The refusal of John Hampden to pay under the writ of August 1635 became a test in which both Crown and gentry sought to establish in law just where real power lay.

By the time the case came to court in October 1637 several points were clear. Ship Money was proving a very efficient tax: a quota was fixed by the Privy Council for county sheriffs to collect. It was in its third year as an all-England levy. About 90 per cent of the assessment was being paid to the Treasurer of the Navy – an extraordinary success by seventeenth-century standards, when a mere 60 per cent could be expected from parliamentary subsidies. (For instance, in 1635–6 Ship Money was assessed at £199,000, and £194,000 of it was collected.) The improved navy was also beginning to deal with the pirates who preyed on English shipping, the reason for the 1634 writ in the first place. To Hampden and his gentry friends Ship Money had become a centralised, Privy Council-authorised collection, and a substantial, permanent addition of money for Crown funds over which the representatives of the landed elite in Parliament had no control.

The essence of Hampden's case was that Parliament should be called to assess Ship Money; the essence of the Crown case was that pirates constituted such a danger that the King was using his legitimate emergency powers in the national interest. The problem then before the judges in Rex *versus* Hampden was to determine the limit of the King's discretionary power to act *pro bono publico*, for the public good. The implications of a legal judgement on this 'limit', concerning *who* exercised *how much* power in the country, would be momentous. For generations Tudor and Stuart monarchs had avoided a too precise definition of the extent of their prerogative powers: a certain vagueness was convenient, in that subjects never quite knew what their sovereigns could do. Parliament, we have seen, possessed important functions, which rightly could be seen as practical restrictions on a despotically-inclined monarch, but its members' biggest problem was to ensure that the King called them with some regularity and then listened to their advice. With no Parliament for eight years the Hampden case would see many of these issues of power being tested. (Sources of following extracts: 6, pp. 109–16; 63, pp. 546–74).

The trial underway, there was some sparring between lawyers on legal technicalities and loopholes in the writ: for instance, that there was no emergency as

> it appears not by anything in the writ that any war at all was proclaimed,

and some judges were embarrassed at trying to explain how Hampden could 'prepare' a ship (the word in the writ), when his county, Buckinghamshire, had no seaboard! But the crucial issues soon emerged from the legal froth. Hampden's defence counsel was Oliver St. John, and he began by granting

> That in this business of defence the supreme power is inherent in His Majesty, who is the sole judge of dangers from foreigners.

Thus there was no challenge to that ultimate right of sovereignty, claimed and acted upon by all governments at all times, to act in a national emergency. Rather St John drove hard at three main arguments. First, that

> His Majesty having declared the danger, they (ie. MPs), best knowing the estates of all men within the realm, are fittest, by comparing the danger and men's estates together, to proportion the aid accordingly.

The implications of this were obvious – Parliament should have been called and Parliament should have decided on amounts and collection procedures, not the centralised Privy Council and its sheriffs. St John then accepted that in times of real emergency, 'the immediate danger' he called it, the King had to act quickly and that summoning a Parliament would take too long. But in this case, he said, the danger (i.e. pirates) did not seem *that* immediate – it was only 'apprehended' – and the writ clearly allowed 'seven months' for the collection of money and the building of a ship. So, St John pointed out, a Parliamentary consent might in that time have been endeavoured for the effecting of the supply.

His third argument concerned property. Others had already taken the view that the powers of the sheriff to collect money, or, if necessary, to seize a person's goods, was contrary to Magna Carta. St John took up this line of attack by raising the fundamental question of a 'limit' to the King's power in this matter:

> If no limit, then no man possesses anything, but at the goodness and mercy of the King.

He went on to say that he thought Statute Law (i.e. an Act of Parliament) protected a subject's property against a tyrant, but he wanted a clearer legal view on this. Could His Majesty, for instance,

> in times of peace, without consent of Parliament, alter the property (i.e. ownership) of a subject's goods for the defence of the realm?

All three arguments presented a powerful case for the existence of some kind of limit or check to a king's power – or so Hampden and St John thought.

Counsel for the Crown dismissed all this reasoning as specious, and rested its case on the simple proposition that the King possessed the power to provide for national defence by virtue of his prerogative. In the end the two cases had to be decided upon by twelve senior judges; they made clear their opinions before passing judgement early in 1638. Three judges said the original writ was defective because of technical errors like 'not any war at all'. So they said there was no case against Hampden. They were, of course, dodging the central and very controversial issue of power and its limits. On this, two other judges declared for Hampden, but the remaining seven gave the Crown a legal victory.

For most judges the critical point was '*pro bono publico*'. They expressed serious reservations about St John's insistence on the need to call Parliament: would it be wise, speedy and generous in a crisis? Recent history had shown otherwise – Parliamentary grants for a war with Spain in the 1620s, of which MPs approved, had been very niggardly. The judges too considered St John's distinction between 'immediate' and 'apprehended' danger faulty: where, they said, would the line be drawn for decision-making; what if precautionary measures for defence were needed? One judge, Jones, using a favourite classical example of Carthage with its leader Hannibal attacking the Roman Empire, said, 'Will you have the danger so apparent as Hannibal *ad portas*? Will you suffer the enemy to come in before you prepare to resist?' Most judges were impressed by this argument. Visions of the King in a legal straitjacket, unable to do anything until armadas of Spaniards or Frenchmen actually beached themselves on the south coast of England, scuppered St

John's case. Several judges had already stressed that the Ship Money Case did not give the King any general right of extra-Parliamentary taxation, so there was some relief in gentry quarters that St John had won his point about the security of a subject's property. But then two of the more extreme judges, Sir Robert Berkeley and Sir John Finch, raised sinister visions of a king with absolute power; using some ill-chosen language they did Charles I more harm than good. On the important issue of 'limits' to a king's power, Berkeley, in what became an infamous phrase, said,

> The law knows no such king-yoking policy. The law is of itself an old and trusty servant of the king; it is his instrument.

Finch said much the same thing:

> No Act of Parliament can bar a king of his regality. Acts to take away his royal power in defence of the kingdom are void.

To the tax-paying gentry and merchants of England the point had been starkly made: the judges had failed to find any definable limits to the King's power; people must rely on the King's good faith. But could he always be trusted? What if he chose to pursue expensive policies, unacceptable to his richer subjects?

The Scottish Policy

The collection of Ship Money continued as before. One historian, S.R. Gardiner, writing at the end of the nineteenth century, saw the Trial as a crucial event leading directly to the Civil War, five years later: 'Ship Money', he said, 'roused furious opposition in the provinces.' But recent research on county histories has proved this to be too simplistic a statement of cause and effect. The evidence shows that people continued to pay well after the trial ended, and the percentage collection was still around the excellent level of ninety throughout 1638 and into 1639. Taxpayers accepted that Ship Money was for a good cause. There was, of course, much grumbling about the fairness of collection, especially as the levy now seemed permanent.

However, thoughtful observers of the political scene in 1638 (and there were many in the manor houses of the counties) could make an ominous and terrifying link. If Charles, without recourse to Parliament, could demand Ship Money, he could demand Army Money too. Disputes across the border in Scotland pointed to such a possibility. It was not long arriving. By 1639 Army Money (or Coat-and-Conduct Money as it was called – a tax on counties to pay for the uniform, training and passage of troops to a battlefield) was being demanded. Coming on top of Ship Money it produced a tax-payers' strike in 1639–40.

The trouble in Scotland had begun with the stool-throwing in Edinburgh in 1637, and events had moved on apace. Charles knew little of his subjects north of the border, and a decade of offence had been given to landowners and religious leaders in Scotland. They were proud and resentful, and would not stomach attempts to centralise and make uniform with England practices in government and worship. In 1580 Charles' father (as James VI of Scotland) had reluctantly accepted a Confession of Faith establishing a Calvinist–Presbyterian doctrine and organisation in Scotland; there were still bishops there but they had little power or wealth. The Confession especially rejected control by bishops and any form of service that resembled the Catholic Mass; in their place the Scots' Presbyterians wanted elder-control and a preaching ministry which would emphasise sermons based on Biblical texts. These characteristics had more in common with the English Puritans than Laud's bishop-orientated authority and Prayer Book services. So in 1638 a National Covenant was drawn up: it restated the 1580 Confession of Faith and ended:

> We promise and swear by the Great Name of the Lord our God to continue in the profession and obedience of the aforesaid religion; we shall resist all these contrary errors and corruptions.

Charles' senior bishop in Scotland, Archbishop Spottiswoode of St Andrews, fled to England, remarking, 'All we have done these thirty years past is thrown down at once.'

Charles did not agree, and prepared to use force after futile efforts to persuade the Scots to give in had been made. Given their cause and determination the Scots speedily raised a well-equipped Covenanting Army. Charles had less success: his was a poorly organised, ill-paid force, stretching over long lines of communication, that appeared on the border at Berwick in June 1639, already demoralised at the rumours of efficient Scots' preparations. Charles accepted the obvious and arranged a truce. He was only playing for time, but the Scots calculated that in the end Charles would have to let them be.

These calculations were based on slowly emerging information of English resistance to Charles' policy, with negligible Ship Money collection and heated opposition to Coat-and-Conduct Money. There had been a number of critics of Crown policies expressing their view in Parliament since Elizabeth's time, but they had rarely exceeded fifty and in no way could they be called a party or an organised opposition. Foreign policy, religious issues, monopolies, Court favourites, had all at times been matters of parliamentary grievance, but 1637 might be seen as a turning point. Until then Stuart monarchs had estimated that the critics were a tiny but noisy minority, referring to them as 'fiery and popular spirits'; normally Crown and gentry co-operated in the general running of the country. By the late 1630s a rapid change of political mood can, with hindsight, be detected. Historian John Morrill has called John Hampden the voice of 'an articulate opposition', and beyond this there existed a deeply-felt emotion that there was something wrong in the treatment of Prynne, Burton and Bastwick – these men were gentlemen!

The key event, however, was the Prayer Book episode. The first forty years of the seventeenth century had proved England's inability to fight a war. MPs were simply not interested in facing up to the true costs, and locally the Crown had failed miserably to raise troops or collect money even for an anti-Spanish policy which was generally approved. So, when the Scottish policy was brought to a crisis point in the years immediately following 1637, Sheriff and JP co-operation with the Privy Council withered away. Few among the gentry and merchants of provincial England could see any sense in imposing by force an order of religious service the Scots manifestly did not want. It reeked of centralised control from London, and looked like a private whim of Charles and Laud: and the taxpayers of England had no intention of paying for either.

Charles, though, would not yield. In desperation in 1639 he summoned Thomas, Viscount Wentworth, from Ireland where as Lord Lieutenant he had imposed a ruthless but successful Crown control. Laud and Wentworth, who corresponded regularly, were under no illusion about how many people felt about Crown policies: 'the minds of men are mightily alienated' (42, p. 116) was a remark from one of these letters of late 1638, and it proved a remarkably accurate forecast of impending doom. Professor John Kenyon speaks of Wentworth arriving in London 'like some great barbarian consul' (64, p. 93). He was the strong man come to save the English equivalent of the Roman Empire from the Goths and Huns; he had already suggested that John Hampden be 'whipped through the streets of London'. He was 'Black Tom Tyrant', and details of Wentworth's harsh methods in Ireland created the fear that these were the blueprint for establishing absolute monarchy in England. The year 1640 was to see a crisis of authority, the like of which Englishmen had not witnessed for many, many generations.

─────────────── *Study 1* ───────────────

The whole of this chapter raises some fundamental points about the nature of government. There is no 'right' or 'wrong' about your reaction to the events of 1637–40, but at the outset of your study of the great constitutional crisis of the seventeenth century, you ought to ask yourself: to whom would you have given the verdict in Rex *versus* Hampden, and for what reasons?

Observations:

Forget the technicalities and consider whom you would have had take care of your safety. Government at that time was about maintaining law and order and the defence of the realm. In face of danger do you think you would put your trust in Charles and his advisers, or do you think MPs would be more sensitive to your needs? The origin of all 'government' is rooted in a community's need for security and peace of mind, but since the days of the ancient philosophers men and women have argued about who shall be the guardians of that peace of mind, how much power over your life these guardians should have, and to whom should they be accountable for their actions?

Two perceptive remarks on this issue have been

Quis custodiet ipsos
Custodes.
> *(Who is to guard the guardians?)*

(Juvenal, *c.* 100 AD.)

Power tends to corrupt, and absolute power corrupts absolutely.

(Lord Acton, late 19th century)

But this book is not about abstract power: it concerns people, and George Bernard Shaw, writing around 1900, tempered Actons's dictum with:

> Power does not corrupt men; fools, however, if they get into a position of power, corrupt power.

In considering your answer to this question ignore modern attitudes and preferences in government. Hampden was no democrat; one-man, one-vote did not exist. And Parliaments from Tudor times had rarely shown themselves to be the admirable repositories of political virtue they claimed to be. Writing of James II (Charles I's son), the historian John Miller concluded he found Parliament 'irritatingly dilatory, inquisitive and bloody-minded.' (36, p. 63) As we shall see, even that great Parliamentarian, Oliver Cromwell, would not entirely have disagreed with this verdict.

A final point: all this, of course, assumes you were concerned with England's security. Those in London and in the southern ports could be assumed to have that concern; but if you were of little-travelled, provincial gentry stock in, say, Leicestershire or Wiltshire, your interest in security might well be local not national. How would this affect your appreciation of the Ship Money Trial issues?

CHAPTER 3

1640 – Crisis Year and a Foreign Intervention

Illusions

The early part of 1640 was one of decision-making and preparation for war. Against a backcloth of climatic misery, with gales, heavy snow and floods, Charles busied himself with matters politic and military. On 12 January Wentworth was honoured, receiving the Earldom of Strafford. For the King it was a most proper appointment, showing confidence in the undoubted abilities of the man. But it is arguable that the timing was a miscalculation. 'Black Tom Tyrant' would now be seen as the most significant of Charles' 'evil counsellors'.

A small council of war had been created in the closing months of 1639, meeting three times a week throughout the stormy winter. Though the King was often present, Strafford was its driving force, and the planning looked impressive. A new commander, the Earl of Northumberland, able if uninspiring, was appointed to command a proposed army of 23,000 men. The provision of equipment was examined and arrangements to manufacture 1000 swords a month were made. Regular, generous pay was offered to experienced middle-ranking officers: Strafford was determined that the bane of previous military expeditions, a severe lack of efficient colonels and captains, should not be repeated.

In February, Charles received a delegation of Scots Covenanters who demanded that he accept decisions of the Scottish Parliament. There was little of an atmosphere of negotiation in the meeting, and it is difficult to judge who was being the more obstinate. Records from the State Papers of 1640 reveal that the Scots were quite openly comparing Charles to a truant schoolboy who would promise anything, until his schoolmaster, Archbishop Laud, caught up with him and made him recant. Charles, for his part, had no intention of making a peaceful agreement. There is sound documentary evidence to support this assertion: in an instruction sent the previous year to his negotiators with the Scots, he wrote, 'flatter them with what hopes you please... until I be ready to suppress them.'

Charles lived in an increasingly unreal world. He inspired little trust and lacked the public sympathy which would have given his expectations a chance of realisation. Local religious grievances, for instance, were brought to the notice of the Privy Council. Catholic priests were openly pursuing their Counter-Reformation work: in an outlying London parish, St Giles, the vicar reported with alarm that twenty-one conversions to the old faith were depleting his flock. The arguments between Laudian clergy and middle-of-the-road parishioners, so much a feature of the late 1630s, continued. A few awkward-minded Puritans could set a manifestly Nonconformist example, as in a parish in Huntingdon where the whole congregation refused to abide by the Prayer Book requirement that they file up to the altar rail to receive communion. In places resentment spilled over into violence. A bishop's official in Herefordshire was killed by a gang of the local poor who discovered he was laying legal claim to part of the common. Numerous other examples are to be found in the records of the time. Yet only on rare occasions did the Privy Council do anything about the complaints or respond to the challenge to royal authority. It is clear that Charles was convinced, as he had been throughout his fifteen-year reign, that the troublemakers were only a minority.

Further evidence that Charles' world was based on illusion comes from the Court. Here a Masque was presented early in the New Year by Inigo Jones. His *Salmcida Spolia* was one of the most elaborate and expensive masques ever mounted. A drama with scenery and music, it depicted the furies of disorder and rebellion being dealt with by a great and wise leader, and the climax − a ritual glorification of the monarch − was intended as a political morale-booster. The gulf between the masque's portrayal of a victorious monarch and the poor military performance of the English against the Scots in the previous year was not lost on some observers.

Court politics were more serious than court frivolities. They were hardly more inspiring. On the Privy Council Charles had an opportunity to strengthen his team of senior advisers with men commanding respect in the political nation. It was not taken. John Finch was appointed Lord Keeper of the Great Seal. It was a strange choice, for he was very unpopular: as Speaker in the Commons in 1629 he had been held in his chair during a turbulent debate; and as one of the judges in the Ship Money Trial we have seen him as an uncompromising supporter of the King's case. The other appointment, of Sir Henry Vane (the elder) to be Secretary of State, showed how strong the Queen and her faction still were at Court, for Vane was very much their nominee. Strafford resented the choice: he did not trust him, thought him self-seeking and, worse, inefficient. Vane's son, who was known to be a Puritan by conscience, was also brought into the ring of key servants of the King; knighted in 1640, he became Treasurer of the Navy, the man who received all the Ship Money payments.

War planning, court frivolities and manoeuvrings could not disguise the problem central to all Charles' aspirations: armies have to be paid, and the Crown had barely sufficient money for its peacetime needs. Charles had already decided, late in '39, that Parliament would have to be called. But already the county communities were incensed. Lord Keeper Finch informed his circuit judges, 'I know not how it comes about that there is not alacrity and cheerfulness given to the obedience of His Majesty's writs for Ship Money.' The payments, despite grumbles, had been highly successful up to early 1639, but by 1640 collections were down to a mere twenty per cent of what had been assessed.

The full picture, however, was not yet clear, and anyway the fragments of information from the counties were not properly evaluated at Court where they were seen as minor irritants. There was in fact a renewed confidence in Court circles, based on two hopes. First, Strafford was going to Ireland. He left in March with Charles' authority to raise money from the Irish Parliament and to enlarge his army there. Such was Strafford's control that within a week he had a promise of both money and men – four subsidies totalling £45,000 and 9000 soldiers. Secondly, Charles' expressed wish 'to meet our people and to demand their assistance in the ancient and ordinary way of parliament' was being fulfilled: elections were under way. The King and Strafford could expect instant supply when the full facts were revealed, as Charles put it to his Council, 'of the huge and insolent carriage and demands of our rebellious subjects' in Scotland.

March 1640, then, was a busy month, full of promise. An order went out to the Lord Lieutenants in the counties. It was crisp and clear. They were to raise 27,600 men into the 'perfect militia', an idea that Charles had long supported. The rather haphazard system of the previous year was dropped in favour of weekly drilling by established army officers; then, after seven weeks, these disciplined forces would move to a county rendezvous, preparatory to marching north to deal with the Scots. At the same time the first serious costs of a campaign had to be met, and the Privy Council made it plain that they would charge coat and conduct money to the individual counties.

The Short Parliament, 13 April–5 May

The elections were fiercely contested. In one way they were traditional: great landowning families exploited local rivalries to get 'their' candidate returned; bribery and dubious vote-counting were common; and there was the usual medley of local issues. In another way this election revealed how deep was the distrust of Charles and his Court. Each county and borough community assessed the effect of past royal policies on it, and to this extent the election was unusual in focusing attention as much on national issues as on local personalities. The result was a rout of the candidates associated with the Court – a mere handful of about forty were elected.

How far the remainder, who prided themselves on being independent country gentlemen, could be persuaded to stand together was to depend on the oratory of a few men. The first Parliament for eleven years opened on 13 April. Charles, aloof, laconic, aware of his stammer, lost whatever chance he had of imposing a majestic, Elizabethan performance on the members. He merely remarked, 'There never was a king that had more weighty cause to call his people together than myself. I will not trouble you with the particulars.' With Strafford still journeying from Ireland, Lord Keeper Finch delivered the major speech on the King's policy. He made three points, and the order was significant. First, ample subsidies must be granted so that rebellion – 'the unspeakable wickedness of the Scots', he called it – could be crushed. Secondly, Parliament must pass a bill, already prepared by the Council, granting to the King Tunnage and Poundage customs duties, (traditional for generations but refused to Charles in 1626) in order, Finch declared, 'to repair the insolencies of previous parliaments'. Thirdly, any grievances Parliament might have would be listened to, this session, if there was time after the Subsidies Bill and the Tunnage and Poundage Bill had been passed; if not, another session would be held later in the year. The pompous tone of the speech, its patronising phraseology, and especially the order of business displeased many members of both Houses.

Three days later the Commons, having reflected upon royal priorities, began discussions. The MP for Colchester, Harbottle Grimstone, a man noted for his middle-of-the-road views, spoke angrily: bad as the Scots' problem was, the attacks on 'the liberties of the subject' at home were more dangerous; an example ought to be made of those men responsible. Here was a direct attack on 'evil counsellors', possibly implying a Commons' demand to control the King's ministers. How far Grimstone represented the views of the other members remained to be seen.

That the political nation had grievances was made quickly apparent when the Commons came to consider the petitions sent in by many counties. For example, the freeholders of the County of Northampton complained,

> of late we have been charged, troubled and grieved in our consciences, persons and estates by innovation in religion, exactions in spiritual courts, molestation of our most Godly and learned ministry, ship money, monopolies, undue impositions, army money, waggon money, horse money, conduct money, and enlarging the Forest beyond its ancient bounds, and the like. (65, p. 168)

Annoyed, but without control or direction, the Commons could have gone on complaining for days. But on 17 April the member for Tavistock in Devon rose: John Pym spoke for two hours. It was an unusually long speech delivered in cold, plain English, and in marked contrast to the many short, colourful, stirringly poetic orations which the Commons were wont to enjoy. The pith of Pym's argument can be seen from the following sentences culled

Matth.15.13. *Every plant which mine heavenly Father hath not planted should be rooted up.*

Loe, here are three men, standing in degree,
The least of these, the greatest ought to be.

Of God,   Of Man,   Of the Divell.

The other two, of men and of the Devill.
Ought to be rooted out for ere as evill.

Above: 'Triple Episcopacie' – a Puritan satire on Laud and the Court bishops. (Mansell Collection)   Below: Laud himself c. 1636 (National Portrait Gallery)

from different parts of the speech:

> I shall offer you a model of the grievances which have disabled us to
> administer any supply until they be redressed. The first are those grievances
> which during these eleven years' interval of parliaments are against the
> liberties and privileges of parliament.
> – the last Parliament was dissolved before our grievances had redress.
> – the Parliament was punished without being suffered to make its own
>   defence. I call the dissolution of the Parliament a punishment.
> The next sort of grievances are those that concern innovations in religion.
> Popish books have been published and disputations of Popish points are
> preached in the pulpit and maintained for sound doctrine: also Popish
> ceremonies, as altars, bowing towards the east, pictures, crosses, crucifixes
> and the like. I shall observe the daily discouraging of Godly men who truly
> profess the Protestant religion. Then the encroaching upon the king's
> authority by ecclesiastical courts, as namely the High Commission, which
> takes upon it to fine and imprison men.
> I now come to grievances belonging to civil matters – the taking of
> tunnage and poundage without any grant or law for to do so – monopolies
> – ship money, and although there be a judgement for it, yet I dare be bold
> to say it's against all former precedent, and laws. Military charges by letters
> only from the Council table whereby soldiers' conduct money and coats
> are to be provided at the county's charge.
> The breach of parliaments is much prejudicial, for by this means the
> great union and love which should be kept betwixt king and his subjects is
> interrupted. They cannot make known their petitions, nor the king his
> wants, to have supplies. If Parliaments had been more frequent the king
> had had more supplies.
> I now come to the last thing, the remedy of these grievances. First, I
> advise to present them to the House of Peers, that they may join with us to
> go to the King, and pray that these grievances, being clear in fact, may be
> voted [i.e. turned into statute law]. (6, p. 197)

The speech was received with cries of 'A good oration!' The issue between
Pym and Finch can be simply stated: Charles faced an emergency and wanted
supply before redress of grievances; Pym echoed members' sentiments by
sticking ruthlessly to redress before supply.

Strafford returned to London the day after the speech to find the Commons
already drafting bills implementing Pym's proposals. He saw the possibility
that the Commons' obstinacy might annoy the House of Lords, so he
persuaded Charles to speak briefly but personally to the Upper House. On 24
April Charles appealed for subsidies: his necessities, he said, were too serious to
admit delay. The vote was crucial. Out of 86, 61 voted that supply must
precede redress. The Commons were furious at the Lords' decision, and a

conference between the two Houses was arranged, but it failed to resolve the matter. Events of the next few days only served to blur the position. Certainly a degree of ambivalence could be detected when further discussion in the Lords showed the King's majority of 36 dwindling to 20; yet in the Commons at one point 148, a substantial minority, revealed themselves in sympathy with Charles' urgent need for money.

The confusion was compounded by manoeuvres in the Council. Strafford favoured cajoling Parliament by open or devious means; Vane thought a bargain ought to be struck – if twelve subsidies (about £80,000 each) were immediately granted, the King would abolish Ship Money. Charles was unresolved for several days. Vane, perhaps on his own initiative (the documentary evidence is unclear), put the bargain to the Commons on 4 May. Tactless as usual, even politically inept, Vane used language more likely to inflame than cool the situation: the bargain, he said, was an offer made by His Majesty's 'grace and favour'.

In the debate that followed the few moderate voices such as that of Edward Hyde (the future Earl of Clarendon) were drowned. For the first time the strong emotions felt in the county communities about the preparation for the Scots War were revealed. Ship Money alone was not by now the key issue. It was the *extra* military charges, like Coat-and-Conduct Money, that rankled. Sir John Hotham, member for Yorkshire, put it bluntly: Ship Money had cost his county £12,000, the other military charges £40,000. Information was coming in from sheriffs throughout the country that they could not possibly be expected to collect Ship Money *and* Coat-and-Conduct Money. The Council was being monstrously insensitive to local feeling. That nightmare of the gentry – the breakdown of peace, quiet and order in their county communities – seemed imminent. (8, pp. 26–8) It might fairly be concluded that Coat-and-Conduct Money was the last straw – the one that broke the Ship Money camel's back. In turn this produced that phenomenon so central to the events of 1640: a taxpayers' strike.

Far from being interested in Vane's bargain, the Commons began drawing up a petition for a reconciliation with the Scots. Charles was angry and dismayed. On the night of 4–5 May he brooded over three matters. It seemed to him that Pym, showing considerable capacity for organisation, had the initiative: through Commons' committees he and his friends such as Hampden and Oliver St John were examining the multitude of complaints which members brought from their counties, instead of directing the Commons to the King's urgent requirements. Rumours had reached him that Pym's friends were in correspondence with the Scots.

Charles summoned a Privy Council meeting for 5 May – at 6 a.m., a most unusual hour. Strafford, hampered by chronic gout, and Laud arrived late, to hear Vane telling the King there was no hope that the Commons 'would give one penny'. Strafford was unconvinced, but others shared Charles' anger.

Before noon Charles went to the Houses of Parliament and dismissed the members. So ended the Short Parliament after only three weeks.

Study 2

As the Crisis of 1640 unfolded the decision to dissolve the Short Parliament may be seen as a significant one. You ought to pause here to inquire why this was so.

1 Lord Keeper Finch's speech has been much criticised. How would you have handled the speech? Examine its tone and content.

2 Write a brief assessment of Pym's 17 April speech, pin-pointing the task he faced, his qualities as a speaker, and how he differed in one very precise sense from Grimstone's attitude.

3 Was the dissolution of the Short Parliament on 5 May a lost opportunity, or inevitable given the circumstances?

This question provoked controversy and historians have offered the following conflicting verdicts:

It seems unlikely that Strafford could by any exercise of skill or bribery have brought this intractable Parliament under control. He had, however, no time to do so.
C.V. Wedgwood, (18, p. 283.) Note: the phrase "intractable parliament" is also used in 62, p. 325.

It was a potentially tractable body, with which the King might have come to terms... open to criticism is Charles' failure to negotiate and his over-hasty action in dissolving it... at least there was a lack of tact and patience.
G.E. Aylmer, (2, p. 101).

The Short Parliament failed by a narrower margin than many people, including Charles, supposed... There was a real split, which Charles might well have managed to exploit. Even the most irresponsible of country members were patriotic, and, Puritan or not, they did not like the Scots.
Conrad Russell, (19, p. 109)

The King's exasperation is excusable, but he had acted rashly. A few ostentatious gestures might have got a generous reward... But Charles' whole experience told him that appeasement brought nothing but further trouble... The hearts of the critics were hardened, and the King had done nothing to encourage mugwumps to jump down on his side.
Ivan Roots, (25, pp. 29–30).

Bearing these opinions in mind, review the evidence from the narrative of this chapter and give *your* verdict on whether the dissolution was inevitable or really a lost opportunity.

Observations

1. If you regard politics as the 'art of the possible', then you might have been very critical of Finch. He was one of the agents of that change in political atmosphere which modern historians (for example, R. Ashton, 44), have

labelled 'From Consensus to Confrontation'. The general spirit of co-operation – with important exceptions, of course – which existed between Crown and Parliament in Elizabethan and some early Stuart meetings was fast evaporating. In its place a new 'consensus' could be discerned: the political nation (the 'Country') united in distrust of the King and the 'Court', and in fear that the Crown's policies would lead to royal absolutism. At the moment, early in 1640, this unanimity was negative – Ship Money was disliked, for instance, but there was no agreed substitute. The 'Country' was amorphous, lacking organisation and leadership, its only common ideal being a desire to preserve the political, economic and social health of the county community.

Could Finch have had a more accurate appreciation of this position? Laud and Strafford did: hence the remark we have noted, 'the minds of men are mightily alienated.' Finch might have avoided the politics of confrontation in favour of persuasion. Some disarming of critics was required by concessions, generously made, not in the spirit of resentment. This tone of conciliation could have been supported by a consideration of matters conspicuously absent from Finch's speech. What were these? Examine Pym's speech for guidance.

2. Pym's task was not easy: remember that Parliament had not met for eleven years. A contemporary, Thomas May, noted that the people were 'almost amazed, so strange a thing was the name of Parliament.' The elected members had no parties or even loose groupings. The old hands were out of practice, and new members lacked experience.

But Pym had important qualities. One has been well described by Ivan Roots: 'His capacity for organisation was shown in the way in which he brought under a few convenient heads the sprawling mass of grievances amid the mutterings of less articulate men' (25, p. 29) Another was his moderation, for Pym's speech could cause no real offence to the hesitant, even timid, country gentlemen. It is here that Pym steered a more politic course than Grimstone. Read the final paragraph through carefully.

3. You probably found this puzzling. If two such respected modern historians as Dame Veronica Wedgwood and Professor Gerald Aylmer can come to diametrically opposed verdicts on the same evidence ('intractable'; 'tractable'), you might well feel bemused. But the point about May 1640 is that *no one* can be certain whether Pym, who was in no mood to compromise, really did have the more independent-minded country gentlemen supporting him or not; and even if they were, whether they would continue to on all issues. Again, it is difficult to judge how many of them would have reacted to what Roots calls 'a few ostentatious gestures' from the King. On both counts we are in the realm

of 'might have been' where evaluation on the basis of even thoroughly researched evidence becomes sticky. The evidence is clearer regarding the wooing of the House of Lords: both Strafford and Pym laboured to win its affections. But the time-scale is short: Charles dissolved Parliament before the allegiance of the Lords was properly settled. On balance, it seems reasonable to have expected Charles to allow the session a few more weeks of life.

Urgent alternatives, May – August

The Short Parliament ended late in the morning of 5 May. In the early afternoon Charles called a meeting of a group of eight Privy Councillors who were his special advisers on Scotland. Strafford, fearing loss of national honour, argued for a vigorous offensive against the Scots; Northumberland, the army commander, was lukewarm. What actually was said during the meeting is difficult to establish. What documentary evidence we have is in the State Papers of 1640: its authenticity, accuracy, even its meaning – right down to devious and partisan assertions, and to denials relating to a single adjectival pronoun – were to be questioned within twelve months on a quite spectacular occasion. For the moment suffice it to say that we have jottings made by Sir Henry Vane the Elder, who was acting rather inefficiently as secretary. Beside the abbreviation 'LLt.Ir', which could only mean Lord Lieutenant of Ireland (i.e. Strafford) were the words:

> ... go on with an offensive war as you first designed, loosed and absolved from all rules of government... You have an army in Ireland you may employ here to reduce this kingdom. Confident as anything under heaven, Scotland shall not hold out five months. One summer well employed will do it. (6, pp. 481–2)

Charles accepted Strafford's counsel. Preparations for war with the Scots would go on, and the search for alternative sources of money acquired a desperate urgency.

Strafford spent the late afternoon of 5 May at home meeting with some representatives from Spain. Within a few hours it seemed all Charles' money problems were over: four million ducats, an enormous sum of money which would have certainly paid for an efficient, though short, campaign in Scotland, were part of a bargain leading to an Anglo-Spanish Treaty. In return Charles' navy would escort regular movements of Spanish transport ships up the English Channel to Flanders, thus enabling Spain to prosecute her struggle with the French and the Dutch (part of that confusing contest for European hegemony, the Thirty Years' War). Strafford's dream never materialised. Within a week he was seriously ill again, gout and dysentery bringing him close to death; his absence from matters of state allowed the Dutch diplomatically to outwit him. It was made very plain to Charles that if any English help was given to Spain, the Dutch would declare war on England; such a prospect alarmed him, and relations with Spain were allowed to grow cold. C.V. Wedgwood concludes: 'Strafford's vision of rebuilding royal authority on the foundation of Spanish gold faded into a remote future.' Yet, she goes on, 'Nothing that the King did could stifle the continuous whispering of the old story that he was in some way selling England to Spain'. (62, pp. 335 and 337) The Scots were quite convinced on this point: some letters have survived which state, 'His Majesty has absolutely taken the King of Spain by the hand'.

Efforts made elsewhere brought in mere pittances compared with the Spanish offer. Irish enthusiasm for Strafford's extra soldiers and money began to wane, and the army promised for July together with subsidies assumed a mirage-like expectancy. At home Convocation, the Anglican Church 'parliament', offered a grant to last six years of £20,000 per annum; in view of Charles' needs perhaps it should have been called a mite. The Lord Mayor of London was informed that the Crown required a list of citizens rich enough to contribute to a 'loan' of £200,000. A cargo of pepper was taken for a nominal sum from the East India Company and sold – at a profit to the Crown. Finally a fresh issue of Ship Money writs was made. Nothing illustrates better the desperate straits of Charles' position, coupled with the dangerous political impossibility of doing anything about it. Roots refers expressively to Charles' 'thrashings about in deep waters'. (25, p. 30)

How deep were these waters? Charles needed half a million pounds for a quick campaign, an amount previous monarchs had normally been able to borrow from merchants without much difficulty. In 1640, though, two factors combined to reduce him to near penury. The first was a crisis of credit: Crown policies had created such animus and censure that neither taxation nor borrowing could generate sufficient funds to fight a successful war. The 'mighty alienation' of the late 1630s had deteriorated even more. Merchants were particularly outraged by some of Charles' recent actions – the inept handling of the East India Company was an object lesson in how to lose friends. The second factor related to the lean trading years of the early seventeenth century, for there had been several slumps and the late '30s was one such period. A contemporary wrote, 'the decay of trade is in everybody's mouth from the sheep shearer to the merchant.' Plague, bad harvests, the dislocation of continental markets because of the Thirty Years War, severe Dutch competition in the wool trade – all meant a reduced ordinary income from customs duties.

Then came the Southwark riots of May: they should have warned Charles that his policies embittered not just gentry and merchants. Lower down the social order were apprentices, poor and often provincial adolescents in London to seek their fortunes. As hopes faded in the economic gloom of the time, resentment at both their poverty and the harsh discipline imposed by masters produced a turbulent force which was angered immediately the Short Parliament was dissolved. Rumour spread that Laud was the man responsible, and the 'hunting of William the Fox' became the centrepiece of three days of 'tumults' as contemporary accounts called them. A march from Southwark by several hundred apprentices, dockhands and sailors on Lambeth Palace produced a sharp reaction from the authorities. A young seaman who had tried to force the door of the Archbishop's home with a crowbar was arrested and charged with high treason! His sentence was to be hanged, drawn and quartered, and his head spiked on London Bridge.

Whether this was the mindless mob violence which for centuries had erupted occasionally, or whether there was a clear 'alliance' of popular radicalism with the Pym-like critics of the Crown's policies was at that moment an open-ended question. Yet among propertied men fear of 'the multi-headed monster' of social discontent was to rumble on throughout the 1640s.

While 'hunting the Fox' was going on, Laud escaped westwards to continue to preside over Convocation – still sitting, even though it was usual to dissolve it with a parliament. If Strafford's advice was for a vigorous military preparation, this was reflected in Laud's restatement of the Anglican position. In June, the Canons of 1640, as they became known, were issued under Charles' authority. The following extracts reveal them to be resolute and unyielding; that they might also be insensate and inflammatory does not seem to have concerned Charles and Laud:

> Our good subjects imagine... that we intend to bring some alteration of religion here established... How utterly we detest every thought thereof...
> Concerning regal power: The most high and sacred order of Kings is of Divine Right, being the ordinance of God Himself... and clearly established by express texts both of the Old and New Testaments. A supreme power is given to this most excellent Order by God Himself in the Scriptures, which is that kings should rule and command in their several dominions all persons of what rank and estate... and that they should restrain and punish with the temporal sword all stubborn and wicked doers...
> An oath for the preventing of all innovations in doctrine and government: all archbishops, bishops, and all other priests and deacons shall swear:

> 'I do approve the doctrine and discipline, or government established in the Church of England, as containing all things necessary to salvation, and that I will not endeavour to bring in any Popish doctrine, contrary to that which is so established; nor will I ever give my consent to alter the government of this Church by archbishops, bishops, deans, and archdeacons, etcetera.' (6, pp. 166–71)

Such assertions of authority failed to move the nation at large, though Charles and his Council, amid these discontents and still short of money, pressed on with the war plans.

Bellum Episcopale: the Scots invade

We left the actual gathering of armies in March, when some hope still existed: by May the army should have been poised to march north, funded from a variety of sources, not the least being a patriotic grant of subsidies from Parliament. By mid-summer such hopes were bereft of any substance. Strafford was driven to comment to a friend, 'Pity me, for never came any man to so lost a business. The army altogether unexercised and unprovided of all necessaries.' Charles' foolishness in promoting a war he could not pay for was never more evident.

The air of decisiveness about the early planning evaporated at the county level. Deputy Lord Lieutenants were at one moment urged to hurry; then instructions to postpone arrived – even the post broke down in outlying areas. In Somerset 2000 men were kept at a rendezvous for ten days, costing nearly £700, yet an order to disband temporarily should have been received *before* any movement to assembly points. Renewed efforts to enforce the Ship Money writs and to collect Coat-and-Conduct Money were made. The Privy Council issued a statement complaining of 'the great and supine negligence of the high sheriffs of divers counties', and it commanded that 'the names of every man' who refused to pay be listed – the numbers ran into many hundreds in most counties. Such threats had little effect. We have already noted the percentage decline in Ship Money collection; the actual figures for 1640 were: demanded, £214,000; received, £43,400.

By June the money ran out. Desertion from the gathering soldiery was common. Wiltshire soldiers broke open the county gaol to release those committed for not paying Coat-and-Conduct Money. Pressed men from Dorset straggled northwards, but then turned on an officer and hanged him before deserting. Professor Barnes in his standard work on Somerset in this period comments, 'The army on which rested all the King's hopes had become in a matter of days the greatest law enforcement problem in living memory'. (41, p. 277)

What had gone wrong? It is easy to point to the lack of pay, to the parochialism of the rural 'soldier' who refused to fight outside his county, to the Puritan unwillingness to combat Scottish Presbyterians. Barnes argues, however, that Charles' ideal of the 'perfect militia' had never been achieved. There was no discipline. In expecting amateur squires to fashion an army out of often hostile countrymen, Charles I paid the price in 1640 of failure by his servants at the county level to execute his orders.

The upshot of the whole operation came on 9 July when Sir Jacob Astley, the senior officer responsible for collecting all the levies into an army at Selby in Yorkshire, reported three facts to Charles: a mere 4000 had arrived; they seemed 'the arch knaves of the country'; and he had monies only to pay them for a week.

Then Charles was upstaged: on 20 August the Scots invaded England. Zealous, well-equipped, led by officers experienced on the continent, they numbered over 25,000. They were also well-disciplined. As they crossed the River Tweed at Coldstream they issued a manifesto assuring the people of Northumberland that they would not take a chicken or a pot of ale without paying for it.

By now Astley had a few thousand more to send north. Charles decided to take personal command, and at the end of the month he led his 'army' out of York towards Newcastle. But the failures and confusions of the past months took their toll: Charles moved too late, his meagre forces were far inferior to the enemy's, and when the Scots crossed the River Tyne at the ford of Newburn, four miles upstream from Newcastle, the city had to be abandoned for fear of being caught in a trap.

For a while Charles still thought he had some things in his favour. The Scottish Covenanters were not wholly united – news of bickerings over what to do now, and who should make the decisions reached his ears. In any case he felt he had only to wait for northern England to resent a Scottish military presence for old patriotic instincts to revive. Then there was Strafford's Irish army, admittedly not as large as expected. Much publicity had been given in London to the way 'the wild Irish Macdonalds would eat the Covenanters alive'. But unbeknown to Charles many on the Privy Council had serious reservations about using Irish soldiers, so the ships necessary to transport them were never sent. Charles finally acknowledged that a military solution was impossible – for the moment. An armistice was arranged at Ripon in October. The Scots' army would occupy the Border to Newcastle area, and be paid £850 a day for expenses; discussions would move to London in order that a final peace treaty could be agreed.

It all seemed dismally humiliating. Yet Charles' mind was already busy with fresh strategies. Conciliation, not intimidation, would now be the watchword. He would concede, he would procrastinate – all in the hope of eventually dividing his opponents in Scotland and in England. Then he would set about restoring that authority which was the proper right of kings.

It was already rumoured that he intended calling a new parliament. Strafford became the scapegoat for the failure of *Bellum Episcopale*, the Earl of Bristol going as far as to accuse him of being the author of the war. Charles did nothing to protect his senior minister. Thoughtful observers raised a question in their minds: was Charles about to discard Strafford?

Meanwhile elections for a new parliament were under way. It met on 3

November 1640 and became known as the Long Parliament, initiating such a train of events and raising such questions central to the stability of the government of England that historians have applied the labels 'The English Revolution' or 'The Great Rebellion' to the coming decades. Solutions to the issues raised in 1640 (these were not yet closely defined or related to matters of constitutional principle until the Long Parliament met) were hard to come by. Over half a century passed before a final, albeit piecemeal, settlement was achieved.

--- *Study 3* ---

What had gone wrong? Your argument, plus evidence to support your assertions, should result in a short essay of one to two thousand words as follows:
Why was there a crisis in 1640, and who bears the responsibility for its seriousness and lack of solution?

Observations

1 Central to your argument will be the connections between such factors as Ship Money, Coat-and-Conduct Money and the Scots' war. You will also have to include a statement on Conciliar Government, its strengths and weaknesses; to review the later 1630s and to ask yourself whether the general alienation of the 1630s had anything to do with dislike of the specific policies of the Crown in 1639–40, and what exactly were the fears of the county communities in the summer of 1640. Further, you must assess whether it was Charles' *policies* (e.g. enforcing his authority on Scotland), or his *style of government* (e.g. conciliar decision-making, the image of Strafford as Black Tom Tyrant, and the fear of Ireland as a blueprint for England) or the *institutions* of government (e.g. the executive's only partial control over a local bureaucracy) which were to blame. You should be able to detect clues to the answer in the words of Finch, Pym and Strafford.

2 Who was to blame? Was it Charles, or Strafford and Laud, or the Privy Council collectively? Charles seems an easy target, perhaps too easy! You may regard him as foolish, and certainly his tactics are open to question on some occasions. But was he given the best advice? (Find precise examples of this.) Some general points to remember: his Council advised on the May dissolution and on the implementation of war plans; Laud with his Canons and Strafford in pursuing the Spanish connection were important agents in the decision-making process. C.V. Wedgwood declares Strafford 'was unquestionably the councillor responsible for the persistence in war after the Short Parliament failed'. (18, p. 303)
    Charles, in the final analysis, was responsible for choosing his ministers,

and we shall have to see whether this 'prerogative right' emerges as a key issue in the Long Parliament. Why was Charles so stubborn? Is this the right word? Was he being blindly masochistic in not recognising the obvious (that he could not 'win') and not making immediate peace? Others had done it before: Henry VIII cut taxes and ended an unpopular war in 1525. Or do you regard Charles' stand as being properly defiant and courageous, even responsible? Remember, he *was* king and had a firm belief in the political and religious authority which such a position had given him and his predecessors for generations. Determination to persist in unattractive and seemingly untenable policies has sometimes been the hallmark of statesmen and women. (What if Charles had offered his people what Churchill offered on 13 May exactly three hundred years later: nothing but 'blood, toil, tears and sweat'?)

3 Was there a conspiracy? In view of the seriousness of the crisis both the Crown's supporters and Pym's friends charged each other with machination. First, there were those of the 'Country' who had a genuine fear that Charles and his advisers at Court were the real revolutionaries. Solid evidence was hard to obtain, but Strafford and Laud's activities seemed to point to arbitrary government with little chance if any of Parliament having some voice in the realm's affairs. Word spread that in Laud's Canons the mysterious 'etcetera' could mean a return to papal influence. S.R. Gardiner, writing at the end of the nineteenth century, regarded the evidence as damning:

> The subjects held that all that had taken place was the result of a settled conspiracy to replace law and liberty by an absolute despotism at home, whilst the political despotism brought into existence was to be subjected in turn to the ecclesiastical despotism of the Pope. (66, p. 218)

Secondly, Strafford and Laud certainly felt that Pym's group were not only conspirators, but, worse, guilty of treason. Strafford warned the King of 'the peevishness of some few factious spirits', and as 1640 progressed suspicions were aroused that some parliamentary radicals were in touch with the Scots. When did this become a factor of political consequence? Later there was the £850 a day demand: in what way was this so 'convenient' to the radicals that it must increase a suspicion of collusion?

4 What happened was nothing less than a disintegration of the Caroline regime – a collapse under pressure from a foreign war of the Tudor ideal of conciliar government. Modern historians are in remarkable agreement about what went wrong in 1640. Here is a selection of opinions from four authorities on the period; how do they measure against your own observations?

The government was brought down by a revolt of the tax-payers. In 1639, encouraged by the presence of the Scots' army, they went on strike; and the government was shown to be unable to exist (in 1640) without their goodwill.

Christopher Hill, (56, p. 107)

Although not a single hand had risen against it in England, in the face of universal subordination and disaffection, Charles and his Council were powerless to rule. What occurred was possible only because the King had no independent force at his disposal with which to scourge and chastise his refractory subjects.

Perez Zagorin, (42, p. 116)

Charles' structure of local government still depended heavily on exactly the same county gentry whom he could not trust to help him in Parliament... In the circumstances it was possible to produce something approaching a taxpayers' strike...

Conrad Russell, (19, pp. 108–9).

What produced the collapse of cooperation in 1639–40 was not a growing awareness of great constitutional issues raised by Hampden's lawyers, but a growing fear of the consequences of ship money for the economic and social stability of each county community.

John Morrill, (8, p. 26)

CHAPTER 4

Restraining the Prerogative
1640-41

'A design to alter the kingdom...'

The first session of the Long Parliament met from 3 November 1640 until 9 September 1641. It proved one of the most significant sessions of any parliament, before or since. Of its membership of around 500, only 64 could be clearly grouped as Court sympathisers. The vast bulk were united in resentment of Charles' government, particularly its ecclesiastical and financial policies, coupled recently with its conscription demands. These men were the 'Country', gentry whose ambitions are easily summarised: to assert the liberties of parliament, to reform the Church, and, most importantly, to restore to the county communities freedom from Court interference.

Once again John Pym seized the opportunity to channel more effectively indistinct appeals to 'Magna Carta', 'a Reformed Church', the 'Ancient Constitution' and so on. He delivered his second major speech of 1640 on 7 November. It is instructive to compare it with that of 17 April: no longer would a catalogue of grievances suffice, for in Pym's opinion something far more dangerous was now apparent.

The distempers of this kingdom are well known; they need no repetition. There is a design to alter the kingdom both in religion and government... The Papists' party alter religion, and this by setting differences between the King and his subjects.... The designs are carried on four feet:
1. Religion – ecclesiastical courts, and the discountenancing of forward men in our religion....
2. Policy for the State – the Council endeavouring to make a difference between King and People by taxes against laws... no imputation to be laid upon the King for any irregular actions, but upon them that he entrusted.
3. Breach of Parliaments – and by moulding the Irish government into an illegal course, with intent to do the same here.
4. Military steps – papists into command of armies... and the Irish army to bring us to a better order; we are not fully conquered!
There might be a settled committee to find out the danger the King and kingdom is in. (6, pp. 204–5)

34

Study 4

Pym's 'settled committee' will have to draw up a programme of change. The main issues raised by the crisis of 1640 will have to be isolated, and in each case a practical reform enacted. At the same time an order of priorities will have to be established: some reforms will be uncontested, others could provoke controversy. Draw up your own programme: issues, reforms, priorities, and note any problems you think might arise. This is an exercise in political strategy, and you have been given in the last few chapters as much information as the committee would have had before it.

Observations:

If you agree that the average MP would be especially concerned with grievances, then the first steps in your programme look straightforward. The removal of the personnel and destruction of the machinery of prerogative government will be high on the list: Strafford, Laud, the Star Chamber, etc., must go. Also Parliament must meet regularly to counter the threat of Charles' personal government becoming absolute. What financial and religious matters ought to be included? For instance, something has to be done about what was called by contemporaries 'the delinquencies of bishops'. A proper enforcement of these points would reduce the central government's excessive meddling in the localities.

But your programme must now face a looming, uncomfortable question: how far along the path of reform does the parliamentary leadership want or need to go before the measures take on a distinctly radical, even seditious, prospect? Complaints about the abuses were convenient in that most members agreed on their removal, but positive suggestions would open up a wide spectrum of opinion, part of it too advanced for some to accept. For instance, some members would be startled by and apprehensive of Pym's persuasive reference to 'a design to alter the kingdom'. Why do you think this might be so? Others might ask: would a mere reform of abuses eliminate Pym's accusations of a 'design'? Some of the leaders clearly thought not; you will have to take account of this, that in their minds they were moving towards the idea of some share in executive power. How much support both in the Commons and Lords, and in the county communities would there be for such an idea? And if the 'share in executive power' was made effective by some of the Parliamentary leaders entering the Privy Council, might not, for instance, Pym and Hampden become the next 'evil counsellors' in the tradition of Buckingham, Laud and Strafford?

Your programme might highlight the five central issues of the 1640 crises: in view of their importance throughout the rest of this book, you are advised to commit them to memory.

1. The royal prerogative power to summon, prorogue and dissolve Parliament.

2. The appointment, power and accountability of ministers of the Crown (and generals).
3. The efficiency and acceptability of taxation arrangements.
4. The question of conformity in religious opinion.
5. Respect for county community prejudices.

And pervading all five was the willingness of both the Crown and the political nation to accept any proposed solutions.

Parliamentary Insurance

The Parliamentary leaders expected to achieve workable answers to all the major problems well within a year. The cost of the Scots army mounted daily, yet Pym was unwilling to pay it off — not only did its presence hang, Damocles-fashion, over Charles' freedom of action, especially dissolution, but it was Pym's only guarantee against a possible military counter-stroke. (The remnant of the English army was still in the north, while Strafford's was in Ireland; Charles refused to disband either). The Scots would not remain for ever, though.

To prevent 'the breach of parliaments' in the long term was fairly straightforward. In February, 1641 Charles was persuaded to accept William Strode's measure, the Triennial Bill, ensuring that a parliament would be summoned every three years, and would meet for at least 50 days. The leaders of the Long Parliament were not seriously interested in a Parliamentary sovereignty of annual sessions effectively controlling policy: not all members could afford town houses and long sessions in London were expensive (19, pp. 92–3). But this particular Parliament was crucial. Its leaders did not want a repetition of the snap dissolution of the Short Parliament. So on 10 May a second measure was passed: an act preventing the prorogation or dissolution of the present Parliament without its own consent. Professor Ashton concludes that 'both acts were radical innovations of crucial significance', the second especially so, being an immediate invasion of the Crown prerogative. Charles' alarm was understandable: his fears expressed in 1629 of a Commons with 'universal, overswaying power', were being confirmed. The Parliamentary leaders did not see matters in the same way. In the Lords, the Earls of Bedford, Essex and Warwick, and in the Commons, Pym, St John, Hampden, Holles, Strode, Fiennes and Haselrig stood united in suspicion of Charles, whose prevarication before accepting both bills suggested that he might not honour his signature. Trust was to be an ever-recurring theme over the next decade. Their answer, it seemed, was to try to encase Charles in a corset of such interlocking legal obligations and advisory services that he could never again entertain hopes of being a despot, however benevolent.

But, as we shall see, these men were already in dispute with each other about how constricting the corset need be.

The Trial of Thomas Wentworth, Earl of Strafford

Running parallel with the Parliamentary 'insurance' policies was the attack on the agents of Charles' personal government. The onslaught on 'evil counsellors' was immediate. Within four days of his November 1640 speech, Pym impeached Strafford of high treason. His arrest was soon followed by that of Laud (who was to languish in prison, an old, forgotten, almost irrelevant figure until 1645); Finch and other leading royal advisers fled abroad.

Black Tom was the focus of Parliamentary spleen. His talents, arrogance and ruthlessness meant he could be an effective barrier to any settlement; he could also stiffen Charles' resistance to Parliamentary measures which cut into the prerogative. Pym had no illusions: while Strafford lived the Parliamentary leaders could never feel secure.

Articles of Impeachment were drawn up by the Commons in January 1641, prior to a trial before the Lords. Of the 28 articles, three were to be significant.

> 'Article III: the Lord Deputy intending the subversion of the fundamental laws and settled government of that realm of Ireland... did declare and publish that Ireland was a conquered nation.
>
> Article XX: the Earl did labour and endeavour to persuade, incite and provoke his Majesty to an offensive war against his subjects of the Scottish nation...
>
> Article XXIII: Strafford, with the assistance of the Archbishop (ie. Laud) did procure his Majesty to dissolve the Parliament upon 5 May last... and upon the same day did traitorously and wickedly counsel his Majesty to this effect: he was loosed and absolved from all rules of government... and that he had an army in Ireland which he might employ to reduce this kingdom'(6, pp. 207–10).

The scope of the charges was clear: Strafford's Deputyship in Ireland, his counsel on the Scots' war, and, in England, that fearful phrase, 'loosed and absolved from all rules of government.'

The trial opened on 22 March in the great Westminster Hall. Strafford's appearance revealed how chronic illness had affected him; C.V. Wedgwood describes him as 'a stooping grey-beard, his head sunk between his shoulders, well-wrapped in a warm cloak'. But his mind was clear. He defended himself with a masterly performance.

The trial lasted seven weeks and ranks as one of the great set-pieces in English legal history. The opening days set the pattern. The prosecution, mainly Pym and three young Commons lawyers, recounted details of

Master *PYM*
HIS SPEECH

In *Parliament*, on *Wednesday*, the
fifth of *January*, 1641.

Concerning the Vote of the House of *Commons*,
for his discharge upon the Accusation of High
Treason, exhibited against himselfe, and the
Lord *Kimbolton*, Mr. *Iohn Hampden*, Sr.
Arthur Haslerig, Mr. *Strowd*,
M. Hollis, by his Maiesty,

The true Effigies of Mr. *Iohn Pym*, Esquire

London Printed for I.W, 1641.

Earl of Strafford.

The antagonists of 1641: (above) Thomas Wentworth, Earl of Strafford c. 1640 (National Portrait Gallery); (opposite) John Pym M.P. Pym's picture is taken from a pamphlet of 1642 (dated 1641 by the old form of dating) containing his speech in his own defence against the articles of treason issued by Charles I (National Portrait Gallery)

Strafford's Irish rule, but reliance on assertion and second-hand evidence enabled him to brush many of the charges aside. Two flaws in the prosecution case were soon apparent: many witnesses were motivated by private hate, and too much argument depended on vague references to 'arbitrary government' and 'subverting fundamental laws'. John Maynard, one of the young lawyers, tried to prop up the Commons' assertion of treason by stating that though singly the charges were but little, all together they were unanswerable. Strafford expressed concern at such a flexible view of the law of high treason. Laughter broke through the solemn occasion when he congratulated his old Irish rival, the Earl of Cork, on remembering the exact words of a statement made seven years before!

On 5 April Article XXIII, the lynch-pin of Pym's case was considered. The elder Vane was questioned about the Council meeting of 5 May 1640. Nervously he claimed Strafford had referred to 'an army in Ireland' which his Majesty might 'employ here to reduce this kingdom'. (The word 'here' did not appear in the Impeachment articles). Vane was pressed about the two words 'here' and 'this'; yes, he said, those were the words, not 'there' and 'that'. The impression was thus given at the trial that Strafford had meant England when he referred to 'this kingdom'. A few members of the Lords had already made up their minds – even if he had meant Scotland, a victorious army there would return to England to shore up a royal despotism. For others, though, previous doubts about the prosecution's case were reinforced when Strafford called three other members of the Privy Council who then denied hearing the Lord Deputy saying anything of the sort.

By 10 April Strafford was obviously surviving the charges. On that Saturday afternoon two developments occurred in the House of Commons. First, Pym revealed that he possessed important written evidence. Back in October 1640 Vane's son had found and brought to him the minutes which his father had taken at the 5 May Council meeting (see p. 26 and compare wording with Article XXIII); Pym had taken a copy, and the minutes were replaced. The originals were later destroyed by the elder Vane just before the long Parliament met. Tinged as it was by dishonourable practice, the evidence was produced by Pym only with reluctance. The whole affair stank of collusion. Be that as it may, many members were now convinced of Strafford's guilt, even if it were difficult to prove in court.

Then later in the afternoon came the second development, when members' impatience with the legal process in the Lords was voiced by Sir Arthur Haselrig, as he rose to introduce a Bill of Attainder. This was an ancient but disused practice of condemning a man via an Act of Parliament and without requiring strict legal proof. Historians differ over whether Pym supported this move. C.V. Wedgwood thinks he did; but others have questioned this. The evidence points more to reluctance than support, for Pym knew such a bill would offend the House of Lords, and a few days later he urged in vain that the Commons should 'go the other way' (i.e. impeachment). The American historian, Perez Zagorin, regards this as 'the first political difference to arise among the opposition leaders'. (41, p. 220).

On 13 April Strafford made his final speech on the impeachment charge. No verdict was now likely, but how he performed would influence the Lords in the way they voted on Haselrig's Attainder, assuming it passed the Commons. It was a brilliant, moving, two-hour oration by a man whose face was lined with pain and fatigue. His central defence was phrased thus:

> To make up this treason by accumulation many articles are brought against me, as if in a heap of felonies some prolific seed apt to produce what is treasonable could lurk... How can that be treason in the whole which is not in any of the parts... Neither statute, Common Law nor practice hath from the beginning of this government ever mentioned such a thing. My Lords, do we not live by laws?... These gentlemen tell me they speak in defence of the commonweal against my arbitrary laws; give me leave to say that I speak in defence of the commonweal against their arbitrary treason. (6, pp. 211–13)

John Pym replied with equal force. His main point was that Strafford was an over-mighty subject, conjuring up images of the medieval baronial wars and Warwick the Kingmaker:

> The Earl of Strafford hath endeavoured by his words, actions and counsels to subvert the fundamental laws of England and Ireland, and to introduce an arbitrary and tyrannical government... This arbitrary power is danger-ous to the King's person and dangerous to his Crown; it is apt to cherish ambition, usurpation and oppression in great men. (6, pp. 213–15)

The voting on the Attainder would determine Strafford's fate. The Commons on 21 April passed the Bill by 204 to 59, a verdict delivered amid wild cheering, yet with many absentees, troubled over the manner of the destruction of the man. In the next fortnight attitudes hardened. Charles wrote to Strafford in the Tower of London, saying that he should 'not suffer in life, honour and fortune', and then made an impassioned speech to both Houses of Parliament in a vain effort to save Strafford's life. In the Lords the Earl of Essex was implacable: 'Stone dead hath no fellow.' Fear of even an exiled Strafford was too much for some Parliamentary leaders. Oliver St John angrily attacked him: 'It was never accounted either cruelty or foul play to knock foxes and wolves on the head because they be beasts of prey.'

Notions of justice and calm appraisals of evidence evaporated in those weeks. Developments made certain that Strafford's judicial murder – for that is what a Bill of Attainder meant – should take place. Early in May Pym spoke to the Commons about an army plot. Officers of the northern army were discontented over delays in pay (especially as the Scots seemed to be receiving their £850 in regular sums), and rumours of these officers' negotiations with royal advisers reached some of the Parliamentary leaders. They expressed fears of military counter-revolution, so that on 8 May the Lords followed the Commons' lead and passed the Attainder by 26 to 19. To political decision was now added the passion of turbulent crowds; respectable citizens as well as angry, leaderless mobs clamoured around Westminster. On 9 May a crowd stormed into Whitehall, and the Queen feared for her life. Charles delayed for hours, but at 9 p.m. he agreed to sign the Attainder. Strafford was told immediately. He exclaimed, 'Put not your trust in princes!' (18, p. 380). Yet it is arguable that Charles had no choice: the capital city was nearly out of control and the royal family evidently in serious danger. Strafford was beheaded on 12 May 1641 at Tower Hill before a vast crowd who had come to witness the end of Black Tom Tyrant. A deafening noise of approval rose from the people as the executioner lifted the bleeding head.

The State Papers for 1640 in the Public Records Office in London contain a contemporary broadsheet on the occasion:

> Here lies wise and valiant dust
> Huddled up 'twixt fit and just,
> Strafford who was hurried hence
> 'Twixt treason and convenience...
> The prop and ruin of the State;
> The People's violent love and hate. (18, p. 395)

Bridge appointments?

The instruments of personal government followed Strafford to destruction. On 5 July a statute removed the Privy Council's judicial powers. The Court of the Star Chamber was abolished as contrary to law, and the Council of the North and the Council of the Marches of Wales ceased to function. On the same day a second statute abolished the Court of High Commission.

If prerogative government via its personalities and its machinery was so effectively being dismantled, the question arises, what in a more positive sense did the Parliamentary leadership want? The answer was to get important members taken into Crown office and especially on to the Privy Council. The surviving papers of the Earl of Bedford, a powerful but conciliatory voice, make it plain that early in 1641 he would support neither the sovereignty of the King nor that of Parliament: he believed in the sovereignty of the Privy Council, (19, pp. 28, 111). Yet this was *not* to be a scramble for power for power's sake, a sort of 'palace revolution' where one set of villains, the 'outs', merely take over from another set of villains, the 'ins'. Rather, Bedford, Pym and their friends would use their presence on the Council to force radical changes in policy – in religion, in foreign affairs, in financial matters. They saw themselves as 'bridge appointments', effectively spanning the gap between the Crown and its 'Court' on the one side and Parliament and the 'Country' on the other.

Such appointments were widely expected in the months *before* Strafford's trial. Charles was not so foolish as to ignore this opportunity for lowering the political temperature. Rumours spread that Bedford might be Lord Treasurer, Holles Secretary of State, and Pym Chancellor of the Exchequer. Indeed the first appointments raised hopes that others might follow: St John was made Solicitor-General, and Bedford and Essex were nominated to the Privy Council, though not given senior office. Here matters stuck. Appointments as bargaining counters for Strafford's life foundered in the critical weeks of April – May 1641, when Essex and Pym made it plain that Strafford must die. The early appointees also found they had no say in policy: Zagorin concludes that because 'Charles gave the shadow and withheld the substance, his appointees effected nothing' (42, p. 215). Then Bedford died of smallpox at the end of the first week in May. The exit of this essentially moderate, influential voice was a tragedy to those hoping for a compromise settlement.

After Strafford's execution Charles abandoned any idea of bridge appointments, turning instead to men who had opposed Attainder, such as the Earl of Bristol and his son, Lord Digby. Bristol, earlier one of Bedford's group, now found himself spoken of as the new 'evil counsellor'. A voice of despair was heard in the Commons: Vane the younger declared in June 1641, 'We are still in the labyrinth and cannot get out.' The Parliamentary leaders feared the worst, and now sought fresh guarantees against future royal 'misrule'.

Obtaining appointments on the Privy Council remained the chief priority. On 24 June Pym presented his Ten Propositions to the King. The third one demanded that Charles

> Take into his Council, and for the managing of the great affairs of the Kingdom, such officers and counsellors as his people and Parliament may have just cause to confide in. (42, p. 247)

This was a vital revolutionary step: if Charles would not make bridge appointments freely, then he must be forced to. It went far beyond the original ideas of reform. Kenyon has argued forcibly that 'control of the executive had not even been on the opposition's programme of reform in November 1640; henceforward it was the only serious point at issue between them and the King' (6, p. 193).

Charles simply ignored Proposition Three.

Finance

Money had been the main reason for summoning the Long Parliament in November 1640 – the Scots army had to be paid. Parliament did not shirk the issue: subsidies which they had denied Charles were now quickly granted, and immediate loans raised in the City. The administration of these funds became the responsibility of Parliamentary committees, not the usual Treasury officials. Pym, that master of committee work, busied himself almost unnoticed to involve these committees in the sphere of government. The financial policy of the first session was two-fold, one negative, one positive.

The members of both Houses cried out for financial blood. The abuses of the '30s had to be publicly removed, though more urgent matters, such as Strafford's trial were given priority. In May 1641 an act granting the King tunnage and poundage was passed, but only for two months; it then had to be renewed at intervals with Parliamentary consent. In August a series of statutes annulled the Ship Money verdict and made the tax illegal; and declared void all the dubious ways of raising money of the 1630s.

A constructive set of proposals to resolve the government's financial problems, now at least half a century old, was worked out. Bedford was the architect of the whole scheme, but he had a range of specialist advice available from sympathetic officials in the various Exchequer departments. It was a long job covering detailed revenue balances and estimates, customs administrations, Crown lands, Navy expenditure and the Court of Wards. By the spring of '41 a variety of solutions was ready to be implemented as part of the general settlement with the King. First, Parliament would vote money to pay Crown debts. Secondly, a document now in the Public Records Office contains a clear statement by Bedford that, 'It will be very difficult... to make the King subsist upon his own revenue without supply from his people in Parliament' (67, p. 629). Here was the germ of an idea that could end once and for all the anachronistic 'live of the King's own' convention. The old subsidy system, based on getting a proportion of taxpayers' income would be replaced by a fixed sum voted by Parliament; there would thus be a closer relation between how much the Crown ought to get and how much it actually received. Thirdly, the Great Contract idea of 1610 was revived, and the old wardship and feudal dues would disappear in favour of calculable sums. Fourthly, tunnage and poundage, the Crown's main source of income, would be run by Parliament men and voted for three years at a time (i.e. linked with the Triennial Act).

There is no doubt that these were sensible ideas. They would have revolutionised government finance and placed it on a secure footing. The certainty of £x coming in from taxation would have given Charles such credit in the City that loans would have been available at low rates of interest; the 'canker of want', as James I called it, would be no more. Domestic, foreign and commercial opportunities for expansion undreamed of by previous monarchs would have been feasible.

Yet the whole scheme foundered. Why? The tragic death of Bedford in May 1641 removed the man whose personal vision and aristocratic position might have given it a chance. The King, too, had to be convinced, and it is unlikely that he would tie himself so closely to Parliament's apron-strings; instinct told him that together with bridge-appointments the scheme represented an unacceptable diminution of his prerogative power. Conrad Russell, however, has suggested a third, possibly determinant factor: it foundered 'on the rock-like obstinacy of country members' refusal to accept the real cost of government.' The first hint of this came when Pym tried to use Bedford's idea of a fixed-sum assessment to pay the Scots army: the attempt was defeated in the Commons early in 1641. Then, after Bedford's death in May, Pym fought hard against Holles and Strode over the idea of farming the customs by Parliament-men: he lost. Thus Pym experienced great resistance from colleagues in the Parliamentarian leadership as well as from 'Country' figures like the Phelips family and Seymour, the West Country gentry members, whom Russell condemns as having an 'irresponsible distrust of the executive... a rooted distrust of government for its own sake... men not ready to accept the responsibilities of power'. (19, p. 116) Perhaps Pym should not have been surprised – the fixed-sum assessment plan looked remarkably like a camouflaged version of Ship-Money!

By the end of the first session the financial difficulties had not been resolved. English government and administration continued its traditional fiscal hand-to-mouth existence.

Religion: Pandora's Box

On 28 November 1640 Prynne and Burton, released from prison, were fêted by thousands of Londoners. A Puritan witness described it as 'the return of the captivity from Babylon'. In the Commons, soon after Pym's denunciation of 'the Papists' Party', the Canons of 1640 were attacked as contrary to law.

Suddenly 'Godly Rule' became a possibility and within weeks a wave of religious hysteria swept the country. Separatists, hitherto persecuted and numerically insignificant, began to flourish. Preaching to the House of Commons placed constant emphasis on the opportunity for religious reformation. John Milton, the poet and Puritan pamphleteer, called the time, 'an age of ages wherein God is manifestly come down among us,' Visions of a new Jerusalem were abroad. A London MP, Alderman Pennington, began organising a monster petition which focused all criticism of the Church on one issue: the delinquency of bishops. This became the famous Root and Branch Petition, presented to the House of Commons on 11 December 1640. It demanded

> That the government [ie of the Church by bishops], with all its dependencies, roots and branches, may be abolished, and government according to God's Word may be rightly placed amongst us. (6, p. 172)

Also out in the county communities a vigorous Puritan campaign was being conducted. In Cheshire, for instance, the Prayer Book was attacked 'as bad or worse than the mumbling of the Mass upon beads, that the Book of Common Prayer doth stink in the nostrils of God'.

But this gives only one side of the picture. The impression which the radicals were giving – that revolutionary reform of the Church had widespread support – was simply not true. There was a strong undercurrent of moderate opinion critical of the activities and policies of the extremists. In Kent a petition supposedly voicing the views of 2500 local villagers was found to be based (including signatures) on a copy of the London Root and Branch document. Sir Edward Dering MP, one of the Kentish gentry, was angered at 'finding it a parrot' (48, p. 86). Gradually a serious division of opinion became evident in many counties; idealists were chastened to find that far from a 'Godly Reformation' taking place, a babel of discord was developing.

This babel worried John Pym when it was reflected in the Commons debate on the Root and Branch motion in February 1641. Haselrig, Fiennes and Holles were for the abolition of episcopacy, i.e. the institution; some, Hyde and Falkland for example, desired only a reduction in 'lordly prelacy'. Others in the debate asked what would take the place of bishops? The general assumption was that authority in the church would be by Presbyterian elders; yet hostility to the ruling elder idea soon appeared. Digby spoke of the Root and Branch as 'a comet with a terrible tail... pointed to the North [i.e. Scotland]'. He went on, 'I am confident that instead of every bishop we put down in a diocese, we shall set up a pope in every parish.' Such fears of extremism were echoed in many counties. In Kent a new petition pleaded: 'Give us a severe reformation, but not an absolute innovation.' In Somerset a plea that 'the bad clergy may be rejected and the good retained' was made.

Pym sensed serious division both in the Commons and in the counties. This would wreck whatever slim hopes he had of a constitutional and financial settlement. As the spring and summer wore on fresh efforts to abolish bishops were made, but by August Pym got his way – the bill was quietly laid aside, when it became known that the Lords would not touch it. Yet the nettle of religious discord would have to be grasped some time; also Pym realised that things had already gone too far for some who were reconsidering their loyalties. Dering was one: not yet a Royalist, he nevertheless voiced a powerful anti-Parliamentarian sentiment in Kent. As the historian Robert Ashton has written, Dering was a would-be reformer 'who consented to the opening of a religious and social Pandora's Box, and is horrified at the awful consequences of his action. All certainties were gone' (44, p. 155).

After months and months of Parliamentary work in London there was pressure from members for a respite; the first session of the Long Parliament came to an end in September 1641. The hopes of the Westminster members and the distant county communities was for a speedy settlement. Much had been done, of course: enough to pay off the Scots army in August and send them home; some would also argue that a constitutional revolution had taken place. But distrust of the King meant that divisions in the Westminster ranks must be healed so that further guarantees could be forced from Charles on oustanding issues like ministers, money and religion. In the counties a different view was held. A settlement was certainly wanted, but only as a prelude to the restoration of economic and social order. It was not to happen.

Study 5

The approach adopted in this chapter has been analytical rather than narrative. Revolutionary periods can present difficulties for students in that events and issues covering a short time-span crowd in upon themselves. The approach adopted should enable you to make sense of what was going on; yet it has the danger of being too schematic. To gain some appreciation of the confusion and lack of direction and priorities as it seemed to contemporaries, a necessary exercise at this stage is to draw up, from the details scattered through the chapter, a month-by-month chronology of the period November 1640 to September 1641. Note in what way May was a significant month.

Some important matters cannot be dated exactly (e.g. the working out of the Pym-Bedford financial scheme); so for imprecise trends and developments use lines marking several months.

CHAPTER 5

A House Divides

1641 - 42

The Long Parliament met for a second session on 20 October 1641. In view of the serious divisions of opinion which the first session had only papered over, Pym decided to restrict demands to two matters: the expulsion of bishops from the House of Lords, and the Parliamentary approval of ministers.

On Monday 1 November news arrived in Westminster of an Irish Rebellion, in which Catholics had risen against their Protestant rulers. The effect was electricifying. English political life would never be the same again. The rebellion arose from a mixture of religious and land grievances, and was serious enough to require an army to be sent to restore order. Thus, into the already confused melting-pot of English politics was thrown a totally new factor: who would command this army? The military dimension was the most alarming matter yet considered. Both Crown and Parliament agreed on the necessity of an army, raised in the usual way; yet such was the suspicion and distrust that two premises and conclusions were formulated. First, *if* the King commanded and appointed the senior officers (as tradition held), and *if* the rebellion was crushed (as expected), *then* a victorious army could return to assist Charles in a military-style counter-revolution – Parliament would be dissolved, its constitutional measures ignored, and the despotic rule of the 1630s restored. Secondly, *if* Parliament's leaders should demand (as they were doing so over the question of ministers), that the army be commanded only by approved officers, and, again, *if* the rebellion was crushed, *then* a victorious army could return to assist Pym, Hampden, Haselrig and their friends in compelling Charles to accept a much extended invasion of the Crown prerogatives. Quite how far this invasion would go was not known, but Root and Branch abolition of episcopacy and centralised parliamentary taxation were highly controversial possibilities. Each argument offended enough people to produce a massive increase in tension. Whatever unity Pym had managed to maintain in the first session vanished overnight.

The Irish Rebellion seemed to confirm Pym's claim of a papist conspiracy. Within a week he proposed to the Commons an *Additional Instruction* to be placed before Charles: that unless he 'take such counsellors as might be approved by Parliament, we should account ourselves absolved from this engagement' [i.e. not support the king in raising an army]. (6, p. 226). Members thought this too irresponsible, so on 8 November Pym amended it to read that if the King did not accept the condition, 'we should take such a course for the securing of Ireland ourselves'. Without doubt this was the most revolutionary proposal so far. In effect it would deprive the King of the most ancient of his prerogative rights, to raise and command forces in defence of the realm. Pym secured the vote: 151 to 110.

Almost at once Pym revealed the product of a twelve-month investigation into the state of the kingdom. This was the *Grand Remonstrance*, a massive indictment of Charles' misgovernment since he came to the throne, followed by a summary of Parliament's achievements so far, and ending with a series of recommendations for further reform. In all it had 204 clauses. The first hundred or so were propagandist and aggressive in tone; among the recommendations two issues stood out. There were three clauses on religion, and one on ministers of the Crown.

> 183... to reduce within bounds that exorbitant power which prelates have assumed.
> 184... it is far from our purpose or desire to let loose the golden reins of discipline... to leave private persons or particular congregations to take up what form of Divine Service they please, for we hold it requisite that there should be throughout the whole realm a conformity to the Word of God.
> 185... And the better to effect the intended reformation, we desire there may be a general synod of the most grave, pious, learned and judicious divines of this island, assisted with some from foreign parts.
> 197. His Majesty to be petitioned to employ such councillors, ambassadors and other ministers, in managing his business at home and abroad, as Parliament may have cause to confide in, without which we cannot give His Majesty such supplies for support of his own estate. (6, pp. 228–40; in full in 43, pp. 202–232)

The debate, often angry, took seven days; the final draft was put to the vote, and in the late hours of 22 November 1641 the Grand Remonstrance passed the Commons, 159 to 148. Immediately quarrelling broke out when a member called for it to be printed; swords were drawn as tempers rose. Sir Edward Dering commented, 'I did not dream that we should remonstrate downward; tell stories to the people.' He was not alone in rejecting printing as an appeal to the common people – the clauses were controversial enough for the elite of the nation, without involving the many-headed monster.

Charles ignored the nastiness of the Remonstrance when it was presented to him. He declared that he would choose his own ministers, and would preserve the Church, reiterating a declaration of some months before, that he would 'live and die in the maintenance of it.' It was a reasonable answer, taking its stand on known laws.

Meanwhile the question of Parliament's security from 'army plots' (rumours were still rife), and the problem of the relief of Ireland kept members' attention on Charles' control of the militia. In essence it concerned the power of appointment, and in principle senior army officers and Privy Council ministers were the same: both 'counselled' the King, on military and political matters respectively. Thus far humble requests to the King, even veiled threats, had achieved nothing. So on 7 December Haselrig introduced a militia bill: it intended to use statute law to give command of England's armed forces to a general and an admiral nominated by Parliament. Once more Parliament proposed to take a step down the revolutionary road. Haselrig's bill passed its first reading in the Commons by 158 to 125.

───────────────── *Study 6* ─────────────────

1 Construct some brief notes on the significance of the voting figures and the wording of the various measures from May to December 1641 (Attainder, Ten Propositions, Additional Instructions, Grand Remonstrance, Militia Bill). It is worth noting at this point that 300 + was a very high attendance in the Commons.

2 Discuss briefly the three religious clauses of the Grand Remonstrance in relation to the religious debates in the Commons in the first session and to popular pressure from outside. Why do you think Kenyon argues that the Remonstrance 'tried to smother the Church question'(6, p. 194)?

Observations:

1 The questions ask you to detect trends in a year's crowded story. Beware of labelling Pym a revolutionary. It is arguable that he began as a moderate (even in his eyes a conservative), but as Aylmer points out, 'the logic of the crisis itself' may have forced him, against his wishes, 'to adopt radical and eventually revolutionary policies in order to secure [his] conservative objectives'. (2, p. 105) On the issue of ministerial and military appointments, note that until December, Parliament with phrases like 'cause to confide in' was asking for a *veto* over the *King's choice*. How did the Militia Bill differ in the powers it gave Parliament? The voting trend is crucial. Pym's organising talents have failed to preserve even the semblance of unity. But take care not to generalise: 'First session = unity; second session = division'. The evidence points to a more complex and longer alienation process: the 'Straffordians' (those voting against Attainder) were gradually increased as members became disillusioned with Pym and his group's policies, and the image of 'King Pym' as he was called, offended many. Hyde, Falkland and Dering are examples of anti-Court men who were now hostile to Pym.

2 The *Grand Remonstrance* has always been seen as a vital document in this period. Historians have not always agreed why. Gardiner, writing in late Victorian times, was convinced that religion was crucial in creating the

split. Modern historians no longer accept this conclusion. Root and Branch plans and fears of sectarianism and Presbyterianism, so publicised early in 1641, were emphatically blurred in the Remonstrance. How? The real significance of the Remonstrance vote was that it confirmed a trend already apparent – a split in the 'Country' over the extent of possible radical measures. Hyde was deeply offended by Pym's invasion of the Crown's legal rights, and Dering, with many others, was alarmed by the appeal for popular support by printing the Remonstrance – conservative gentry and merchants felt Pym was playing a dangerous game in stirring up the 'many-headed monster' of unrest among social inferiors.

A bungled coup

If Charles had been cautious, maintaining a conciliatory approach, there is little doubt that Pym could have found himself isolated in a minority group in the Commons. A number of members, such as Hyde and Falkland, were already seeking Court favour and being granted advisory positions. They signalled the emergence of a group best labelled 'Constitutional Royalists', who would endeavour to keep the King within the bounds of existing law (a corset, but not laced too tightly). They liked to see themselves as the party of order, and quickly gained support from several county communities. A remarkable document now in the Bodleian Library in Oxford, emerged from Hereford in 1642, a county manifestly opposed to the extremes of both Royalism and Parliamentarianism:

> 'Whereas the kingdom for many years past hath groaned under taxes of loans, Ship-Money, and the like dismal effects of an arbitrary government and a high-stretched prerogative: for the Cure of which distempers a Parliament was held to be the only good old way of physicke to cleanse the body politic... but not by over-strong purgations to weaken it in the principal part... which instead of restoring it to its primitive vigour and health, must needs drive it to a fatal period. Such is our misery.'(8, p. 149).

Kent, too, emerged early in 1642 with an anti-Parliamentarian sentiment, producing another protest against extremes. The Kentish Petition became celebrated because leaders of the Commons burned the document and imprisoned some leading county gentry, including Dering and his cousin Sir Roger Twysden. As no cause was given for the arrest, Twysden drily commented, with Charles' arbitrary imprisonments of the late 1620s in mind. 'I am sure I have heard this practice enough condemned in others' (48, pp. 94 and 99).

Consistency, however, was not in Charles' character. If the image of constitutional monarchy was to be fostered, royal behaviour had to be beyond question. Yet Charles had toyed for some time with the idea of using force; opinions at Court, especially the Queen's, encouraged the idea. Charles wavered; then developments late in December 1641 panicked him. The annual elections in the City of London for the local Common Council removed many royal sympathisers; new councilmen were militants who offered support to the Parliamentary leaders. London was proving far more radical than some of the counties. Tumults, too, were becoming common. Three days of rioting against bishops disturbed the peace of the capital city as the year drew to a close.

On Monday 3 January 1642 Charles acted. He issued an order:

'Articles of High Treason: against the Lord Kimbolton, Mr Denzil Holles, Sir Arthur Haselrig, Mr John Pym, Mr John Hampden and Mr William Strode.

... that they have traitorously endeavoured to subvert the fundamental laws and government of the kingdom of England, to deprive His Majesty of his regal power...'

[plus six other charges]. (6, pp. 240–1)

The Commons refused the Speaker's order for their custody, so on the next afternoon one of the most dramatic episodes in English political history took place. Charles appeared in the Commons, walked to the Speaker's chair and called for the five members (Kimbolton, later the Earl of Manchester, was in the Lords), but they had departed a few minutes before by boat down the Thames to seek sanctuary with their new allies in the City. Not only had the King entered the Commons' chamber, where centuries of convention decreed he should not go, but he had arrived with several hundred armed men. This was the royal coup which many feared might happen. Robert Ashton has written, 'Here in all too solid flesh were the courtly villains, the threatening, trigger-happy, Cavalier ruffians – many of them allegedly papists – of popular rumour.' (44, p. 147). Yet Charles left the Commons empty-handed. Bungled coups offer the worst of all possible worlds to their perpetrators.

The King's self-evident weakness was deeply humiliating. Hyde was appalled: the image of a lawful king, which the Constitutional Royalists were building, lay for the moment in ruins. Charles, faced with a hostile capital, suddenly left Whitehall with his family for Hampton Court on 10 January; the same day the 'Five Members' returned to Westminster with vast crowds applauding their journey.

The events of December and January had done nothing to reduce the tension. Yet, although the idea of two 'sides', King Charles *versus* King Pym, was beginning to gain currency, a closer analysis reveals that each had its 'hawks' and 'doves'. For the Crown the Queen (vigorously in favour of a resort to arms) and Lord Digby did not favour the more conciliatory policies of, say, Hyde and Falkland. Divisions in the Parliamentary ranks were also well-known: with many independent country gentlemen members still not committed, and with radicals like Haselrig and Holles in full voice on occasions, Pym and Hampden occupied a middle position. Labelling Pym as an extremist was a royalist jibe that did not fit the evidence. The absence of St John from the Five Members list was curious; and it was foolish of Charles to tar Pym and Haselrig with the same brush. An approach of 'divide and rule' might have paid better dividends for the Crown.

The inevitability of conflict?

The English Civil War is conventionally dated from August 1642, when Charles raised his standard at Nottingham. This over-simplifies what was really a hesitant drift, from the political confrontation between two minority groups early in 1642, through a summer of 'cold war' propaganda and sporadic violence, to the clash of two small field armies at Edgehill in October. Selecting the point of inevitability of conflict is not easy. Conrad Russell argues for 10 January: 'hard to see any way of avoiding it [war] after the King's withdrawal from London'. (4, p. 339) But some contemporaries thought fighting was avoidable: ten days after the 10th the perceptive Symonds D'Ewes was expressing concern in the Commons lest 'the misunderstanding between us and His Majesty grow into a flame.' Also the King could, under Hyde's influence, still make concessions – early in February he agreed to the expulsion of bishops from the House of Lords.

A more obvious point of no return was the *Militia Ordinance*. The Commons had already petitioned the King on the matter of Haselrig's bill. Charles' reply was adamant: the military prerogative was 'an inseparable flower of the Crown'. Holles and Strode responded with a measure to control the militia through Lords Lieutenant who would be named and appointed by Parliament's authority. This was an ordinance, not a statute, for the King resisted all efforts to change his mind. On 2 March the Commons voted to put the kingdom in a state of defence against, as the Ordinance said, 'the blood counsels of papists and other ill-affected persons... for the safety of His Majesty's person.' (43, p. 245) Parliament still clung to the notion that the 'enemy' was not the King, but evil counsellors. The original intention of the militia bill – to suppress rebels in Ireland – was now merged with concerns nearer home!

Charles, who had moved from Hampton Court to York, decided to go to Hull, with its massive arsenal, enough for a 16,000–strong army. Sir John Hotham, its commander and a Parliamentary sympathiser, refused Charles admittance; shots were fired, and first blood was drawn on 23 April. Charles began raising troops in Yorkshire to assert his authority: ghosts of *Bellum Episcopale* moved silently across the north.

Meanwhile a vigorous propaganda war developed. Except in solidly-Parliamentarian London, every county community had small groups committed to each side; the uncommitted were pressed throughout the summer of 1642 by speeches, pamphlets and even newspapers (in 1641 the first regular, weekly newspapers devoted to English affairs had begun to appear). Few relished involvement: 8000 Cheshire people, for instance, signed a petition deploring 'that dangerous and disloyal distinction, viz. for the King or for Parliament'. Fear of social disruption had been a creeping phenomenon in the counties over the past two years, and all but tiny minorities now viewed the prospect of plundering armies with horror. Neutralism gripped provincial England, while a militant minority began raising troops (8, pp. 35–6).

June 1642 was a significant month both in the propaganda war and in the enlisting of county militias. On 1 June Parliament (now devoid of Royalist sympathisers who had been returning to their counties to muster their apathetic supporters), drew up the *Nineteen Propositions*. These implied a complete surrender by Charles: in summary, using key words from the document they demanded that

1. Privy Councillors and ministers of state shall be approved of by both Houses of Parliament.
2. The great affairs of the kingdom are proper for the High Court of Parliament.
4/5. The education of the King's children shall be approved by Parliament, and no marriage for any of the King's children without the consent of Parliament.
6. Laws against Popish recusants strictly in execution.
8. Such a reformation be made of the Church government and liturgy, as both Houses of Parliament shall advise... and a sufficient maintenance for preaching ministers throughout the kingdom.
9/16. Your Majesty be satisfied with that course that the Lords and Commons have appointed for the ordering of the militia... The military forces now attending your Majesty be removed.
13. [The King be satisfied with] what Justice Parliament may pass upon all delinquents.
17. A strict alliance with the States of the United Provinces (the Dutch) and other neighbouring princes of the Protestant religion.
... our humble desires being granted, we shall forthwith apply ourselves to regulate your present revenue. (6, pp. 244–7)

These propositions would, as Charles put it, make him 'a mere phantom of a king'. The main issue of 1641 was a *reduction* in royal power; now in the *Nineteen Propositions*, Parliament claimed the right to solve *all* the big problems of 1640: from ministers (now clearly first in order of priorities) and policy-making to religion, military and foreign affairs, and finance.

Moderates who could not stomach such extremes read evil things into Clause 13...

The King's *Answer to the Nineteen Propositions* came on 18 June. It was a calculated appeal to moderates, who had long reasoned that no one person or group was ever going to have the monopoly of political virtue and truth – so why should those chosen by Parliament to run the country necessarily be more efficient than those chosen by the King? The *Answer* became an eloquent statement of Constitutional Royalism.

There being three kinds of government among men: absolute monarchy, aristocracy and democracy *... [all these are efficient] as long as the balance hangs even between the three estates... [Each on its own]: the ill of absolute monarchy is tyranny, the ill of aristocracy is faction and division, the ills of democracy are tumults, violence and licentiousness.

In this kingdom the laws are jointly made by a King, by a House of Peers, and by a House of Commons... The government according to these laws is trusted to the king... The prince may not make use of this high and perpetual power to the hurt of those for whose good be hath it... The House of Commons (an excellent convener of liberty, but never intended for any share in government, or in the choosing of them that govern) is solely entrusted with the levy of money, and the impeaching of those who for their own ends have violated the law... The Lords, being trusted with judiciary power, are an excellent screen between the prince and the people, to assist each against the encroachments of the other. (6, pp. 21–3)

June was also the month when the rival 'authorities' began presenting demands to the counties. Parliament's *Militia Ordinance* already being circulated, was countered by the King's issue of *Commisions of Array*, the medieval writ commanding 'gentlemen of known loyalty' in the counties to muster and arm the able-bodied for royal service. The competition for a county's support dragged on through July and August; both *Ordinance* and *Array* were unpopular in the provinces. In Cheshire violence was threatened against Parliament's man - he 'had been pulled to pieces by the citizens had not the Mayor and Recorder conveyed him away with a guard'; yet the King's men were equally disliked. In Somerset, because the *Array* was in Latin, Parliamentarians translated it into the frightening prospect of crippling taxation and compulsory work for the King.

Parliament had the better initial response, and by October 1642 a force of over 20,000 was in being, claiming 'to live and die by the Earl of Essex', its Commander-in-chief. The King had a much poorer start, but a Parliamentary

---

* 'democracy' means, here, the people represented by a property-owning Commons of gentry, merchants and lawyers.

Declaration on 6 September spoke of:

> persons as have been voted by both Houses to be delinquents [to be left] to the justice of Parliament

This, of course, recapped on Clause 13 of the *Nineteen Propositions*. But an alarming statement followed:

> ... well-affected subjects who by loans have assisted the Commonwealth (ie Parliament) may be repaid out of the estates of the said delinquents. (6, p. 250)

The Declaration of the 6th could not have been more misguided or mistimed. It was a well-known fact that Parlimentarians regarded anyone not *for* them as *against* them. Many would-be neutrals took fright: uncertainty over what 'delinquency' meant led them to wonder if it included any remarks critical of the Parliamentary leadership made during the past year. With property at stake waverers suddenly moved into active support for the King. Soon 10,000 were under arms. The unwanted conflict, the English Civil War, was now unavoidable - the King not only had a party, but an army as well.

Study 7

1 Write an essay on the following:
   Trace the emergence of the King's ability to resist Parliament's encroachment on his prerogative by political argument and force.

2 Conrad Russell asserts that the start of the war was accidental, the product of 'sheer fear of the intentions of the other side... of chronic misunderstanding, terror and distrust.' (4, p. 339; 19, p. 1) Select what evidence you can to support this view from the period May 1641 to September 1642.

Observations;

1 In the 1640/early 1641 period there could have been no Civil War, as the King was isolated. Thus the clue to the immediate origins of the English Civil War lies in the emergence of a Royalist Party with both a cause and military support. Before November 1641 there is some evidence of alienation from the parliamentary leadership, but this seems more anti-parliament than pro-Charles. In what way was the Irish rebellion a catalyst? And why was the Five Member's Episode a setback? Remember the propaganda war by two minority sides to secure the allegiance of the uncommitted majority. Were the *Nineteen Propositions* too extreme? If so give examples. The King's *Answer* (though too late) was to undercut Pym's priority issue of ministerial appointments by arguing that Parliamentary power of impeachment was an effective control. Later in the enlistment

stakes it is arguable that the Parliamentary Declaration of 6 September was a disastrous blunder.

2 Russell's argument provides a useful antidote to that blood sport of historians, the hunt for the origins of the Civil War. Here it would be useful to distinguish between 1640, when the Tudor polity collapsed – which has already been explained – and 1642, when Civil War occurred – and now needs a separate explanation. There are two problems: even at the point which most historians pick as the point of inevitability, the Militia Ordinance, neither side had an army; and how does one explain the occurrence of something nobody wanted. The only explanation which makes consistent sense is that people turned to force out of apprehension – fear of what the other side might do. Your 'selections' might include:

– the 'judicial murder' of Strafford (how far would Parliament's leaders go to achieve their ends?), and the Army Plot revelations (how far would Charles' counter-revolutionary instincts take him?).
– Root and Branch – shelved, but for how long?
– suspicion in the counties that the Bedford/Pym financial settlement could be 'worse' (i.e. more expensive and more efficiently collected) than Charles' financial devices of the early 1630s.
– the Irish Rebellion: proof of Pym's claim for a papist conspiracy?
– would an army to deal with the Rebellion under either King *or* Parliament, when victorious, be used against the other?
– the Grand Remonstrance: did the 'synod of divines' herald Presbyterianism and a 'pope in every parish'?
– the Five Members: royal extremism – the emergence possibly of the King's *real* advisers? 'Cavalierism, red in tooth and claw', as Ashton calls the event.
– Ordinance versus Array: in the counties a lack of understanding and legal doubts – which to obey?
– the 'many-headed monster': the use of mob violence and where it might lead, and in particular the fear in the counties of social upheaval.
– Charles: could he be trusted to play a part in any settlement?

CHAPTER 6

The First Civil War

1642 - 46

The military outline

Summarily, the military aspects of the war were two-fold. First, a well-nigh continuous struggle for control in each county by small armed groups, some shires in the broad sweep of territory between Wessex and the Humber changing 'sides' during the war. Secondly, there were efforts by larger field armies to achieve a strategic objective – the Royalists to regain Charles' capital city, Parliament to bring an opposing army to battle and destroy it. Each year a major trial of strength took place (see map on p. 67).

At Edgehill in October 1642 two very amateur forces met each other in a drawn, confused battle; the Earl of Essex's Parliamentary army, though, had prevented the King from moving immediately to London, and a little later a small cavalry foray down the Thames by Prince Rupert halted at Turnham Green. Caution, or even loss of nerve, by the Royalists meant a long winter of planning for the next summer's campaign. Despite an excellent paper scheme, Charles' three-pronged plan to seize London with armies moving from York, Oxford and Cornwall foundered; of the four key ports, Bristol, Plymouth, Gloucester and Hull, held by Parliament and supplied by the navy, only the first fell to the King. Whether viewed as myopic parochialism or understandable self-interest, Royalist troops from Yorkshire, South Wales and Cornwall refused to move until pillaging Roundhead attacks from these ports on their families and land had been dealt with. Charles had to give up the siege of Gloucester to deal with Essex's relief army coming from London: yet another drawn engagement occurred at Newbury in 1643.

In the effort to break the deadlock by improving their forces in quantity and/or quality Parliament proved the more successful. Charles found recruitment progressively more difficult, and the prospects of help from an Irish army or the Scots Highlanders under Montrose were rendered minimal again by Parliament's naval supremacy. With the Thirty Years' War preventing either side getting significant continental support, Parliament too had to seek men from the British Isles: they found them in the Presbyterian Lowlands of Scotland, and under the Solemn League and Covenant of late 1643 a 20,000–strong Scots army moved into England. Combining with Parliament's army in Yorkshire under Sir Thomas Fairfax and its Eastern Association forces under Manchester and Cromwell, they defeated Charles' northern army reinforced from Oxford by Rupert, at the biggest battle of the war, Marston Moor near York in July 1644.

Rifts already evident politically in Parliament's cause now extended to the battlefield because its divided command failed to capitalise on Marston Moor: Essex lost in Cornwall at Lostwithiel and another drawn affair at Newbury meant 1644 was only a partial Parliamentary success. Fairfax and Cromwell, insisting now on a single, well-paid, equipped and trained force, led by determined and successful officers, obtained political support at Westminster for the Self-Denying Ordinance, which eliminated all members of the Lords (including the half-hearted Manchester and Essex) and Commons from army command; they then assembled the New Model Army in the spring of 1645. A decisive rout of Charles' remaining forces occurred in the Naseby–Langport campaign of June to September. After mopping-up operations by Parliament, Charles surrendered to the Scots in April 1646.

Allegiances

The reason for the Civil War may be briefly stated: on the critical issues which emerged from the Crisis of 1640 some progress had been made, but on three of them – ministers, finance and religion – agreement had been nil. Political deadlock developed into military confrontation when the Irish Rebellion provoked the question of the King's generals. The two 'sides' were labelled Parliament and the King.

The key division of opinion and precipitating cause of the War was over the constitutional matter of power. Leading Parliamentarians demanded that the King relinquish his executive authority; it seemed the only way they could feel secure and be sure the gains of 1640–41 were permanent. Leading Royalists regarded the Crown's concessions as sufficient, and the demands of Pym and his friends as outrageous, opening the door to unacceptable revolutionary changes in England's traditional constitution. This was the unbridgeable gap for those who felt passionately about it; but they were a tiny minority only of the political nation – insufficient to wage a civil war.

It was religion which raised the political temperature to the point where, through commitment or fear, each 'side' found enough support and the will to take up arms and fight. Some historians, like Anthony Fletcher in his very detailed book, published in 1981, *The Outbreak of the English Civil War*, go as far as to isolate this as the real cause: 'What was really at stake at the deepest level of this crisis was not the issue of the militia or appointment of councillors, the immediate expressions of political distrust, but the future of the Church.' (68, p. 416) For Parliament the general label 'Puritan' covered those who hated Catholicism, disliked bishops and Church ceremonies, and pleaded for more preaching and less emphasis on Prayer Book services. For the King were those who upheld the existing established Church, despite its imperfections. Essentially the split was 'a Godly Commonwealth' (Puritan-Parliamentarian) *versus* 'the Church of the Elizabethan Settlement' of 1559 (Anglican-Royalist). But no one quite knew what these terms meant, for each had its extremists who fell foul of moderate opinion. The thesis presented at the end of the last chapter, that war occurred because of what people *feared* the other side's radicals would do, still holds. Men like Sir Thomas Aston of Cheshire fought for the Royalist cause, because he so disliked extreme Puritans who

> under the pretext of reforming the Church... shake off the yoke of all obedience, either to ecclesiastical, civil, common, statute or customary laws of the kingdom, and introduce a more arbitrary government. (8, p. 49)

For Parliament, Puritan pamphleteers and preachers found hatred of Catholicism an easy whipping-boy. Francis Cheynell wrote in his *God's Alarum*:

> To what end should we waste time about a discourse of Hull and the militia? Come speak to the point. If a king of the Protestant profession should give his strength and power to his queen, a papist, and she give it to the Jesuits, to the Beast, it is neither rebellion nor treason to fight for the king, to recover his power out of the hands of the Beast.★ (47, p. 120).

The fact that neither Parliament nor the King intended respectively to promote anarchy and papal sovereignty was irrelevant. That they *might* do so engaged people's emotions sufficiently for enough of them to fight a war. A contemporary, Edward Walford, remarked, 'Kings and parliaments might have been quiet this day, if they would have left Israel alone.' ★★

Two opponents, each with positive support and agreed ideals, struggling for the constitution and inflamed by religious passion, has long been the conventionalised representation of the English Civil War. Yet a close analysis of people's attitudes will show that this was never really so. Each 'side' was merely an umbrella of convenience sheltering a wide spectrum of opinion on how to resolve the deadlock. More importantly, even though religion increased the numbers, those who actively pledged their honour and their estates in a trial by battle remained small. It is easy to 'count heads' at Westminster: 236 members of the House of Commons eventually became Royalists (not all at the start of the War), leaving the rest, just over half, supporting 'King Pym'. Recent research at the grass roots level of the county communities has done much to recast traditional views of the War. John Morrill concludes from all the evidence that 'side-taking for the great

---

★ The idea that Parliament fought *for* the King to remove evil counsellors and papal influence (i.e. the Beast, the Pope) was a powerful generator of support.
★★ Religious enthusiasts seeking the 'Promised Land.'

majority was largely arbitrary' (8, p. 46). David Underdown, another county historian, takes the point further: the War was 'fought between two minorities, struggling in a sea of neutralism and apathy' (46, p. 117). Religious and political argument was still crucial to the committed but not, it would seem, to the majority. The turmoil of emotions is well illustrated in the famous exchange of letters between two important military commanders, Sir William Waller and Sir Ralph Hopton. The Parliamentarian, Waller, wrote in June 1643, to his Royalist opponent:

> Hostility itself cannot violate my friendship to your person... I detest this war without an enemy... We are both upon the stage and must act the parts assigned us in this tragedy. (42, p. 341).

A strong case can be made out that the interest of the local community commanded a bigger allegiance than either of those 'abstractions', King or Parliament. Many instances of this exist in the records. Throughout the War there was a reluctance in the local militia to move beyond the county boundaries. Norfolk men stipulated in writing that any help they gave should be 'for defence of this county, not to be sent out'. Again, the power of local families exerted an almost semi-feudal influence in determining county loyalties. The Stanley family wielded enormous power in Lancashire: its head, the Earl of Derby, Lord Lieutenant and avid Royalist, ordered people to support the King's cause, 'upon pain of death to appear at general musters... and (his officers were) to shoot such as lagged behind.' In Leicestershire, as in Wiltshire, rival families whose feuds long pre-dated 1640 split each county.

Elsewhere families themselves divided or realigned. Sir Edmund Verney died at Edgehill carrying the King's standard; his son, Ralph, chose to serve Parliament, though later quarrelled with its policies and went into exile abroad. Disillusion and fear of extremists produced some remarkable changes of side. Forty-four members of the Commons who stayed to support Pym in 1642, defected to the King at various times in the next two years. The most famous were the Hothams, father and son, who joined Charles in 1643. It is an interesting speculation that had they not denied Hull to the King in the summer of 1642, (see p. 53), the Royalist fortunes of war might have been very different.

Local loyalties and self-interest drove many to opt for peace at any price. Research has revealed that neutrality pacts were attempted in twenty-two counties and in many towns. At the start of the War Devon and Cornwall seriously proposed that their 'interest' should be Parliamentarian and Royalist respectively and each would not interfere with the other! The gentry of Cheshire in August 1642 pleaded that

> The King and Parliament being like Hippocrates twins, they must laugh and cry, live and die together; and both are so rooted in our loyal hearts that we cannot disjoint them. (8, p. 159).

Evidence too has been found of a strong current of neutralism in East Anglia, once thought to be the bastion of Puritan/Parliamentary power. Elsewhere boroughs, Salisbury, Worcester and Lincoln, for example, regarded the war in terms of a trading disaster rather than a conflict of ideals, and sought to shut their gates against *all* 'foreigners'. Individual efforts to avoid commitment verged on the comic. Lord Dacre in east Sussex retired in late 1642 to his yacht in the seclusion of the Pevensey Marshes, and replied to letters requesting his active support with vague references that 'the highways were extremely clogged with snow'; yet throughout the war he entertained lavishly senior Parliamentary *and* Royalist guests. In Cheshire several of the gentry paid money to both sides, only to find themselves persecuted by both sides.

If anything neutralism grew as the war progressed. While bitterness and venom engulfed the upper strata of county society, at the lower levels also a most remarkable development occurred in 1645, known as the Clubmen (8, pp. 98–111). In ten counties in the midlands and central southern England a militant peasant–yeoman farmer movement gathered force. It began spontaneously as villagers lashed out at marauding soldiers: quite ordinary men of Dorset got together in May 'to preserve ourselves from plunder'. Then the local gentry took up the leadership and formed Clubmen Associations with positive aims. Each claimed widespread support: Dorset and Wiltshire said they could raise 20,000 men in 48 hours, while Berkshire Clubmen had 16,000 on its lists. Possibly exaggerated, these numbers still presented serious problems for the campaign plans of both King and Parliament. Clubmen petitions found a ready audience. The nation was 'bleeding under the devouring sword', said one. A Somerset Clubmen document commented pointedly on Parliament's claim to be fighting against the King's 'evil counsellors': 'for it is possible that a Parliament may err (and that foully) as well as a general Council'. The Clubmen demanded a withdrawal of field armies from their counties and a restoration of their customary local rights. The best exposition of this came on 26 September 1645 when the Sussex Clubmen published a 'humble remonstrance', complaining of:

1 The want of Church government, whereby our churches are decayed, God's ordinances neglected.
2 For three years we have through much labour and God's blessing gained the fruit of the earth, and had hoped to enjoy the same, but by free quarter [billeting] and plunder of soldiers our purses have been exhausted... we are disabled to pay our rents, just debts and to maintain our wives and families from utter ruin.
3 The insufferable, insolent, arbitrary power that hath been used amongst us, contrary to all our ancient known laws...
4 Now we shall endeavour to defend the frontiers of the county, that all the taxes imposed by Parliament we may be abated in a moderate way. (59, Tanner Ms. 60. fo. 254)

The Clubmen, then, were as hostile to Parliament's centralising policies as the 'Country' of 1640 to those of the Crown. Concern for local autonomy, one of the key issues of the 1640 Crisis, had become a casualty of war. Of those who sincerely and actively defended this concern by proclaiming 'a plague on both your houses', most found themselves swallowed by the war machine; the Clubmen suffered worst, defeated in numerous skirmishes by the more disciplined and experienced soldiers of King and Parliament alike.

Few subjects have perplexed historians more in recent years than the issue of 'the choosing of sides' in the English Civil War. In 1954 Brunton and Pennington spelt out the essence of the problem:

> Men are not usually in the habit of weighing in their minds a pennyworth of political liberty against an ounce of religious freedom, and assessing the effect of either on their bank-balance before engaging in an armed struggle, and we can hardly disentangle for them their own confusion of motives. (69, p. 1).

Parliament's hollow military victory

Parliament 'won' the Civil War in the strict sense that, by 1646, after four years of fighting, Royalist armies had been defeated on the battlefield, pockets of armed resistance had been overcome, and Charles had surrendered. The reasons for this military victory, overwhelming and inevitable as it seemed from the vantage point of 1646, lay in the slow emergence of three factors: first, the Royalist failure to solve the problem of provincialism; secondly, Parliament's political and military leadership; and thirdly, the effective Parliamentary marshalling of resources. The issue remained in doubt until the summer of 1645, when within one month the campaigns of Naseby and Langport destroyed the King's field armies.

In the beginning the Royalist chances looked reasonable. The King at least had a clearly defined purpose: the recovery of his capital city. Perhaps only timidity after the harrowing experience of Edgehill in 1642 prevented a successful Royalist seizure of London. In the event a winter in Oxford planning a three-pronged assault on the capital gave the King what on paper seemed a great opportunity. Early successes in the spring of 1643 raised his hopes as three thrusts from the south-west, from the Oxford area and from Yorkshire got under way. But each was halted within months by currents of localism: because of Parliamentary control of key garrisons in Plymouth, Gloucester and Hull, Royalist soldiers with strong local ties would not agree to fight beyond their region. The fear that their families and homes would be subject to rape and plunder by forces from the three ports was not an idle one; yet besieging them meant delay which Charles could ill afford.

Provincialism struck twice at the Royalist military effort. The abortive execution of the 1643 plan was serious enough, but over the next two years a more insidious form of localism affected the Royalists. The preservation of county interests bedevilled attempts to establish a well-paid national force commanded from the King's headquarters at Oxford. As the war proceeded Charles acquiesced and allowed local control of parts of his army. Its impact on the King's forces was soon apparent: the money required from the counties to maintain field armies slumped. As John Morrill concludes, 'Financial thrombosis killed the Royalist cause' (8, pp. 113–14).

Parliament, of course, faced the same problems. But in the political arena the leadership until his death in 1643 of John Pym, and then of Fairfax and Cromwell on the battlefield, brought sufficient energy, ruthlessness and centralised direction to the cause to allow an effective use of Parliament's considerable resources. Pym's difficulties were enormous. An executive capable of directing the war had to be created from scratch; this problem was at the root of Charles' contemptuous reference to his enemy's War Council: 'that committee of 400!' Pym's leadership was never fully assured: rather he led a middle group between two others, best labelled peace and war factions. The peace faction of Denzil Holles and the Earl of Essex viewed the war with horror and pressed for a negotiated settlement on the basis of the measures of 1641. The war radicals included Haselrig, Sir Henry Vane the Younger and the most extreme figure of all, Henry Marten (whose republican views led to his expulsion from the Commons in 1643); their policy was the King's unconditional surrender followed by a dictated peace. The middle group led by Oliver St John after Pym's death wanted a compromise peace based on the 1641 measures plus the safeguards of control of the militia and the nomination of Charles' councillors. Each of the three groups had about thirty supporters in an active Commons' membership (i.e. regular attendance) of about 200 (23, pp. 59–64). Yet Pym in the early part of the war held this discordant crew together; he became, as a contemporary recognised, 'the director of the whole machine'.

C.H. Firth, the early twentieth-century historian, wrote, 'The history of the Civil War is the history of the evolution of an efficient army out of chaos.' The verdict survives, but with reservations. There was little military experience available in 1642 and, with only a short defensive war expected, most 'armies' were county-based and very amateur. Later groupings such as the Earl of Manchester's Eastern Association were additional to the main force of the Lord General, the Earl of Essex, and produced tangled lines of command; the entry of the Scots early in 1644 as an independent army with its own commanders made matters worse. The hesitant behaviour of Essex and Manchester angered Cromwell, who reckoned Marston Moor had been bungled. What was needed was a national force, free of local county loyalties, drilled, well-paid and uniformed. What emerged was the New Model Army under Sir Thomas Fairfax. It was not immediately characterised by Cromwell's ideal; rather it was a hastily put-together body of reluctant conscripts. Its later invincible reputation was far from apparent in June 1645 when it narrowly defeated the King at Naseby. Cromwell's cavalry on the New Model's right wing and the absence from the King's army of 3000 horse (which had to be dealt with later at Langport) were the vital ingredients of victory. The 'efficient army' of Firth's assessment was only fashioned *after* Naseby. (Note that Cromwell was never an army commander in the first Civil War; yet his military advice at Westminster, his superb cavalry tactics, and his remarkable training and leadership of men contributed much to Parliament's victory.)

The third factor was resources. These have often been summarised: Parliament controlled London with its 'supply' of men, its city monies, its great port attracting trade like a magnet, and its Tower armoury; the fleet, in fair shape ironically because of Ship Money, declared for Parliament in July 1642 – its eighteen men-of-war and twenty-four armed merchantmen crucial in supplying beleaguered ports like Hull and Plymouth; the economically prosperous East Anglian and Yorkshire woollen areas gave Parliament much support. Stated thus the wonder is that the Royalists lasted so long. Yet these points were not all that they seem. Neutralism certainly restricted Parliament's effective use of resources. John Kenyon makes two further points. The navy was 'more ornamental than useful', as it was never employed in the really dangerous function of transporting soldiers for combined operations behind enemy lines. Also 'the City was a fickle and unruly jade, difficult to control and expensive to feed'; cheap bread became a regular mob demand (3, p. 147).

Only one factor emerges as fundamental and undisputed in an evaluation of Parliament's victory: financial organisation. It was Pym's achievement to lay the foundation in 1643 for the centralised and often ruthless acquisition of enough money to feed the war machine. County Committees of leading Parliamentary gentry were set up to supervise the collection of the Weekly Pay (later called Monthly Assessment). This was a fixed amount from each county with local assessors dividing the total among all householders. Though it was essentially the same as the Bedford/Pym financial scheme of May 1641 (modelled, as we have seen, on Ship Money), the exigencies of war removed much of Parliament's previous hostility. Begun in February 1643, it was remorselessly collected, with arrears never being written off, and was to continue until 1660. In Kent, one of the most heavily burdened counties, it averaged £100,000 per annum in 1645–46, and represented an equivalent income tax of 12p in the pound. Comparisons were staggering. Kent paid more in Assessment in a *month* than it had paid in Ship Money in a *year*; it was equivalent to paying an Elizabethan or early Stuart Parliamentary subsidy every *fortnight*. Yet generalisations are difficult: its success in Kent and Sussex had no parallel in Cheshire and parts of East Anglia, where delays were chronic. Sequestrations were also supervised by the County Committees, enabling them to seize estates and the personal effects of 'delinquents' – now defined simply as known Royalists and Papists. Again the differences in efficiency between counties was remarkable. In Cheshire they were the most significant source of revenue for the Parliamentary cause; in Sussex the whole process was dogged by administrative difficulties; while in Kent, in Alan Everitt's pointed phrase, 'the mountains laboured and brought forth a fiscal mouse.' (48, p. 160) Another device of Pym's was the Excise, a kind of sales tax on goods like tobacco and beer (even home-brewed beer); it was effective in some areas, though it was grossly unpopular. Given the reservations of untidiness, delay and resistance, the provision of cash for the Parliamentary cause was a great achievement. Over a million pounds per year was the lifeline which kept the armies in being. Unwillingly, provincial England found its wealth, in unparalleled measure, realistically being harnessed to the needs of Parliament's version of central government. The architect of it all was John Pym, whose ghost presided in magisterial fashion over Parliament's eventual victory in 1646.

Parliament won the war, but lost the peace. The Royalist, Sir Jacob Astley, commented on his enemy's 'triumph': 'Go play... unless you fall out amongst yourselves.' He was not making an inspired glimpse into the future, because the alliance of individuals called 'Parliament' was widely known to be under extreme strain. We have seen that from the start of the war Pym and St John's Middle Group had held together quite discordant views on Parliament's aims. Also new factors had emerged as a *result* of the war – to such an extent that any attempt to measure 'victory' in 1646 against the aims Parliament set out with in 1642 becomes impossible. Three examples may be cited.

A celebrated open quarrel between the Earl of Manchester and Oliver Cromwell in the Council of War in November 1644 revealed how two years of military frustration could produce savage argument about Parliament's role and aims.

> *Manchester*: 'It concerns us to be wary, for in fighting we venture all to nothing. If we fight a hundred times and beat him [the King] ninety-nine times, he will still be king. But if he beat us but once, or the last time, we shall be hanged.'
> *Cromwell*: 'If this be so, why did we take up arms at first? This is against fighting ever hereafter.' (58, nos. 148–60)

The Scots' alliance too caused much heart-searching. The Solemn League and Covenant of 1643 was the price Pym paid for a 20,000-strong Scots army to help Parliament. The Scots, little concerned with English constitutional arguments, pressed for the establishment of Presbyterianism in England after the war. However in its final version the Solemn League's first clause referred

Map 1: The English Civil Wars, 1642–46 and 1648

to the intended reformation as being 'according to the Word of God, and the example of the best reformed churches' (6, p. 264). The disparity between this convenient vagueness and the precision of Scottish expectations promised only mischief when the time came to honour pledges. Besides, Cromwell was not alone in claiming that the religious exclusiveness of Scottish Presbyterian theocracy was not what was being contended.

A third factor was the New Model Army. Its centralised control raised fears in the county communities, as did the presence in it of Cromwell's 'plain russet-coated captains'. These men were not necessarily of gentry status and mutterings about social upstarts rumbled through the traditional ruling households of England. Denzil Holles recalled in his 'Memoirs' his fear of social revolution, of that 'great evil, that servants should ride on horses' (23, p. 59). He was referring not only to the army, but to ominous trends in the County Committees. The old gentry leadership in many shires was being thrust aside by energetic new men, the lesser gentry and urban citizenry from lower down the social scale.

Thus, when the fighting petered out in the summer of 1646 the county gentlemen in Parliament pondered the legacy of the Scots connection, their distrust of the New Model Army, the base membership and power of the County Committees, but most of all how to deal with a king who would concede nothing. Charles, defiant in defeat, had informed Prince Rupert: 'I must tell you that God will not suffer rebels and traitors to prosper, nor this cause to be overthrown.' It augured ill for a peaceful healing of the kingdom's divisions.

―――――――――――――――――― *Study 8* ――――――――――――――――――

1 You will need to make notes on the military conflict; an atlas is essential. Avoid an over-simple list of a score or so of encounters. Bear the following points in mind. Wars are rarely 'won' on the battlefield; campaigns are more important than battles, and the logistics of a campaign are as worth investigating as the leadership qualities on each side. The errors of Edgehill, 1642; parochial attitudes and the King's Plan of 1643; the lost opportunity of the great 1644 Marston Moor campaign and its clash of personalities; how Naseby and Langport proved decisive – a study of these themes will give a pattern to the war. But wars have to be paid for, soldiers trained, allies recruited, talented leaders discovered – all within a framework of political decision-making about how best to secure victory. The best accounts are those which take these factors into account. There is a short, stylish account in Ivan Roots, *The Great Rebellion*, pp. 73–101; but for length Austin Woolrych's *Battles of the English Civil War*, chs. 2–6, will repay study.

2 The most important historical writing on the Civil War period over the past twenty years has been on the local and regional aspects, i.e. the county communities. How important this research has been in modifying long-held opinions can be seen by taking two remarks from one of the standard works on the seventeenth century – Christopher Hill's *Century of Revolution* (first published in 1961, slightly amended in 1981). On page 121 he writes: 'If we want to understand the Civil War a glance at maps... [shows that] support for Parliament came from the economically advanced south and east of England.' Hill's problem was that none of the important county surveys had been published when he was writing his book, whereas today it is fair comment that maps showing the south and east 'for Parliament' and the north and west 'for the King' are misleading. In this book check back, for instance, to references to Kent, Sussex and East Anglia. You will also find it an instructive exercise to examine at least one of the four most significant publications in this field (up to 1983), and see how it compares with earlier views of Civil War issues and loyalties:

Alan Everitt, *The Community of Kent and the Great Rebellion*, Leicester U.P., 1966.
David Underdown, *Somerset in the Civil War and Interregnum*, David & Charles, 1973.

John Morrill, *Cheshire, 1630–1660*, OUP, 1974.
Anthony Fletcher, *A County Community in Peace and War: Sussex, 1600–1660*, Longman, 1975.

Everitt has also written a 30-page pamphlet on 'The Local Community', published by the Historical Association in 1969; Morrill's *The Revolt of the Provinces* (Allen & Unwin, 1976, second edition, Longman, 1980) is the best one-volume survey. Only three urban areas have been researched, London by Pearl, 1961, Newcastle by Howell, 1967, and Norwich by Evans, 1979. There are some specialist surveys, but most books published before 1960 tend to emphasise only military affairs. If you find these themes interesting, a visit to your local county library could begin a profitable enquiry.

Christopher Hill's second remark (on p. 60) was 'Papists were solidly Royalist in the Civil War'. Keith Lindley, writing in 1973 (47, p. 174), has challenged this verdict by surveying many of the local studies. In Suffolk, a strongly Parliamentarian county, only four per cent of all known Catholics were Royalist; this was remarkable as the county had in past years witnessed some bad anti-popery rioting. In a leading Royalist county, Yorkshire, of 110 Catholic gentry families in the North Riding, only 45 supported the King. Lindley examined 1,511 Catholic families in nine counties: 82 per cent preferred neutrality. Whichever county you have chosen to study, find whether or not it fits Lindley's findings. Hill's book is still a valuable and challenging survey of the century, and is especially good on economic issues and on Puritanism; but criticisms of some of his conclusions show how much specialised research has been and is being done. Lindley has himself been criticized on some of his findings (70, pp. 26–38), so you will understand how uncertain and controversial some of these matters are.

CHAPTER 7

A Recalcitrant King
1646-48

The Newcastle Propositions

The war solved nothing because solutions to unresolved issues of the 1640 Crisis were not directly contingent upon the defeat of the Royalist field armies and the personal surrender of Charles. Yet Parliamentarians had gone to war in precisely that expectation: the 'war party' believing that total defeat would leave Charles no option but to sign proscriptive terms; the 'peace party' believing that a show of strength would bring Charles sufficiently to his senses for him to negotiate terms. These terms should provide some kind of answer to questions

- of the legislature's voice in restraining the executive's power (particularly in the appointment of ministers and control of the militia)
- of the raising of revenue and its disbursement
- of religious diversity and conformity
- of the amount of central control which the county communities would tolerate.

An illusion existed. Parliament's belief was that Charles would keep not only to the letter, but also to the spirit of any agreement. How pathetically naive this was revealed itself when Charles, having surrendered to the Scots in the North, received the *Newcastle Propositions*, sent to him by Holles, St John and other leading Westminster politicians in July 1646. In essence the terms were Nineteen Propositions of 1642 plus the Scots agreement of 1643:

Clause 2 required Charles 'to swear and sign the late Solemn League and Covenant';
Clause 3 called 'for the utter abolishing and taking away all archbishops and bishops';
Clause 5 for the 'reformation of religion according to the Covenant be settled by Act of Parliament';
Clause 12 required an act 'for the raising of money as shall be agreed on by both Houses of Parliament';
Clause 13 stated 'that the Lords and Commons shall during the space of twenty years arm, train and discipline all the forces of the kingdom.';
Clause 16 was lengthy and precise on the matter of the King's advisers: it

named 57 leading Royalists as 'persons who shall expect no pardon for treason'; and 48 others who would 'be removed from His Majesty's counsels'. The first group included Prince Rupert, the Earl of Bristol and Lord Digby, the Earl of Newcastle, George Goring, Sir Edward Hyde and the Earl of Montrose. The feelings of the county communities were not mentioned (43, pp. 291–300).

The King, aware of the unease which existed in the ranks of his late enemies and of the opportunities for bargaining in the Propositions, evaded an immediate answer. Charles, who enjoyed a game of chess and played much while he waited until January 1647 for the Scots and Parliament to arrange his transfer to London, might well have meditated on the manoeuvrings around him. Five pieces on the political chessboard could be distinguished. Some regarded Charles as a mere pawn, but he ought to have been seen more properly as the King, at the moment bereft of power, but still the key to the ultimate end-game. He was convinced of this role and with some justification. His efforts to wrest something from the ashes of military defeat were certainly not hopeless: to many of the gentry, fearful of some of the radical ideas current at the end of the war, the King was still the guarantee of stability, custom and social order. In attempting to play off his opponents he was perhaps guilty of prevaricating too long, but, as Aylmer has argued, it was only 'a narrow miscalculation' (28, p. 4).

What made a permanent settlement difficult, even unlikely, was the existence of four other 'chess-pieces'. The Scots had limited power of movement; they could only react to the changing English political scene. They were the knights of the board, for they began moving, albeit uneasily, with Holles and the Newcastle Propositions, but later changed direction and struck their own, private, bargain with the King. For the moment in 1646, they were critical of the Propositions, and even Charles understood the vague implications of lay control in Clause 5, which did not suit the strict theocratic ideas of the Scots. Another 'piece' was a London group called Levellers, attempting to make some ideological sense out of the formless, shadowy appetite of the 'many-headed monster'. Again we shall see its leaders divided in personality and interest, especially as the Levellers acquired support from the rank-and-file of the New Model Army. These leaders were the pawns in the power-game, potentially exceedingly dangerous for they could become queens and dominate the board. How they grasped the revolutionary opportunity in November 1647, but lost it through lack of ruthlessness and support will emerge as an interesting side-show of the years 1646–48.

The 'Peace Party' and the 'War Party', papered-over cracks in the Parliamentary side during the war, now became explicit divisions. Denzil Holles led the 'peace' majority in the House of Commons (now enlarged by the 'Recruiter' elections of 1645, when the seats left vacant by the exit of the Royalists in 1642 were filled – even so the average attendance was a mere 150). On the face of it Parliament's victory should have resulted in Holles negotiating a settlement with the King based on the Newcastle Propositions. But the existence of the other 'pieces', plus the fact that Scottish Presbyterianism and the continuation of the County Committees were most unpopular policies, meant that Holles' freedom of movement was restricted. Many of his old colleagues were no longer there: men of the stature of Bedford, Pym and Hampden were dead, and Essex was to die in 1646, Holles' party, then, can only be regarded as a castle on the board: important, but limited in role.

The real power in the kingdom belonged undoubtedly to the chess Queen: the 'War Party' of Vane, Haselrig, Cromwell and Henry Ireton. Its single-mindedness might be said to have brought the war to a successful conclusion, and their possession of the sword, i.e. the New Model Army, would give it a powerful voice in any real settlement, despite being in a minority in the House of Commons. It was bitterly hostile to the Covenanting clauses of the Newcastle Propositions. Even this group could hardly claim to be united: Fairfax, the army commander, was not interested in politics; an important colonel, Thomas Rainsborough, supported the Levellers; while Henry Marten's womanising and republican views made him a social outcast. There were, of course, no bishops on the political chessboard; episcopacy was abolished by Parliamentary ordinance in October 1646.

With five competing elements on the political scene a stalemate seemed inevitable. But perhaps the chess analogy is too neat. Despite Charles' wishful thinking there was no chess-master controlling the pieces, and demonstrably there was no simple black and white choice of options. Serious rifts in groups and hesitancy in individuals produced a confused three-year period. It was a time of leaden immobility and irresolution punctuated by mercurial conduct and precipitant events. At the end of it a recalcitrant King would face accusers intent on regicide.

Presbyterians and Independents

In explaining the course of events an involved problem for historians is the provision of sensible labels. We have already noted that 'Parliament' during the Civil War was merely a convenient title for a coalition representing a spectrum of opinion. 'The Scots', too, did not represent a single policy: in the twelve months after the end of the war internal political manoeuvring brought to power men who wished to be more accommodating with Charles. In England the terms 'War Party' and 'Peace Party' quickly ceased to be useful once the fighting ended; contemporaries, however, used words which bristle with ambiguities. For instance, 'Presbyterians' and 'Independents' seem acceptable labels for religious groups which had developed since 1640 from the more general term, Puritans – the one favouring a strict, centralised, elder-controlled church government; the other believing in congegationalism, which meant that each congregation should be independent of superior authority. But widely varying opinions existed within each group: there were tolerant and intolerant Presbyterians; some Independents accepted the idea of a national church but not the sectarian offshoots like the Baptists; some, like Nathaniel Fiennes, straddled both, claiming the names were invented 'by the Devil to cast a ball of contention and division in all companies, stirring animosities' (23, p. 22).

The most confusing problem was the use of Presbyterian and Independent as *political* labels. They emerged as party terms late in the Civil War and they stuck after the War was over. The linking of Holles Peace Party with the Scots, and of the radical War Party with congregationalists like Oliver Cromwell in the New Model Army gave birth to the Presbyterian Party and Independent Party respectively. These were political groupings, but their membership did *not* coincide exactly with the religious ones. For instance, Edward Hyde said Haselrig was 'as to religion perfectly presbyterian', yet he was a political Independent. And between the two Parties lay St John's Middle Group, plus an important bloc of uncommitted country gentlemen. The policies of these loose political units are summarised as follows.

The Presbyterians, the biggest party in the Commons, were fairly conservative constitutionally, believing in a negotiated, compromise settlement on the big issues with the King. However devious and dilatory Charles might be, it was crucial to keep pressing for agreement through proposals and conferences – it was believed that the use of force would not produce an acceptable working relationship between the executive and the legislature. On a Church settlement, by and large they favoured a state-controlled Presbyterian Church, not simply because of the Scots Covenant, but because of its exclusiveness: control in the parishes by elders of gentry origin represented the best hope for social peace in the localities. Its immediate objectives were the King's signature on the *Newcastle Propositions*, and the disbandment of the expensive New Model Army.

The Independent Party, with a regular fifty or so attendance in the Commons, depended for its survival on support from the Middle Group. This radical – moderate alliance was to be the key to the events of the next decade. It was anti-Scot, favoured liberty of religious conscience, and demanded that the New Model be kept in being as a guarantee that Charles would accept important checks on his prerogative. The radicals in this alliance were difficult to contain: we shall see sectarian idealism and militant political demands from parts of the army appearing in these years. For some supporters of these views the position of the King on the political chessboard was seen as an irrelevancy. 'Should anything happen to disturb the alliance, the Independent Party would be destroyed. The army and the radicals would be out of control, and the result would be revolution,' writes Professor Underdown (23, p. 75). Unrest in the provinces and a scheming king would do just that.

Unrest in the provinces

The gentry of provincial England were shocked by what they regarded as the pointlessness of the Civil War. The ideals of 1642 had been brutalised by the needs of military conflict. There was a desperate irony in the complaints of the post-war years, which mirrored the complaints of the 1630s: Coat-and-Conduct Money, Ship Money and Church canons had gone; but the New Model Army, County Committees and something approaching ecclesiastical anarchy now replaced them as targets for displeasure. Centralisation *versus* local autonomy was still a struggle as rancorous as ever. A jury petition from Devon in 1647 declared that the War had brought,

> after so large expense of blood and treasure, only the exchange of men in places, but not of manners, old burdens with new names, and new men with old corruptions. (8, p.53)

The official cost of armies during the War was bad enough. Quartering and plundering were just as burdensome: the first compelled private householders to give a free room and food to soldiers (it cost Cheshire £120,000 during the War, more than all taxation); the second meant the seizure of a person's possessions (one small Cheshire village had 51 horses taken). There was thus a high expectation that army costs would cease immediately the war was over. The New Model Army was still there, however, early in 1647. With the Independents at Westminster wanting to keep the army for political reasons, and the Presbyterians facing huge arrears of pay before demobilisation, the prospects of England being rid of it as a problem looked thin.

The County Committees were just as unwanted. The new men who had encroached on traditional gentry family preserves offended many with their radical attitudes, the range of their functions (e.g. control over militia, tax collection and church appointments), and their power of arbitrary arrest. The War could no longer be used as an excuse for ruthlessness. William Strode (one of the Five Members of January 1642), in declaring in February 1647 that Committeemen were 'all rogues', was appealing to traditional county sentiment. Strode came from Somerset, as did another MP, Clement Walker, regarded as the typical conservative voice of the gentry, the old 'Country'. In a tract he wrote,

> If there be any intention to restore our laws and liberties, and free us from arbitrary government, it is fit that these Committeemen be laid down...

[their power] was far higher than ever Strafford or Canterbury (Laud) durst advise the King to exercise. (44, p. 287)

A third factor in provincial discontent was religion, because the gentry saw control of the pulpit as essential for secular propaganda as well as spiritual purposes: it circulated information carefully designed to preserve law and order and maintain the old social hierarchies. So when Parliament endorsed a presbyterian form of worship and the use of the *Directory of Worship* in June 1646, the way seemed open for lay control and stern moral discipline exercised through elders, who would most likely be of the gentry. In places this occurred. In Bolton, in Lancashire, two ministers worked with twelve lay elders in examining people to see if they were 'morally fit' to receive communion; tickets were issued to those who 'passed', which had to be given in to an elder before an act of communion. This provoked much hostility. Elsewhere the substitution of elders for churchwardens never took place. Many ministers were episcopally ordained from pre-war days, and decided to conform to the new system but in practice they conducted their services much as always.

It was evident that English Presbyterianism differed importantly from the strict Scots version in that it was a voluntary system, dependent on the initiatives of the local clergy and laity (28, pp. 107–110). Yet in thousands of parishes serious practical problems existed. Were tithes still to be paid? How much toleration should be allowed? Should a separatist church, or 'gathered congregation' as it was called, be allowed to exist in a parish parallel with an official Presbyterian system? Who should be expelled (there was a committee for testing 'scandalous ministers', which in practice meant the removal of Royalist sympathisers), and how should empty pulpits be filled? In Somerset 100 ministers were ejected, and yet by July 1646 a complaint was recorded that 'our Committees have filled many churches with vile, wretched men, worse than some they put out' (46, p. 145).

Doubts about the right answers to these questions produced many versions of the 'godly'. With the ecclesiastical courts gone, and presbyterian elder control patchy, conservatives could only witness with horror the impact of the wilder ideas. A contemporary, Thomas Edwards collected in his book *Gangraena* examples of many 'heresies' and scandals: he found some people rejecting the idea of sin and hell – 'There is no Hell, but in this life'; 'Adultery was no sin'; and being drunk was 'a help to see Christ the better by' (4, p. 362). A sect called the Ranters denied the existence of sin, and their appearance confirmed in Presbyterian minds that toleration was misguided. Over the next decade Independency splintered further: other groups like the Fifth Monarchists and the Quakers held ideas which suggested anarchy, because they denied all civil authority. But there were limits. Leading Independents preached liberty of conscience, but excluded Papists, Ranters and Quakers. In 1648 General Ireton, Cromwell's son-in-law, raised the question of toleration in the Army Council: should there be liberty, he asked, 'to practise idolatry, to practise atheism and anything that is against the light of God? (4, p. 370).

Unease at the continued existence of the army, resentment of the Committees and fear of radical religion combined to produce, says John Morrill, 'an England more clearly on the verge of anarchy than at any other time in the century,' in the summer of 1647. Over the past year petitions had been pouring into Parliament from the moderate gentry in the counties. For instance, Dorset presented a 10,000-signature Petition in June 1648:

> We surviving inhabitants of the much despised and distressed County of Dorset, having, like the rest of the kingdom, long groaned under the oppressive tyranny of those whom we reputed our redeemers... demand the speedy introduction of our imprisoned King to sit personally in the House of Peers... That we may have a just and speedy account of all our monies and estates, cheated or wrested from us by taxes, excise or plunder... That we may no longer subjugate our necks to the boundless lusts and unlimited power of beggarly and broken Committees, consisting generally of the tail of the gentry. (8, p. 203)

Revolt was at hand. It broke out first in Kent. Parliament had in 1644 passed an ordinance proscribing festivals, especially the blatantly pagan rites of Yuletide, which had been grafted on to 'Christ's Mass' in early medieval times. It was unevenly obeyed, and late in 1647 the Kent County Committee issued an order requiring strict observance of the Ordinance. On Christmas Day Canterbury rioted: pagan holly was hung on doors, a puritan minister was pelted with mud, and cries of 'For God, King Charles and Kent' were heard. Order was restored, but by the time the rebels were put on trial five months later, the Committee found itself isolated; the jury refused to convict. A Committee pamphlet spoke despairingly of 'the malignity of the humour of Kent (which) had putrefied and corrupted almost the whole county, gentry and all.' Meetings and petitions were supported by 600 of the county's leading families: it was a massive protest against Parliamentary rule, with its Army, Committees and over-taxation. It was, says Everitt, 'the last of the great local insurrections of English history' (48, p. 241), and formed a significant element, as we shall see, in the Second Civil War of 1648. Its fortunes were merged with a revival of royalism and of the King's expectations; its outcome must await a consideration of national events which ran parallel with the local unrest of the years 1647–48.

The Army Revolt 1647

Early in 1647 the Scots handed Charles over to Parliament, who placed him in elegant custody in Northamptonshire, at Holdenby House. He quietly worked on his final answer to the *Newcastle Propositions*, which he presented on 18 May. He would like the twenty-year militia control reduced to ten, and offered to discuss a form of Presbyterian church settlement; he would not, however, allow his supporters to be persecuted, as suggested in Clause 16. It was clear that Charles had no intention of giving up his right to choose his ministers or of accepting a permanent loss of military appointments. Expectation of a compromise settlement rose at Westminster; but by now Holles was no longer in control. The army intervened.

Many legends have grown up about the New Model Army at the end of the War – its discipline and high morale, the fiery godliness of some of its chaplains and rank-and-file, its political consciousness and Leveller influence, the iron determination of leaders such as Cromwell. Most were hindsight creations of later years. In fact Naseby was unexpected ('the success is hardly imaginable', wrote a contemporary); only a few radical preachers have been identified in the army in 1646, and their roles were certainly overplayed; as were the roles of the Levellers, who until 1647 never expected much from the the soldiers. And Cromwell was not even a soldier: his army commission lapsed in July 1646, and he was not invited to rejoin until June of the following year.

However, this army had a grievance: pay. The most recent and authoritative estimate has been made by Dr Ian Gentles (71, p. 49) – the whole arrears of all armed forces in the period 1642 to 1647 was, he says, a massive £3 million. More immediately the New Model itself in March 1647 was owed 18 weeks for its foot soldiers and 43 weeks for its cavalry, though army records indicate that the soldiers would have been willing to settle for 16 weeks 'on account'. At about £180,000 the City bankers could have been approached for a loan. Yet these were figures which Holles and his Presbyterian Party in the Commons did not wish to contemplate. Parliament was in a precarious fiscal state. Assessment and Excise collection had fallen off badly since Naseby. How could it impose *extra* demands to clear the arrears or pay-off loans? In any case Holles was busy plotting: first, to be rid of the New Model, partly by disbanding and partly by sending it to Ireland, still unsettled since 1641, which would mean the reduction in the Independent Party's influence, and secondly, to form a new army uninfluenced by Cromwellian Ironside tradition to secure his own position of power.

The first event gave no hint of the revolution to follow. It was merely a petition in March 1647 by the soldiers to Fairfax to get Parliament to settle their pay and to provide for warwidows as a pre-condition of service in Ireland. When Holles heard of it his response was provocative. The House of Commons *Journals* record his statement:

> the petition tending to put the Army into distemper and mutiny; to put conditions on Parliament, and obstructing the relief of Ireland... (those supporting it) were enemies to the State and disturbers of the public peace.
> (Commons Journals V, 127)

Holles quickly followed this up by naming eight known Presbyterians to command key regiments. Then, on 25 May, the Commons voted for an immediate disbandment of the New Model infantry, beginning with Fairfax's regiment, and offering only eight weeks' back pay.

The effect was spectacular. The New Model Army turned in the space of a few months from a mere fighting force into a political animal. Its resentment at Holles' remarks on its petition galvanised the rank-and-file. Declarations were issued: one gave a view of MPs as 'foxes who lurk in their dens'; another described the Irish expedition as 'a design to ruin and break this Army into pieces'. Militants in threatened cavalry units elected regimental representatives called 'agitators', who would publicise complaints. For the moment the senior army officers could but follow or be driven out as suspected Presbyterians. Fairfax later said,'We were carried away as in a torrent.' He invited Cromwell to return to the army as an active senior officer, but Cromwell hesitated.

Then, on 3 June, Cornet George Joyce with a body of soldiers took charge of Charles at Holdenby, and on the following day removed him to the army's custody at Newmarket, near Cambridge. The catalyst behind this seizure of the King has never been satisfactorily placed: Joyce, with his rank of Cornet (equivalent to a Second Lieutenant today) claimed he came 'with authority from the soldiers' to prevent Charles being used in 'some design against the Army'. Fairfax knew nothing and expressed horror at such an open political coup. Holles accused Joyce of acting under Cromwell's orders, but it is unlikely that a senior ranking officer would have entrusted a Cornet with such a task. Cromwell, in any case, did not accept Fairfax's invitation to chance his fortune with the army until 4 June.

Events moved on apace. Immediately at Newmarket an Army Council was proposed and agreed to, consisting of the generals, with two officers and two privates from each regiment. Eleven leading Presbyterian MPs, including Holles, were accused of treason, and preparations were begun for an army descent on London. On 14 June a major *Declaration of the Army* was issued: it demanded arrears of pay, a purge of opponents of the army from Parliament, the reduction of County Committee power, and then new elections. It was the army's first political programme:

> We shall before disbanding plead some provision for our and the Kingdom's satisfaction and future security... considering that we were not a mere mercenary army, hired to serve any arbitrary power of a State, but called forth and conjured by several declarations of Parliament to the defence of our own and the people's just rights and liberties. (6, pp. 295–301).

The *Declaration* hid for the moment serious divisions of opinion in the Army. To many rank-and-file it *was* 'a mere mercenary army', concerned as they were with pay and little else; but Fairfax and Cromwell made desperate attempts to control the passionate agitations of some of the radicals, now under the influence of Leveller ideas, which asserted royal (not ministerial) responsibility for the war and oppression of liberty. The seeds of a revolution far more fundamental than that of 1640–42 were being sown. In London army movements created panic. The eleven accused members hastily withdrew from the Commons. The City merchant supporters of Holles began to waver. The mobs came out once more and proved difficult to control. A large number of MPs., including the Speaker, fled to the army. Fearing the many-headed monster of social revolution, the men of property dropped their support of Holles and his party, deciding that Fairfax, Cromwell and the discipline of the New Model were lesser evils than popular anarchy. As a cynical pamphleteer wrote at the time, 'Money was at the bottom of the business.' By 3 August 1647 Fairfax was in control of the capital.

The Heads of Proposals and the Agreement of the People 1647

The army, now in power, had to solve the political problems and produce a settlement acceptable to the majority of the political nation. But could the moderate and radical wings agree, and could Charles be deterred from once again playing off his 'enemies', one against the other? Since June and the seizure of the King the officers of the Army Council, led by Fairfax and Henry Ireton, a talented lawyer-soldier and confidant of Cromwell, had been working out their version of a settlement. *The Heads of Proposals* were presented to Charles, and published on 1 August. These 'headings' suggested:

Parliaments be biennially called...

Elections of the Commons be proportionable to the rates the counties bearing the common charge (i.e. taxable wealth), to render the House of Commons as near as may be an equal representative of the whole...

The power of the militia by sea and land during the space of ten years next ensuing shall be ordered by the Lords and Commons...

An Act be passed disposing the great offices for ten years by Lords and Commons...

To take away all coercive power, authority and jurisdiction of bishops... to repeal Acts enjoining the use of the Book of Common Prayer... the taking of the Covenant be not enforced upon any...

His Majesty's person, his Queen and royal issue may be restored to a condition of safety, honour and freedom without further limitation to the exercise of the regal power. (43, pp. 316–26)

While Charles considered them, the defect in the *Heads* became apparent. It was an officer-solution. The agitators were impatient and suspicious – where was the expected impeachment of the eleven leading Presbyterians? It was all too accommodating to the King: the last clause implied that he still retained his legislative veto. The republican, Henry Marten, now back in the Commons, jeered at Cromwell as being 'King-ridden'. Charles, aware of the dissension, yielded to the temptation to deceive. He told Ireton, 'You cannot be without me; you will fall to ruin if I do not sustain you' (27, p. 92). While overtly demanding better terms, he was covertly hoping for something from the Scots, who now viewed the turn of events in England with some concern.

The radicals at this point offered their solution. The Levellers had been born in mid-1646 from the campaigning of John Lilburne, Richard Overton and William Walwyn, who expressed deep disillusionment at the prospects of a settlement. Lilburne spoke to the House of Lords:

> All you intended when you set us a-fighting was merely to unhorse our old riders and tyrants that you might get up and ride us in their stead. (22, p. 44)

Overton and Walwyn castigated 'King Charles and his wickedness'. These London-based civilian radicals found, after the New Model revolt of May 1647, a receptive audience in the army rank-and-file. In the *Heads of Proposals* the ordinary soldier could see a possible betrayal. In October a manifesto, written by one of Lilburne's friends, John Wildman, was presented to Fairfax. *The Case of the Army Truly Stated* was an indictment of:

> The present manner of actings of many at Headquarters... and the supine negligence of many whom we did trust... Whereas all power is originally and essentially in the whole body of the people of this Nation... that people may be equally represented; that all the freeborn at the age of twenty-one years and upwards be the electors, excepting those that shall deprive themselves of that their freedom by delinquency (i.e. Royalists). (22, pp. 58 and 111; 28, p. 67)

The Case of the Army was long, repetitive and offensive to the senior army officers (now becoming known as the 'Grandees'). The agitators, in pressing for discussions on their ideas, produced a much shorter, less impolite document: the celebrated *Agreement of the People* of 28 October 1647. Whether it was less provocative was a different matter.

> The people do chose themselves a Parliament once in two years... the power of all future representatives of this nation is inferior only to theirs who choose them, and doth extend to the enacting of laws, EXCEPT – that matters of religion are not entrusted by us to any human power; – that the impressment to serve in the wars is against our freedom. (6, pp. 308–10)

No reference was made to the 'freeborn' electors of the *Case of the Army*, and ominously, the King too was ignored.

The Grandees were in an unenviable position. On the one hand they had to contend with unrest in the counties, murmurings from Scotland and a recalcitrant King; on the other, they had a rift in the army with revolutionary ideals being posited that went far beyond the earlier radical demands of the old Independent 'War Party'. Late in 1647 solutions to England's constitutional problems were being voiced which would have been unheard of five years earlier.

The Putney Debates, 28 October–8 November 1647

Fairfax being ill, Cromwell agreed to meet army representatives and some civilian Leveller representatives in a church at Putney, just west of London. It was an historic meeting. Never before in recorded verbatim discussions at length, had those normally outside the political decision-making arena been allowed to state their views. Among others, General Ireton and Colonel Rich spoke for the Grandees, Trooper Sexby and Colonel Rainsborough for the army radicals, and Wildman and Petty for the civilian Leveller Party. The meeting opened with a reading of *The Agreement of the People*. Cromwell, in the chair, made a blunt comment:

> Truly this paper does contain in it very great alterations of the very government of this kingdom.

There followed a series of statements and counter-statements, which established two irreconcilable points of view. Rainsborough on the second day argued:

> ... the poorest he that is in England hath a life to live as the greatest he; it's clear that every man that is to live under a government ought first, by his own counsel, to put himself under that government; I do think that the poorest man in England is not at all bound in a strict sense to that government that he hath not had a voice to put himself under.

Ireton was deeply offended by the franchise implications:

> No person hath a right to an interest or share in the disposing of the affairs of the kingdom or choosing those that shall determine what laws we shall be ruled by, that hath not a permanent, fixed interest in this kingdom... We talk of birthright [Rainsborough's opening point]: but that, by a man's being born here, he shall have a share in that power that shall dispose of lands here and of all things here, I do not think it sufficient ground.

Rainsborough was adamant, and in an emotional outburst said,

> I do hear nothing at all that can convince me why any man that is born in England ought not to have his voice in election.

Ireton would not compromise; he regarded the vote as a piece of property:

> I would have an eye to property.

Rainsborough retorted:

> I would fain know what we have fought for.

Petty sought some middle ground:

> I hope that they may live to see the power of the King and Lords thrown down, [who] yet may live to see property preserved... And of changing those that choose the representatives, making of them more full, taking more into the number than formerly.

Colonel Rich returned to Ireton's argument:

> You have 5:1 in this kingdom that have no permanent interest. Some men have ten, some twenty servants. If the master and servant shall be equal electors, then clearly those that have no interest in the kingdom will make it their interest to choose those that have no interest. It may happen that the majority may by law destroy property.

Wildman now presented the Rainsborough case in powerful language, and took the Leveller beliefs to their logical conclusion.

> We have been under slavery; our very laws were made by our conquerors [i.e. Normans]. We are now engaged for our freedom. Every person in England hath as clear a right to elect his representative as the greatest person in England. I conceive that's the undeniable maxim of government: that all government is in the consent of the people.

Trooper Sexby took up the purpose of the late fighting.

> We have ventured our lives, and it was all for this: to recover our birthrights... But it seems now, except a man hath a fixed estate in this kingdom, he hath no right in this kingdom. I wonder we were so much deceived. We were mere mercenary soldiers... Yet the poor have been the means of the preservation of this kingdom. We will not lose that which we have contended for.

Cromwell intervened, as tempers were rising.

> I confess I was most dissatisfied with that I heard Mr Sexby speak, because it did savour so much of will.

Ireton, Cromwell and Sexby tried to find a compromise on the key point of the franchise, modifying both Rainsborough and Wildman's earlier pleas.

> Those that shall choose the law-makers shall be men freed from dependence on others. (Ireton)

Servants while servants are not included; you agree that he who receives alms is to be excluded? (Cromwell)

Yes: servants and apprentices are included in their masters. (Sexby). (6, pp. 310–17, and BBC Radio 1980)

After this small success, arguments by the third day were becoming circular, with speakers asserting and challenging from entrenched positions. Cromwell rapidly tired of the whole operation. Within a few days he moved a resolution that the entire army be called to a rendezvous for consultation. The Levellers naively supposed that voting on their debates and the *Agreement* would take place; but Cromwell and Ireton announced three meeting-points, thus splitting the agitators. At one, on 15 November at Corkbush Field, near Ware north of London, there was even a mutiny. Two regiments arrived with copies of *The Agreement of the People* slotted into their hatbands. The Army leaders however, were determined that radical social ideas should not undermine what Fairfax called 'the ancient discipline of the Army'. Martial law was imposed, ringleaders were arrested, and one, Richard Arnold, was shot. The Grandees revealed how shallow was the base of Leveller support, for there was no more immediate trouble.

The Engagement and a Second Civil War

Four days before Corkbush Field, Charles slipped away from the army's loose custody, and made his way to the Isle of Wight where he received a Scots delegation. (With everything once more in the political melting-pot Fairfax and Cromwell treated the restoration of New Model discipline as most urgent.) Charles signed the *Engagement* with the Scots on 26 December 1647.

His Majesty will confirm by Act of Parliament:
– Presbyterian government and the Directory of Worship for three years...
[after three years] a free debate on how church government shall be fully established...
– The suppressing of the opinions of Anabaptists, Separatists, Independents...
– All armies may be disbanded, and in case this shall not be granted, an army shall be sent from Scotland into England for the preservation of religion, for the defence of His Majesty's person and authority, and restoring him to his government, to the just rights of the Crown and his full revenue. (43, pp. 347–52)

Many people felt they could not trust Charles ever again, and even his supporters might agree he had been disingenuous in the political manouevrings to date. There was now a scent of hypocrisy in the air. Charles had refused to take the Covenant personally, and plainly the Scots and the King expected opposite results from the three-year span of the religious clause of the *Engagement*. It must be said Charles seemed to have the better of the bargain: three years was no time at all for the Scots to see Presbyterianism firmly rooted in England before the 'free debate'. And a Scots army should be a match for the quarrelling New Model. Charles, isolated as he was in the Isle of Wight, was however cut off from political and military realities: he did not grasp the significance of Corkbush Field where army discipline was re-asserted; he failed to understand that, by refusing to take the Covenant, the really efficient, Covenanting part of the Scots army would not be very enthusiastic in the royal cause; and he had no appreciation of provincial unrest which was *against* County Committees rather than in *favour* of the King.

For Cromwell, Ireton and Fairfax this was the moment of truth. Hitherto they had been deeply committed to negotiating with Charles, because the Grandees with the Independent MPs genuinely believed in government by King, Lords and Commons. It was on the precise balance of power and on religious forms that they differed from Holles and his friends, and even from the Constitutional Royalists like Hyde (now abroad with the Royalists). Amid high emotions a revolutionary situation appeared. The army grandees, incensed by Charles' perfidy, threw in their lot with the rank-and-file and some of its Leveller ideas. Suddenly the King ceased to be the corner-stone of the constitution; republicanism became a serious political solution. Cromwell cited scriptures: 'Thou shalt not suffer a hypocrite to reign' (44, p. 316). On 1 May 1648, at a great prayer meeting held at Windsor before the New Model set out to do battle with rebels and Scots, William Allen spoke animatedly of

> Our duty, if ever the Lord brought us back again to peace, to call Charles Stuart, that man of blood, to an account for that blood he shed and mischief he had done. (6, pp. 318–19)

In the House of Commons the moderates (St John's Middle Group, which hitherto had supported the more radical Independents) were alarmed. Civil war was imminent; social revolution just over the horizon. Terrified at the prospect they switched sides and joined Holles' Party. The political possibilities quickly resolved themselves into three: Charles, with all his eggs in the basket of a Scots' victory; the Presbyterian 'Peace Party' desperately trying to detach Charles from the Scots and return in peaceful negotiation; and the revolutionary Independent–Army group now intent on overthrowing the King.

The Second Civil War was an untidy affair with the New Model fighting three opponents. Risings in Kent, South Wales and Essex were essentially a confrontation between the localists of the county communities and centralising Puritan County Committees. Then there were English Royalists emerging once more, but failing lamentably to co-ordinate their efforts with the localists. Both groups were harshly dealt with by the New Model. The Scots came too late and too slowly: Cromwell in August 1648 caught a mixed English–Scots army in Lancashire, and at the Battle of Preston reduced the royalist cause once more to ruins. Charles, carefully supervised in the Isle of Wight, played no part in the war. His fate now rested with a vengeance-seeking New Model Army.

Study 9

1 This is a notoriously difficult period for study. Seeking an accurate chronology, explaining people's motives, understanding shifts of opinion, even labelling the political groupings have all exercised the skills of historians, past and present, to an unusual degree. Basic to everything was the plethora of proposals and declarations (*Newcastle Propositions; Declaration of the Army; Heads of Proposals; Case of the Army; Agreement of the People; Engagement*). Your first task must be to measure each against (a) Charles' hopes of retaining some power, and (b) a possible resolution of any of the four central problems we have been keeping in mind since the chapter on 1640 (appointment of ministers and generals, finance, religion and localism). A ten-point scale is suggested for both (a) and (b). Some of the documents will give you explicit answers; others will only imply an answer or even ignore key issues.

2 There are at least three critical points in the story of these years when events might have taken a significantly different course:

(i) 25 May 1647 – the culminating decision to disband the New Model Army.
(ii) 1 August 1647 – Charles' evasion of an answer to the Heads of Proposals. Set your ideas against Aylmer's judgement that he 'would have done well to accept this' (2, p. 132)
(iii) the abrupt ending of the Putney Debates and the reimposition of army discipline at Corkbush Field on 15 November 1647.

You may find more, and you may speculate briefly with hindsight on how differently things may have turned out if other decisions had been taken. You are asked to assess the prospects of a particular situation, to explain a decision, and to assess whether an issue was handled effectively.

Observations (on 2i):

In view of the revolutionary events which followed, this must seem the most doom-laden decision of the decade! The attempt by Holles and his political Presbyterian supporters in Parliament to rid themselves of the New Model with the promise of only eight weeks' back-pay has been judged shabby, foolish and inept by some historians (e.g. 71, p. 51). Yet at the time it was quite defensible to the Presbyterians. The King's replies to the Newcastle Propositions suggested hope of a settlement soon; if more than eight weeks' money were offered, there might be very few volunteers for Ireland; the prospect of reduced taxes and no more quartering would give them firm support from the county communities. In Holles' scheming mind the orders to Fairfax's 'foot' might separate it from the 'horse' on the principle of divide and rule. Finally he could not know how politically-minded the New Model would become. Yet the whole thing went wrong. Why? Would you agree that it was not the decision to disband, but the conduct of the operation? Holles' appointment of Presbyterian cavalry commanders could be seen as inept in its timing and gave rise to suspicion (correct as it turned out) of his real intention. Failure to negotiate on pay was the central error: a City loan would have calmed tempers, but Holles was over-confident, and, when the Army revolted, his supporters lost their nerve.

Pursue 2ii and 2iii on these lines.

---- CHAPTER 8 ----

Purge and Regicide
1648 - 49

The Purge, 6 December

The army held the key to the future. What had been a purely military force in
1645, and only partly radical in 1647, now in 1648 became fully revolutionary, convinced that it could save itself and the country only by political
change at Westminster.

The politicians refused to face reality. That autumn at Newport, in the Isle
of Wight, a Parliamentary commission led by Holles treated once more with
the King; that they represented the wishes of the gentry of England, desperate
for peace, there was no doubt. Charles was presented with the Newcastle
Propositions as a basis for discussion, and throughout the last months of 1648
they edged towards agreement. Charles made concessions, but resisted
demands that he abandon the Prayer Book for the Presbyterian Directory of
Worship (despite the *Engagement*). He soon decided that it would be a 'mock-
treaty' anyway. He, unlike Holles, had no illusions: a furiously angry Army
would accept no compromise settlement.

With Cromwell still engaged in military mopping-up operations in the
north, and Fairfax unwilling to become too involved in politics, Henry Ireton
seized the initiative. In November an Army *Remonstrance* was drawn up to be
presented to Parliament. It demanded the punishment of Charles –

> that grand and capital author of all our woes... in whose behalf and in
> whose interest only all our wars and troubles have been. (25, p. 131)

Ireton had made a decisive move towards the Leveller point of view, if not as
far as Lilburne and Wildman wanted. There was a second significance: no
longer was the King to be attacked through 'evil counsellors'; as Robert
Ashton concludes, 'The Army at least had moved from the doctrine of
ministerial, to that of regal, responsibility' (44, p. 340). Charles was now taken
into stricter army custody.

Parliament refused to debate the *Remonstrance* and on the fateful 5 December
decided to continue the Newport Treaty negotiations with the King. Ireton had
had enough. At 7 am on the following morning 1000 New Model soldiers
blocked the entrance to Parliament building, and as Members arrived Colonel
Thomas Pride flourished a list of names 'to be secluded' – that is, barred from
entering, some of whom were to be arrested. All the political presbyterians

were on the list, but so were some Independents who were being squeamish over the implications of the *Remonstrance*. Professor Underdown has produced an analysis of the 471 Members reckoned eligible to sit: 231 were secluded, of whom 45 were actually placed in custody; another 86, including Holles, were so fearful that they stayed away and refused to come near Parliament for many months (Holles went abroad). The gulf between Ireton's revolutionaries committed to the *Remonstrance* and their previous political allies is shown by the names of some of those imprisoned: Grimstone, Waller, D'Ewes and Strode – all have appeared in previous pages as parliamentary opponents of the King. Of the remaining members, only 71, a mere 15 per cent of the House of Commons, can be classified as active revolutionaries, determined to purge Parliament and bring the King to trial. (23, pp. 220, 147, 182)

The evidence, Underdown goes on to argue, suggests that 'hesitant and divided counsels beset the revolutionary leaders'. Cromwell, for instance, seems to have been a very reluctant convert to Ireton's actions. He arrived late in London on the evening of Pride's Purge, and, as in 1647, with Joyce's seizure of the King, he might be regarded as 'waiting-on-events'; yet with the Purge done, he said he 'was glad of it'. He still had doubts: was the Army's cry for Charles' blood the answer? Execution or exile, republic or regency (with Charles' youngest son, the Duke of Gloucester, as 'Harry the Ninth') raised difficult questions. 'Our fleshly reasonings ensnare us,' Cromwell commented to a friend. Suddenly early in January 1649, he threw off all caution: 'We will cut off his head with the Crown upon it,' he answered other waverers.

The Trial, 20 – 27 January

Charles I was the first European monarch to be put on public trial *as King*. No precedents existed and time was taken in preparing the charge and obtaining a body of 'commissioners', a term for those who would in effect act as judge and jury. One hundred and thirty-five were nominated. There were some significant absentees from the list: some, like Sir Arthur Haselrig, were on duty in the north, but Sir Henry Vane and Oliver St John (a Chief Justice) refused because they disliked the army's dominant role. Some, like John Downes, the obscure MP for Arundel, agreed to serve only after veiled threats. Fairfax attended only once and avoided the actual trial completely. Forty-seven on the list never appeared in the Court. Attendance was, however, never less than 67. (Source of following extracts: 45, chs. 6 and 7)

Charles was brought before the Court on the afternoon of Saturday 20 January. A little-known judge, John Bradshaw, was President, and a barrister, John Cook, presented the charge: Charles, he said, had

a wicked design to erect and uphold in himself an unlimited and tyrannical power to rule and to overthrow the rights and liberties of the people.

In putting this design into practice, he had

> traitorously and maliciously levied war against the present Parliament and the people therein represented...

Thus was impeached

> the said Charles Stuart as a tyrant, traitor and murderer, and a public and implacable enemy to the Commonwealth of England.

Charles refused to answer according to legal requirement, 'Guilty' or 'Not Guilty'. Instead, without a trace of his usual stammer, he countered:

> I would know by what power I am called hither; I would know by what authority, I mean lawful... Remember I am your lawful King... I have a trust committed to me by God.

Over the next few days Bradshaw and Cook tried to move the trial along according to proper legal procedures, but without any success. Charles contrived to defy the court authority. Bradshaw then committed a blunder: the Court Commissioners, he said,

> sit here by the authority of the Commons of England.

Charles, who knew his law well, reposted:

> The Commons of England was never a Court of Judicature. I would know how they came to be so.

On the third day he still refused to answer the charge; instead he changed his line of attack on the Court.

> For the charge I value it not a rush; it is the liberty of the people of England I stand for.

'Liberty' normally meant 'privilege' in seventeenth-century usage, and Bradshaw was quick to seize upon Charles' claim.

> How far you have preserved the privileges of the people, your actions have spoke it... you have written your meaning in bloody characters throughout the whole kingdom.

But he lost his advantage by stating once again to Charles,

> You are before a Court of Justice.

Charles replied,

> I see I am before a power.

The King was led away to cries of 'God Save the King!'.

The next days were occupied by hearing witnesses and drafting the sentence

The triptych of Charles I by Van Dyck (Mansell Collection)

– the ultimate purpose of the trial. On 27 January Charles was brought back, and Bradshaw spoke to the Commissioners:

> The prisoner at the bar [is] before the Court to make answer to the charge of treason and other high crimes, exhibited against him in the name of the people of England...

He was interrupted by a masked woman in the gallery of Westminster Hall:

> ... not half, not a quarter of the people of England. Oliver Cromwell is a traitor...

She was hastily moved out by some friends before the guards could detain her. It was not known until later that she was Lady Fairfax; a few, perhaps Cromwell, who knew her well, may have recognised her voice. Later there was another interruption: when Charles was refused permission to speak, John Downes, the reluctant commissioner, shouted to the Court: 'Have you hearts of stone?' Such dramatic interludes created consternation, and a brief suspension, and it was with difficulty that Bradshaw brought the Court back to its purpose. In a final forty-minute address to the prisoner, he returned to the best case against Charles:

> There is a contract between the King and his people... for as you are the liege-lord, so they are liege-subjects... the one bond is the bond of protection that is due from a sovereign. Sir, if this bond be once broken, farewell sovereignty!... Whether you have been a protector of England let all England judge.

Bradshaw then called upon a clerk to read out the formal sentence:

> That the said Charles Stuart, as a tyrant, traitor, murderer and public enemy, shall be put to death by the severing of his head from his body.

Charles was refused permission to speak, and as the guards led him out of the Court he shouted,

> I am not suffered for to speak: expect what justice other people will have.

Execution, 30 January 1649, and Martyrdom

Before his death Charles made a short speech on the scaffold on the theme of 'his people':

> Truly I desire their liberty and freedom as much as anybody; but I must tell you that their liberty and freedom consists in having of government... a subject and a sovereign are clean different things... I die a Christian according to the profession of the Church of England. (45, p. 191)

Then, around 2 p.m. on 30 January, Charles was executed. The man who wielded the axe was masked and to this day it is a matter of speculation who he was. The chief executioner, Richard Brandon, had refused fearing that assassination might overtake the killer of a king.

Charles' death was followed by the abolition of the monarchy and the House of Lords, leaving the remnant of the purged Commons, the Rump, to rule with a Council of State exercising a loose executive power. The Army, whose shadow overlay the trial proceedings, remained. Now a republic known officially as the Commonwealth, England was beset by enemies, abroad and at home. Cromwell and the New Model had a busy two years dealing with the exiled, uncrowned Charles II and Royalists (finally defeated at Worcester in 1651), with Presbyterian Scots, with Catholic Ireland and with renewed Leveller mutinies.

It quickly became clear that only the Army stood in the way of resurgent Royalism. For Charles I, viewed by many during his life as difficult and even untrustworthy in his personal relations and inept in his political decision-making, became on his death a very effective martyr. Within months of his execution a book was published which ran into many editions despite official attempts to prevent circulation: this was 'The Portraiture of His Sacred Majesty in His Solitude and Sufferings', entitled *Eikon Basilike*. In it a portrait of Charles, as a martyr for the Church of England and as a moderate sovereign betrayed by the extreme policies of followers and enemies alike, was cleverly presented. In John Kenyon's judgement, 'it was, apart from the *Bible* and perhaps Foxe's *Acts and Monuments*, the most influential book of the century' (3, p. 165).

Manifestly this was not the time in which Ireton, Cromwell and the revolutionary Independents could quietly contemplate the structure and working of a government without a king. An acceptable settlement would have to wait.

Study 10

Essay: Did those who put Charles I on trial achieve their purpose?

Observations on the structure of the essay:

You will need to quote chapter and verse for each point you make from the trial extracts given. Strangely there are few modern authorities that give fairly extensive treatment to what must be regarded as one the great set-piece trials in English history. The best is the full account in chapters 5, 6 and 7 of C.V. Wedgwood's *The Trial of Charles I*, Collins (1964); G.E. Aylmer, *The Struggle for the Constitution*, Blandford (fourth edition 1975), has a valuable, if brief, commentary (pp. 137 – 39).

Your opening few paragraphs need statements on who 'those' were, and on the general circumstances preceding the trial. You might find the phrase 'revolutionary political Independents' useful, but in need of explanation; so, too, the respective roles of Ireton and Cromwell will require careful choice of words. How far back to go in setting the scene is a common difficulty: here, Charles' provocation of a Second Civil War ('that man of blood') and the defeat at Preston are key events (Cromwell's remark, 'This man against whom the Lord hath witnessed' could be useful here). On the purpose of the trial you must show awareness that Charles was tried *as King*, that it was to declare publicly his guilt and to sentence him. Thus it was not a trial to *establish* guilt. Aylmer makes an interesting point, when he says, 'it was a political not a legal act'. You will need some reference to the reservations which many contemporaries had about the trial: fear of continental reprisals; hope, by some until the last moment, that Charles would accept a figurehead political position; fear that the attack on the King was on the 'Lord's Anointed'; fear of the obvious military power behind the process. Kenyon has caustically observed, 'They would have done much better to have him tried by a court-martial, and shot him' (6, p. 294).

The core of the essay must relate purpose to the happenings at the trial. Mention concern for legal forms, the Army presence, poor security. In the end the contest might be seen as a moral victory by Charles over Bradshaw by 2 to 1. Bradshaw failed to halt Charles' speech-making and counter-accusations (what Wedgwood calls his 'eloquent defiance'); and Charles seized on the central weakness of the presecution case – that the authority of the 'Commons of England' had no precedent. Bradshaw won a crucial point: Charles in making war on them had failed in his obligation to protect his subjects. Do you think such legal niceties were irrelevant and that the power of the sword ensured the verdict and sentence?

For a conclusion you might consider distinguishing between the preposterous *procedure* of the trial and execution, and the actual *principles* at stake. These were of a high order, and provide you with a possible answer to the question. For Charles: beware of the *Eikon Basilike* claims of martyrdom and the trial charges of tyranny – the bias and emotive choice of language is all too plain. He did stand for paternal rule, in which he and his choice of ministers could make the best decisions for the nation. In this he was consistent: compare his 'clean different' speech from the scaffold, with the 'never intended for any share in government' point in the *Answer to the Nineteen Propositions* (p. 55). Aylmer argues that for those who put Charles on trial, the point of the affair, however mismanaged in practice, was 'to prove that kings were accountable to their subjects for what they did.' Did they succeed?

Take your discussion to the date of the execution; you cannot go further at the moment, although there is a case to be made for the essay having a long final paragraph on what happened *after* – the next decade, or even the next half-century. But you will be better placed to tackle this when you come to the end of the book.

CHAPTER 9

The Protectorate: A New Solution?

On 20 April 1653 Cromwell expelled the Rump. Disenchanted by its inattention to long-term political reform and by St John and Vane's resolve to hold elections (far too soon, Cromwell said: the people needed 'to forget monarchy' first), he resorted to military power. Thus the New Model Army, the Long Parliament's instrument to win the Civil War, had in two dramatic episodes – purge in 1648 and dissolution in 1653 – destroyed its creator.

There followed a curious, short-lived experiment, the Nominated Parliament. In a mood of idealism and religious enthusiasm Cromwell set up a legislature of godly men 'of approved fidelity and honesty' from the Congregational churches mixed with some senior army officers. Intended for an interim period of a few years until normal elections were 'safe', this assembly would consider enough practical reforms to satisfy the political nation. Yet in entrusting complete authority to it Cromwell seriously misjudged its zeal. Within six months so many were offended by its proposals – which ranged from civil marriage to economies in the army, from the abolition of Chancery as a court 'bleeding the people in the purse-vein' to the abolition of tithes which many of the gentry controlled – that Cromwell accepted this Parliament must go. He was now convinced that solutions to the country's problems demanded a controlled programme with clear priorities implemented on an evolutionary rather than a revolutionary time-scale. The machinery for such action would be a fresh constitutional framework, the Instrument of Government.

The Instrument of Government, December 1653

The Instrument was the brainchild of General John Lambert and its origins can be traced to Ireton's *Heads of Proposals* of 1647. Its 42 Articles, concerned with the executive, the legislature and the practice of religion may be summarised thus:

The Executive

- A 'Single Person' – Oliver Cromwell – named as 'The Lord Protector' for life (on death a new Protector to be elected by the Council with a quorum of thirteen)... (clauses 1, 32 and 33)

– A Council, comprising the Protector, seven Army officers and eight influential civilians – named as members for life. Few were regicides, and none had been a figure of fame or controversy during the previous decade. (On death a replacement would be decided by Parliamentary suggestions, considered by the Council, then ratified by the Protector)... (clauses 2,25 and 26).

– The Council to be aided by 'Officers of State' (a Treasurer, a Chancellor, Chief Justices) 'chosen by approbation of Parliament'.

The Executive's responsibilities were policy-making, administration and security. Clause 3 stated: the Protector 'shall govern in all things by the advice of the Council.' Clause 27 stated: 'a constant yearly revenue shall be raised for the maintaining of 10,000 horse and 20,000 foot in England, Scotland and Ireland for defence, besides £200,000 per annum for defraying the other necessary charges of administration of justice and other expenses of the government; which revenue shall be raised by the customs and other ways agreed upon by the Lord Protector and the Council.' Clause 39 confirmed the Long Parliament's financial arrangements, which meant that the Excise and Monthly Assessments would continue. Clauses 6 and 30 stated: 'Laws shall not be altered, nor any new law made, nor any tax charge or imposition laid upon the people, but by the common consent in Parliament, save only as is expressed in the 30th article [i.e. that the Protector with consent of the major part of the Council for preventing the disorders and dangers, shall have power until the meeting of the first Parliament to raise money]; and also to make laws and ordinances for the peace and welfare of these nations, which shall be binding until order shall be taken in Parliament concerning the same.'

The Legislature

– A single chamber Parliament 'summoned once every third year' to sit for at least five months, and during that time not to be 'adjourned, prorogued or dissolved without their own consent'... (clauses 7 and 8)

– 400 Members for England and Wales, 30 for Scotland, 30 for Ireland, with a redistribution of seats to make the Assembly more representative.

– The franchise was a new idea: everyone 'possessed to his own use of any estate, real or personal, to the value of £200' (i.e., not the traditional 40 shilling freehold or the household franchise of the Levellers), *except* delinquents (those who 'aided, advised, assisted or abetted in any war against Parliament since 1642') for a period of four Parliaments – i.e. 12 years – and Roman Catholics were debarred for ever.

– Members had to be over twenty-one years of age and 'of known integrity, fearing God and of good conversation.'... (clauses 10,14 and 18)

The effect of the redistribution of seats, which cut out many small boroughs, and the new franchise was to *narrow* slightly the electorate and give more representation to the counties and their independent country gentlemen.

The legislature's function was to act, with the Protector, as the 'supreme legislative authority of the Commonwealth of England'. Parliamentary bills were to 'be presented to the Lord Protector for his consent'; should he disagree or wish to alter he had twenty days, after which 'such bills pass into and become law.'... (clauses 1 and 24)

The Practice of Religion

'That the Christian religion as contained in the Scriptures shall be recommended as the Public Profession of these nations; provision be made for the encouragement and maintenance of able and painful teachers for instructing the people; that to the Public Profession none shall be compelled by penalties; that such as profess faith in God by Jesus Christ (though differing from the doctrine, worship or discipline publicly held forth) shall be protected in the profession of the faith; this liberty be not extended to Popery nor Prelacy [i.e. rule by bishops]'... (clauses 35,36 and 37). (6, pp. 342–48)

Study 11

The Instrument of Government was England's first (and only) written constitution. Within a single document a code of rules was thus drafted which would define the function of the various parts of the body politic and control the powers and duties of the people who made the decisions about the running of the country. This could be seen as a great opportunity to settle once and for all the balance of power between the contending forces in English political life. So what do you think of the *Instrument*? Was it an honest attempt to steer, in Gardiner's words, 'a middle course between the despotism of a Single Person and the despotism of a Single House' (43, p. lvi); or do you have any sympathy with those of the political nation at the time who saw it as a veneer of constitutional consent thinly disguising a self-perpetuating military dictatorship?

Observations:

1. Much will depend on the *working* of the constitution – how different people reacted to the letter and spirit of this code of rules – but the *structure* deserves separate attention, for the opportunity was there to take a fresh look at the purposes, principles and institutions of English government. Since 1640, when Conciliar Government collapsed, many proposals had been mooted, even fought over, in the hope that something generally acceptable would emerge.

Taking a favourable view of the *Instrument* you may be impressed by the attempts to achieve a clear system of checks and balances between the executive and the legislature, undoubtedly one of the key issues to emerge from the 1640 Crisis. You will find support from Professor Kenyon here: he calls it a 'sensible, workmanlike document' (6, p. 333), for it harked back to the 1647 *Heads of Proposals*, now widely judged by historians to be the best of the solutions on offer to the King in the 1640s. Your notes should point to specific clauses (e.g. 27/30/3/24). Professor Ivan Roots says that the Council was 'the keystone of the newly flung-up arch of government' (25, p. 171). How does this relate to your notes? And an interesting discussion is possible on whether Lambert's *Instrument* keeps faith with the ideals and expectations of Pym and Hampden in 1640–41 – remember that they were not interested in parliamentary sovereignty, but wanted the executive's (i.e. the monarch's) policies controlled by the parliamentary leadership having a voice on the Privy Council. If you think they would have objected to the named 'fifteen' being there for life (clause 25), then what would the constitutional royalists have thought? Would Edward Hyde have constructed something all that different in principle from the constitutional clauses of the *Instrument*?

A second favourable view of the *Instrument* is that it was a serious attempt to provide the country with a prolonged period of stability. Why do you think the executive council were hard-headed realistic men rather than enthusiastic revolutionaries? You might find Roots' comment helpful: what they would not do, he says, 'was to extend the revolution. The key word was "settlement". Change expressed in "Overturn, overturn, overturn" was now anathema' (28, p. 147). Also two remarks by Cromwell echo the theme of settlement: the people 'hoped for rest after ten years of civil wars'; he would be, he said later, 'the good constable to keep the peace of the parish' (28, p. 171). To whom do you consider clauses 14,17 and 18 would appeal?

2. There were also some very unfavourable features in the *Instrument*. What storm clouds loomed in clauses 12 and 27? How would Haselrig, Vane and St. John react to certain phrases in clause 27? There was no hiding the fact that the *Instrument* was a sword-imposed constitution, mistrustful of the various groups who were expected to work it. Roots makes the point well: 'Every clause was big with suspicion and distrust, distrust of the people, of parliament, and even of the Protector' (25, p. 171). Check clause 18; clauses 7,8 and 12; and clauses 3 and 24 to see the basis of Roots' argument.

The reason for the *Instrument's* complicated system of checks and balances was, of course, not simply to prevent Parliament or Protector acting despotically; it was to ensure that the religious freedoms (clauses 35–37) could not be modified. In a very real sense this 'liberty of conscience' was at the heart of the army officers' purpose – but how far this was generally acceptable to the political nation remained to be seen. You will remember that since 1647 the

New Model had a powerful Independent–Congregationalist flavour about it; so here, at last, in the *Instrument* was legal denial of those other alternatives – Presbyterianism, Anglicanism, Catholicism – which would claim exclusive control of people's religious beliefs, even to the point of persecuting those refusing to conform.

You may at this point detect a flaw in the *Instrument*, that it was army-inspired *and* army-controlled (i.e. Cromwell, plus seven senior officers on the Council, plus clause 27). What suspicion would this create? Kenyon in his recent book, *Stuart England*, has a useful discussion on what should have been arranged. 'The problem,' he says, 'was to erect a new constitution in which those who were to operate the constitution were divorced from those who had made it' (3, p. 174). You might consider why this would be a better solution. In later years others would find an answer in a constituent assembly or convention which would work out a settlement, then dissolve itself (the Restoration in 1660, and the American and French revolutionaries, for instance), but for Cromwell and the army officers no such answer was considered. The army had to stay in control as a guarantee of liberty of conscience.

But need it be a dictatorship? The clues to the balance for and against have been given, but you must make up your own mind regarding an answer to the question. It echoes, of course, what you were asked in the Ship Money study (see p. 15) – so would you have been happy to have been ruled by the Instrument? Haselrig was not, as we shall see.

The First Protectorate Parliament, September 1654 – January 1655

Until Parliament met, Cromwell and the Council ruled by Ordinance, but no clear programme emerged. They had no intention of antagonising people by radical change. In religion only could a policy-line be detected. For centuries the form of worship in each parish had been set 'from above', by the established Church or State; now diversity of religious practice, the hallmark of the period since the end of the Civil War, was given government blessing, and the form of worship determined 'from below', by local parish ideas. Only a loose state control was exercised. Parallel ordinances of 1654 limited the range of state intervention: the first set up a Commission of Triers in London to check that ministers of the Church were religious, moral and capable; the second set up Commissions of Ejectors in each county to expel ministers and schoolmasters who were 'scandalous in their lives and conversation', and a list of the possible unworthy included papists, perjurers, drunkards, scoffers at the godly, defenders of maypoles and gamblers. Thus there was no particular church organisation to be enforced and no special creed to be accepted. A parish might continue with ministers ordained before 1640, even using the Prayer Book; a few miles away a Presbyterian system using lay elders could be seen; yet further on some 'gathered congregations' would flourish in tiny separatist units, enjoying freedom from the ruthless persecution which would certainly have been their fate in Elizabeth's day. For some, as a contemporary the Rev. Richard Baxter wrote, this was 'the unmatchable paradise of the Earth'; for others, suspicious of such liberties, Cromwell's policy was a recipe for sedition and disorder.

The first legislative meeting of the Protectorate began in September, 1654. The Parliamentary membership was remarkably similar to that of the original Long Parliament, containing over a hundred of its previous members, among a large number of gentry. Only a handful of 'dangerous spirits' were excluded – the Leveller, John Wildman, was one – identified as men *not* of known integrity. Within days Arthur Haselrig, that long-time champion of Parliamentary rights, took the initiative, and, with a small but noisy group of would-be republican supporters, placed a proposition before the House: the 'Single Person' must be limited and controlled as Parliament saw fit. This was an open bid for Parliamentary sovereignty, challenging as it did the basic power-balance of the *Instrument*.

Cromwell acted in an uncharacteristically swift manner. On 12 September he delivered a long, often heated, even rambling speech of self-justification to members, shouting at one point, 'I sought not this place'. Disclaiming personal ambition he referred constantly to the difficulties of his position – 'a burden on my back'. Then with religious resignation he asked members to remember *their* humble position: we are only 'poor, creeping ants on the Earth.' The members were not convinced, especially when the political point of Cromwell's tub-thumping tirade emerged. There were, he argued, four features of the *Instrument* which must be seen as 'not circumstantial, but fundamental, bed-rock things': liberty of conscience, limited-duration parliaments, the existence of the army, and joint executive-legislature powers. These, he went on, were not matters for discussion, let alone alteration. Finally, Cromwell demanded the 'Recognition', a paper to be signed by all members binding them to the fourth 'fundamental', accepting, that is, the clear division of powers between the 'Single Person' and Parliament as stated in the *Instrument*.

One hundred members, led by Haselrig, walked out. It was a dramatic demonstration of non-cooperation. Other critics of the *Instrument* stayed, persisting in their determination to dismantle the constitution, clause by clause if necessary. High on the list of priorities were demands that Councillors be approved by Parliament (shades of 1640!), and that the Protectorate's standing army be replaced by the old pattern of country gentlemen raising the local militia when required. Cromwell struggled against a rising tide of opposition, but, when in January 1655 the second of these priorities produced the resolution 'that the militia ought not to be raised, but by the common consent of the people assembled in Parliament', he had had enough. The five-month parliamentary sitting required by the *Instrument* being up, the members were dismissed for 'fertilising weeds', as Cromwell described the way their quarreling encouraged royalist plotting. In reality it was an admission that the *Instrument* was in tatters.

The Major-Generals

Cromwell returned to rule by Ordinance. Its most notorious feature was the period of the Major-Generals, a still little-understood episode in English history. To divide up England in the summer of 1655 into eleven districts, each with a Major-General, was a sensible security measure to deal with Royalist rebellions, actual (as in the Penruddock rising in Wiltshire), or potential (as in the paper plottings uncovered by Cromwell's efficient network of informers). Also the cutting of the national military establishment seemed inevitable as Cromwell found government costs rising; a return to something akin to the local volunteer militias of old would be cheaper, and had the extra advantage of involving the county communities once more in regional government – the first time since 1640 that local sensibilities had been seriously reckoned. The Major-General scheme would be financed by a tax of one-tenth on the estates of known well-to-do Royalists.

However, the working of the scheme had for many people sinister implications. Royalists could be expected, of course, to respond with distaste to the harsh taxation (introducing a new word into the language: decimation), but the vigorous opposition of the ordinary people, gentry to artisan and yeoman, from whom Cromwell was seeking support for his regime, was something he had not foreseen. Far from involving the county communities, the scheme was regarded as yet another experiment in centralised rule from London, similar in tone to Strafford's and Laud's ideas of the 1630s. Cromwell had intended the Major-Generals and their soldiers to *supplement* local officials, the JPs, churchwardens and the still-existing County Committees; yet the closing down of many ale-houses, racehorse meetings and cockfights, and the suppression in some areas of stageplays created a narrow, puritanical, spoilsport image. Some Major-Generals might defend their actions by saying they were less concerned with the morals of the people than with security – ale-houses were the haunts of the disaffected Royalist plotters – but to no avail. The hostility of the general populace was reinforced by that of the greater gentry to whom the Major-Generals and their military assistants were, in the words of Lucy Hutchinson, wife of the regicide Colonel, 'silly, mean

Map 2: The Rule of the Major-Generals, 1655–6

KEY

1. London – Phillip Skippon
2. Middlesex – John Barkstead
3. Surrey and Kent – Thomas Kelsey
4. Sussex, Hampshire and Berkshire – William Goffe
5. Western Counties – John Desborough
6. Bedford, Huntingdon, Northants – William Botelet
7. Oxford, Buckingham, Hertford, Essex, East Anglia – Charles Fleetwood
8. Lincolnshire, Leicester, Derby, Nottingham, Warwick – Edward Whalley
9. Yorkshire and Northern Borders – John Lambert
10. Lancashire, Cheshire and Stafford – Charles Worsley
11. Wales and Marcher Counties – James Berry

fellows' (60, p. 294), often men of inferior social status to whom the civil wars had given a temporary respectability. The mere division of England into military areas echoed the structure of Norman feudalism; an outcry against the 'Norman yoke' had found expression as recently as the 1647 Putney Debates (see p. 82).

When the detailed record of the period is examined, especially in the provinces, the difficulty of making acceptable generalisations is self-evident. As Coward says in his recent study of Stuart England, 'The striking fact that emerges about the Major-Generals, when some of the myths about them have been stripped away, is the differences among them' (1, p. 232). In Blackburn in Lancashire, Major-General Worsley, perhaps the most enthusiastic of them all, proudly proclaimed that 200 alehouses had been closed; in Nottinghamshire Whalley was equally boastful that, 'You may ride all over Nottingham and not see a beggar or a wandering rogue, and there is hardly a meeting of three Cavaliers, but I am suddenly acquainted with it.' Yet there is evidence that their zeal and efficiency was tempered by human failings. The size of some areas was too great, especially when a Major-General faced age-old local apathies. Desborough, in the West, was a formidable Major-General but he found only moderates among the influential men willing to serve under him in Somerset: traditional west country revels and fairs proved impossible to stop, despite puritan complaints at the crowds and unseemly merriment following the sale of beer; in collecting the decimation tax it was reported to London that 'the gentlemen of this county act very mildly'. Both in Somerset and in Kent the 'particulars of estates and revenues' which Royalists had to provide were in many cases absurd under-estimations, yet the Major-Generals found themselves 'mere outsiders' unable to break the closed circle of local loyalties. (In Kent, for example, only 91 out of 500 Royalist 'delinquents' declared property above the £100 level for taxation!).

The real limits of control by the Major-Generals were revealed when Cromwell, in need of money for a war with Spain, called the Second Protectorate Parliament in September 1656. They were confident that elections could be controlled, and anyway undesirables could be excluded under the rules of the *Instrument*. They were right about the second, but not the first. Desborough reported 'great contendings and strugglings in all parts; I hear of them making parties – my business is to break all such contrivances.' He had only partial success. The victors in Somerset were the moderate, respectable country gentlemen and lawyers of the county, Alexander Popham and John Ashe, for example. Although Desborough himself got in, other 'army' candidates gained few votes. The Somerset gentry had listened carefully to Sheriff Hunt's plea that 'pious, sober, prudent and peaceable men' be elected. Kent went the same way: moderates swept the constituencies with the slogan, 'No Swordsmen! No Decimation!' Of Kent's 36 members, Major-General Kelsey was the only outsider to be elected. Elsewhere, too, the counties closed ranks. The message to Cromwell was clear: military depotism, however well-intentioned, would not resolve the basic conflict between central control and local autonomy. This tension, one of the elements in the 1640 Crisis, remained.

The offer of the Crown

Cromwell doggedly pursued his general policy of 'healing and settling'. He withdrew the Council's support for the Major-Generals and the scheme quietly died away. He knew also he must work with Parliament, though some critics he refused to tolerate. Haselrig and Bradshaw, among a hundred or so, were refused admission to the Parliament building, as were vigorous county critics of the military like Popham. The excluded condemned the rest for accepting 'the daily awe and terror of the Lord Protector's armed men'. A contemporary pamphlet raised an interesting comparison: was not the exclusion of so many 'a crime twenty-fold beyond that of the late King's in going about to seclude the Five Members?'

This political mauling could not go on: it impressed nobody, least of all the county communities of provincial England aching for settlement. Between January and May 1657 some significant steps were taken to achieve this – but they were halting, mainly backward-looking, and in the end blurred. First, old John Ashe from Somerset proposed that Cromwell 'take upon him the government according to the ancient constitution' (46, p. 185). The idea struck root, and within a fortnight Cromwell's supporters drew up an invitation that he assume 'the name, style, title and dignity of King'; and in the debate that followed they argued with conviction from medieval and biblical precedent. Said one: 'It is the ancient way by which good kings were ever made. All Israel gathered themselves together at Hebron to make David King' (40, p. 193). Cromwell's immediate reaction was favourable; he said, 'I am hugely taken with the word "settlement".' He had long been convinced that some reconciliation in the body politic was vital – he had spoken in 1651 of 'a settlement of somewhat with monarchical power in it', and in 1654 of the need to unite 'a nobleman, a gentleman, a yeoman: that is a good interest of the nation'.

Detailed proposals which would modify the *Instrument of Government* were now framed. Cromwell, though, hesitated: a member commented that he made 'a speech so dark that no one knows whether he will accept or not'. In May, after weeks of mental anguish, Cromwell refused the Crown, but accepted the other proposed changes. The Protectorate was henceforth to be governed under a new constitutional set-up known as *The Humble Petition and Advice*. Its features, marking a departure from the Instrument, were:

- on the Succession to the Executive: 'Nothing is wanting to bring us into blood and confusion; your Highness will be pleased during your lifetime to appoint and declare the person who shall immediately after your death succeed you.'
- on Parliament: 'Your Highness will be pleased to call Parliament consisting of two Houses; and those legally chosen by free elections of

WITHAL

Opposite: Cromwell in royal regalia – a Dutch caricature from a contemporary broadsheet (Mansell Collection).   Above: Charles II c. 1680 (National Portrait Gallery)

the people to serve in Parliament may not be excluded from sitting.' (The 'Other House' to be nominated by the Protector).

- on the Council: its powerful position under the *Instrument* was reduced; 'None may be admitted to the Privy Council, but be afterwards approved by both Houses of Parliament.'
- on finance: precision replaced uncertain amounts for the armed forces, which would compel a reduction in numbers; 'a yearly revenue of £1,300,000, whereof £1,000,000 for the army and navy.' (A large sum in view of the current war with Spain).
- on religion: there was pressure to establish something akin to a state church and to limit toleration, especially in view of the Quakers and their much-resented habit of interrupting services with cries to the minister, 'Come down, thou Deceiver.' 'That a Confession of Faith to be agreed by your Highness and the Parliament to be recommended, and that none be permitted to revile or reproach this Confession.' (6, pp. 350–57)

Of the Council only John Lambert refused to accept the new arrangements. His personal hopes of succeeding Cromwell as Lord Protector much diminished, he retired to his Wimbledon home 'to grow tulips'.

A second session of the Second Protectorate Parliament met under the new rules in January 1658. The 'Other House' took away many Cromwellian supporters (about forty agreed to sit, including a few peers of the old House of Lords and a few new upstarts), and as all the excluded now, of course, returned to the Lower House they began to denounce the powers of the hereditary Protector and the 'Other House'. Haselrig took the lead, and in an emotional speech cried, 'The Commons will quake to hear that they are returning to Egypt' (i.e. to the bondage of the executive). Later Sir Henry Vane saw a sinister interpretation of the *Humble Petition*: 'Shall we be underbuilders to the supreme Stuart?' he said, accusing Cromwell of being 'not many steps from the old family.' Cromwell's anger mounted and he took swift action when he heard rumours of a Commons' petition supported by some army grousers demanding the abolition of the Protectorate. After two weeks he dissolved Parliament. In a heated speech he denounced the members' attitude: 'If this be your carriage, I think it high time that an end be put to your sitting; let God be judge between you and me.'

Not despairing, Cromwell and the Council pursued their efforts to conciliate the counties. Here was some promise for the future. New JPs were appointed – radicals dismissed, and the old ruling gentry preferred, even young members of Cavalier families. Not all were persuaded, but one remarked with relief, 'We may bless God that our constitution is come again to a settlement' (28, p. 172).

Oliver Cromwell was visibly dying: he was often ill from nervous tension, and the death of his much-loved daughter, Elizabeth, in the summer of 1658 was a deep personal tragedy. He himself died on 3 September, the seventh anniversary of the Battle of Worcester.

Richard's Protectorate

Cromwell delayed nominating his son, Richard, as Lord Protector until the morning of his death. His options were few. Parliament-men like Vane, St John or Haselrig were too critical of the executive power of the Protectorate to be considered; the army commanders, Lambert and Fleetwood, as well as Richard's brother, Henry, seemed too ambitious for power to be acceptable to the county communities. A fair public speaker, Richard Cromwell had many other qualities: a sincere acceptance of his reponsibilities and an appealing modesty and affability which fronted genuine intelligence. Royalists tried to debunk Richard by calling him 'a country bumpkin' and 'a clown', but their hopes of an immediate restoration of Charles II were baseless. Charles had been King-in-exile on the continent since his father's execution in 1649; his effort to recover the throne in 1650–51 with Scots' help had been crushed at Worcester. With him the exiled Edward Hyde noted in 1658, 'The King's condition never appeared so hopeless, so desperate.' In the perspective of history this was a sound judgement. Had Oliver lived or had Richard been given loyal support from some of the powerful men around him, then the hopes of many that *The Humble Petition and Advice* would be more acceptable to the political nation might have been realised, and thus given durability to the Protectorate.

In the event the Protectorate disintegrated in May 1659, and a year later Charles II was restored; there was, however, nothing inevitable about either occurrence. The Protectorate fell because rival groups in London, none commanding more than minority support throughout the nation, challenged Richard's authority, and Richard proved inadequate in a crisis. The Army was, as it had been for twelve years, the key group. Its middle ranks angrily demanded, as in 1647, arrears of pay and the removal from Richard's Council of 'wicked ministers'; its generals, at odds with each other, were unable to maintain proper discipline. Fleetwood, the senior officer, was apt to cry in times of stress – Oliver Cromwell called him a 'milksop' – and Lambert returned to the political scene early in 1659, bent on using his successful and charismatic army career to further his ambitions. His tulip-growing and his beautiful wife had not kept him long from the centre of affairs.

Early in 1659, too, a second group re-emerged to continue agitation against Richard's executive power. Parliament was called in January and a few well-known names like Vane and Haselrig easily took control. They were determined to undo the Protectorate and indulged themselves with expert obstruction of government business. The coincidence of radical political pressure from the army, Lambert's come-back and Haselrig's time-wasting destroyed Richard. His qualities, from which much was expected, proved illusory; instead he buckled under pressure, and, humiliated at finding no support in London, tamely agreed to dissolve the Third Protectorate Parliament in April. With Lambert biding his time and the rest of the army leadership in disarray, Haselrig's demand for the recall of the Rump of the Long Parliament was accepted. Forty-two rather surprised Rump members assembled at Westminster on 7 May 1659. Richard was never formally deposed; finding his presence an irrelevancy on the political scene, he went into exile a few weeks later. 'Richard ye Fourth hath deserted himself', said a contemporary pamphlet. The Protectorate was dead. It had been, suggested Haselrig, only an illegal interval in the proper exercise of sovereignty by the Long Parliament.

It is arguable that this was not at all what the political nation wanted. For nearly two decades neither Parliamentarian nor army leaders had given the country stability. Solutions to the problems raised by the 1640 Crisis seemed as far away as ever. And the options for the immediate future, as viewed by the gentry and merchants, were most unattractive. A despotic Lambert, a tearful Fleetwood, a radical, slippery Haselrig: none inspired much confidence in the City, up in Yorkshire or down in Somerset.

Study 12

So what went wrong? As in 1640 the same question may be asked. In its original conception the Protectorate had much to commend it, as you have already noted. Yet its five-year history is strewn with failed attempts to make it work. Attempt an analysis if its failure to secure a settlement under the headings: (1) Support and (2) Management. Take into account the flaw in the Instrument and include 'opposition' under Support.

Observations:

Gerald Aylmer has observed that 'the basis of support for the Protectorate was too narrow.' You might expect, then, to find it straightforward to list the Protectorate's enemies: those who gibed at the 'quasi-kingship of the bumpkin House of Cromwell'; those who saw the whole operation as a denial of The Good Old Cause (Colonel Edmund Ludlow asserted that it was 'a re-establishment of that which we all engaged against' – what was this?); and those who angrily turned on Cromwell as a 'dissemblingest, perjured villain.' Who comprised this powerful, but divided 'lobby'? On the other hand, some merchants in the City might give their clear support – mutual self-interest, perhaps: why? And of course the army was the most secure prop of all (25, p. 172).

What about the great mass of gentlemen from the shires? Thurloe, Cromwell's influential Secretary, claimed that the Protectorate 'hath a very general acceptance', but that was at the beginning of 1654. What really substantiates Aylmer's observation is that Cromwell and the Council converted only a small proportion of the county gentry to warm-hearted support for his regime. Most of these came in a period of fourteen months (when?), too short for the promise of settlement to be fulfilled. Cromwell was certainly the only man who could have reconciled the communities; he was, as David Underdown has pointedly commented, 'still as much the conservative Huntingdon squire as he was the Puritan zealot and the exalted New Model commander' (28, p. 170). Yet he failed. Some historians are damning: Wilbur Abbott, the American who produced the standard edition of Cromwell's speeches and writings, thought that his talk of settlement was a smokescreen for Puritan despotism. Do you think this is fair? Suggest evidence for your view. You should find the books on the various counties (p. 68) important sources for provincial attitudes in the mid-1650s. For example, Alan Everitt describes the mood of the Kentish gentry: although most accepted the Protectorate in the hope of some peace on their estates,

> The community as a whole was at heart opposed to him; they longed to return to the old days before the War, which seemed in retrospect, however mistakenly, so placid and secure; days when there had been no Army, no Major-Generals, no restless plotting, no sectarian experimentation, and no incessant spying upon those quiet homes whose unquestioned dominion and ordered tranquil life was, with all its faults, the only kind of existence they understood. (48, p. 300)

What do you make of Cromwell's ambivalence over the offer of the Crown? Roots has an excellent discussion of the pros and cons in his *Great Rebellion* (25, pp. 216–19). Did Cromwell really fall between two stools in wanting to conciliate the army at the same time as winning civilian support for his regime? Perhaps you may wish to conclude from the evidence that the verdict is 'not proven'. He kept his links with the army not only out of loyalty and past comradeship but also political realism – you have seen what happened to Richard who had no real ties with the army. You could also consider the point that Richard deserved better support than he received from the leading figures around him – ironically their selfishness led to their own destruction quite soon. Give examples.

Management was an important factor, too. Some pointers: Professor Trevor-Roper has argued that Cromwell's failure was essentially a lack of parliamentary management:

> Under Cromwell something was missing in the mechanics of parliamentary government – that ceaseless vigilance, intervention and management by the Privy Council. (72, pp. 348–55 and 389–91)

You can pick out several critical stages in the narrative when more care and attention on the part of Oliver and later Richard might have prevented Haselrig and his radical friends from wrecking the working of Parliament.

But Christopher Hill has echoed most other modern historians in challenging Trevor-Roper's contention. '"Management",' says Hill, 'enables good parliamentarians to obtain collaboration in working for agreed objectives' (73, pp. 22–4). You may pursue the argument that Oliver Cromwell's insoluble problem was that leading figures on the political scene did not have agreed objectives, and had not had any since 1640. Elsewhere Hill says, 'Even if Oliver had studied the necessary rules of the game, his enemies were more interested in bringing about the Kingdom of God upon Earth than in playing cricket.' It is arguable that Cromwell's tragedy was that few of the many versions of the 'Kingdom of God upon Earth' current in the 1650s accorded with his own vision of central control and an army presence which alone guaranteed liberty of conscience. How does this line of reasoning accord with Trevor Roper's 'management' thesis?

━━━━━━ **CHAPTER 10** ━━━━━━

The Restoration:
A Failure of Expectations

The threat of a Third Civil War

With the Protectorate gone, the seemingly endless series of proposals and experiments, which had characterised the search for a settlement since 1640, was bound to continue. Neither the recalled Rump of about fifty members nor the army leadership offered real hope; indeed such were the attitudes struck and power sought that the average member of the political nation felt only despair. A chorus of voices expressed itself in pamphlets, diaries, speeches and state papers. 'There is a strange contempt and hatred through the nation of this present Parliament,' commented a member of the Council of State. The only chance of settlement meant some kind of 'free Parliament'; only with this could the political nation accept that they were being governed by *their* chosen representatives. Yet though their concerted temper was manifestly fraying they were leaderless and scattered. One small rising, Sir George Booth's 'rebellion' in Cheshire, called for a 'Free Parliament', but was easily suppressed by Lambert's regiment. Political initiative still lay with the Rump politicians and army men.

Debates were, however, sterile. The Rump still saw itself as the predestined instrument of God's Will. Vane's low view of the political instincts of his fellow human beings was bluntly stated: a solution was needed to the central issue of

> how the depraved, corrupted and self-interested will of man, in the great body which we call the people [could be kept on the right road] by the balancing and ruling motion of God's spirit. (28, p. 197)

Some army officers felt the same; they too saw themselves, in the words of Lambert, as safeguarding 'the fundamentals of our Good Old Cause' – by now a nostalgic catch-phrase of only vague meaning. It clearly implied, though, a continuation of the army's political role. The Rump, however, would not brook any army expression of political will. Fleetwood was told that as Commander-in-Chief he could not act without the Rump's authority. Lambert was the more feared: his popularity among the troops, his career and ambitions pointed towards a military coup. Haselrig rashly tried to get him arrested and put in the Tower of London, while other Rumpers appealed for support from the possibly less politically involved part of the army, the regiments maintaining law and order in Scotland under General Monck.

Late autumn 1659 was critical. Lambert's retort to Haselrig was to blockade Westminster and disperse the Rump in October. It was April 1653 come again – with one key exception. The army was no longer a coherent fighting or political force. As Lambert prepared to take his regiments north to 'discipline' Monck's Scottish forces, the political nation realised that the worst of all prospects loomed ahead: not just a military coup, but as Aylmer has succinctly put it, 'competing military despotisms' (2, p. 149). A third civil war was about to begin. The capital city was certainly drifting towards anarchy: citizens clashed with soldiers claiming free quarters (they had not been paid for weeks), and a violent riot took place early in December. The City goldsmiths began moving out of London. News-sheets spoke of 'shops shut, trade gone, fears and jealousies multiply', and one appealed to Monck: 'We are here in great disorder, and expect to be in blood every hour.' While Fleetwood dithered outside London, the Navy declared against Lambert and Haselrig and some republicans seized Portsmouth. Disillusion and fear spread throughout the provinces. At Taunton in Somerset rioters tried to seize the castle in the name of a 'Free Parliament'. Bells were rung and bonfires lit at Christmas in many areas, in direct challenge to the 'godly men' in supposed authority.

Civil war did not develop. The saviour of the gentry was, unexpectedly, an army man. General George Monck, with his soldiers, crossed the Scottish border into England at Coldstream on 1 January 1660.

Monck and the Rump; Hyde and 'Breda'

Monck was the crucial figure in the dramatic events which led to the restoration of Charles II as King of England in May 1660. In fluid and often very dangerous political circumstances he survived the test of nerve. He had several advantages. First, army authority in England was visibly disintegrating. Lambert's men deserted in their hundreds as he moved towards Scotland; they could not see who would pay them in the forthcoming civil war. Fleetwood's rank-and-file joked that they would not join a fight themselves, but would be 'happy to make a ring' in which their officers could slay each other. Fleetwood panicked, handed over the keys of Westminster to the Speaker of the Rump and went into retirement.

Secondly, Monck's character, background and policy were all admirably suited to the times. He was a professional soldier at heart, believing strongly that military men should be subject to the government; he served Dutch, Royalist, Rump and Protectorate governments in turn in a military career spanning thirty years. To the difficult period of the late 1650s he brought a useful trait: caution. One of his contemporaries said he was 'of a great natural prudence and cunning'. He stated his policy in brief yet ambiguous terms – he wanted to restore the civil authority, which in late 1659 could mean to support the Rump, *or* to bring back the purged members, *or* to restore the King. He kept, it was said, 'dark counsel' on these matters. With hindsight, historians have judged this to be Monck's masterstroke; not until the air was clearer and support guaranteed did he declare – in mid-March 1660 – for the restoration of Charles II. Until then he carefully built up his image as the protector of the nation against anarchy and particularly the military despotism of over-mighty subjects, such as Lambert whose ambitions smacked of the great feudal barons of the past. 'I am engaged,' Monck said, 'to see my country freed from that intolerable slavery of a sword government.' Lambert was arrested and sent to the Tower. But Monck needed more advantages than those already noted.

A third asset was his 10,000 strong army in Scotland. Monck had been there for eight years of the 1650s, latterly as an army administrator, ruling with a moderately firm hand and collecting taxes with fair efficiency. His rank-and-file were regularly paid, and the remoteness of Scotland meant that his officers were not lured by London politics. Monck showed his talents in no better fashion than in military management. He chose his junior officers with care and watched their duties closely; by this means he secured loyalty and discipline in his army.

Fourthly, Monck waited on the tide of public opinion – at least of those articulate members of the political nation who could be relied upon to give expression to their views. There were plenty of them, and as the historian Austin Woolrych, has remarked, 'The contrast between the tepid response to the Royalist call to arms in August (Booth's rising of 1659) and the enthusiasm at the end of the year is striking' (28, p. 201) A contemporary, Gilbert Burnet, noted in his papers that people wanted the King back, 'so that matters might again fall into their old channel.' Monck, however, had no intention of issuing an Army invitation to Charles: that had to come from a 'Free Parliament'.

Even with these four assets, Monck had to act with delicate timing. Two of his actions, one late in February and the other in mid-March 1660, directly led to the Restoration. Monck would have admitted he was lucky with the Rump, now, of course, back at Westminster again. Its members played directly into his hands; contemporaries and historians have been amazed at its suicidal tactics – Haselrig actually proposed to demote Monck! As Roots has said, 'the Rump's lack of political sense after all the vicissitudes is almost incredible.' Monck acted swiftly: he sought out many of the old purged (from 1648) Presbyterian MPs, told them they could re-take their seats, and suggested with some force that they use their majority over the Independents to dissolve the Long Parliament – thus keeping the legal forms and paving the way for elections on something like the old franchise for a Convention Parliament. This would work out a constitutional settlement, and its obvious feature would be the restoration of the monarchy. These purged Political Presbyterians expected to be the chief beneficiaries of the new political climate, and as they had been in favour of negotiating with Charles I (see p. 87) right to the bitter end, it was Monck's reasonable and accurate assumption that they would do the same with Charles' son. Such was Monck's first action; familiar names to be seen again at Westminster included Denzil Holles, William Prynne and even Thomas Fairfax. A comment in the Parliament records says that many were 'well-affected to kingly government.' They did what they were told. After twenty years of admittedly interrupted sessions the Long Parliament, according to the May 1641 Act, dissolved itself, and called elections. The writs to the counties made interesting reading, being issued 'in the name of the keepers of the liberties of England'; who 'the keepers' were was not stated.

Meanwhile Monck acted again – covertly. As yet no contact, let alone invitation, had been made with Charles, the exiled King. Early in March Royalists were as disillusioned as ever, and were sure Monck would set himself up as some kind of Lord Protector. But on 17 March Monck sent an agent to Charles who was in Brussels; the agent carried two pieces of advice: Charles should get out of the Spanish Netherlands and go to protestant Breda, a port in Holland, and from there issue a generalised statement referring to a pardon and a Parliamentary-based settlement.

At this point Monck could do little but wait on events. There was still nothing inevitable about Charles' return. Stupid advice, perhaps pressing for controversial terms, could destroy the delicate fabric of opinion in England which had so transformed the King's position. However, Charles and Edward Hyde, so long his adviser on the continent, played a masterly game, made up mostly of inactivity (despite temptation, Hyde kept Charles silent, working on the old truism in politics that the less said the more room for manoeuvre later on), but also when the time came, of a superbly drafted *Declaration of Breda*. Issued on 4 April by 'Charles Rex, to all our loving subjects of what degree or quality,' it was short, yet gave much encouragement to different people, variously expectant or fearful of a royal restoration. He appealed to all men possessing 'a desire and longing that those wounds, which have so many years together been kept bleeding, may be bound up.' To this end, Charles offered four things:

> The fear of punishment may not engage any: we do grant a free and general pardon (excepting only such persons as shall hereafter be excepted by Parliament). Let all our loving subjects how faulty soever rely upon the word of a king... Our subjects we invite to a perfect union among themselves for the re-settlement of our just rights and theirs in a free Parliament, by which upon the word of a king we will be advised...

And because the passions and uncharitableness of the times have produced several opinions in religion, we do declare a liberty to tender consciences, which do not disturb the peace of the kingdom; we shall be ready to consent to such an Act of Parliament offered to us for the full granting of that indulgence,

And we are likewise willing that all things relating to grants, sales and purchases of land shall be determined in Parliament.

And we will be ready to consent to any Act of Parliament for the full satisfaction of all arrears due to the officers and soldiers of the Army under the command of General Monck. (12, p. 57)

The Declaration was a beautiful package: it seemed to contain something for everyone. Its timing was equally important, for elections to the Convention Parliament were under way. Pamphlets recorded that 'the Cavalier spirit breaks out very high'. No one associated with the old Rump or with military rule got in to a county seat and very few in the towns. Significantly, Haselrig failed to get in. There was no serious chance of military intervention: none of the potential military despots, however attached they were to the Good Old Cause, had enough soldiers. The last clause of the *Declaration of Breda* was merely the final stage in the scramble to desert to Monck. Lambert escaped from the Tower in the middle of the elections, but he was easily recaptured when he found no army to command. Evidently disillusion with the politicking of officers had spread through the ranks, and the assertions of 1647 that this was 'not a mere mercenary army' (see p. 78) no longer had any substance. The army's thirteen-year intervention in politics was over.

The formalities of the Restoration of the Monarchy were quickly done. The Convention assembled on 25 April, Charles' *Declaration of Breda* was presented, and on 1 May a rightly famous resolution was adopted by the MPs: 'that the government was and ought to be by King, Lords and Commons' (25, p. 255). Samuel Pepys watched the rejoicing and celebrations that evening, but he had reservations: he thought it 'a little too much' when people drank the King's health on their knees! Charles was proclaimed King, invited to return, and some members of the Convention went to greet him in Holland in mid-May. Charles landed in England at the end of the month, and on 29 May 1660, his thirtieth birthday, he entered London. Popular rejoicing, bells and bonfires reflected the general excitement. Civil war had been averted, and there was high expectation that settlement and stability must follow. John Evelyn, Anglican, former exile and diarist, noted, 'I stood in the Strand and beheld it and blessed God.' John Milton, Independent pamphleteer and poet, regarded the Restoration as a return to bondage, however; he feared for his stated philosophy, 'Give me the liberty to know, to utter and to argue freely according to conscience.' Whether Pepys' doubts, Evelyn's euphoria or Milton's fears were a better guide to the future had yet to be seen.

Study 13

1 Breda was perhaps all things to all men: Royalists at home and abroad, Independents, Presbyterians, sectarians, soldiers, Parliamentarians, gentry. How did Hyde achieve this?
2 Establish some order of importance in the factors which produced the Restoration.

Observations on 2.

You will need to keep in mind the timing (very late on), when the return of Charles became practical politics. There was a groundswell of discontent and fear from early in 1659 – the legacy of the Protectorate (Oliver's narrow base of support and Richard's inadequacy), and the 'competing military despotisms' – which produced a threat of a third civil war, not the Restoration. What it did do, though, was serve as a backcloth to the remarkable swing of public opinion to royalty (evidenced in pamphlets and the Convention elections). On its own it is doubtful if this would have been enough. Three other factors must be seen as determinant, together, not separately: Monck's position, attitudes and the timing of his actions; Hyde's flair for open-ended constitutional phraseology; and the army rank and file's weariness with its officers' political ambitions.

The Convention, 25 April – 29 December 1660

The duty of the Convention was to achieve 'a settlement' – decisions acceptable to the political nation on the major problems of government: its monies, its control over religious practice, its authority over the county communities, and crucially the balance of executive and legislative power. Expectations were high, perhaps impossibly high, for the same problems had remained unsolved by successive regimes since 1640, and members of the Convention proved no more united on the kind of settlement required than, for instance, the 1646 victors of the First Civil War. Again, there were people who did not care for too much precision in the coming decision-making – some could rightly point to the failure of recent legally-worded efforts to produce a constitution of checks and balances; others with less praiseworthy, cynical motives saw more room for profitable manoeuvre and power-mongering in vaguer arrangements.

The Convention dealt with certain of the more immediately pressing problems with speed, moderation and, superficially, with some success. Concern with legal forms required Charles to recognise the Members as a proper Parliament; this was done quickly in June. Yet no amount of juggling with words could alter the fact that the King had not called this Parliament, that it had invited Charles to return, that it was in Roots' expressive phrase, 'an illicit king-making parliament.'

A Navigation Act was framed and passed. It tried to make more efficient previous efforts of the Commonwealth to impose a code regulating the commerce between the American colonial plantations and England. Its crucial clause required commodities to be moved only in ships built, owned and three-quarters crewed by Englishmen. By design and effect it stimulated English commerce at the expense of powerful Dutch rivals. The Act was later condemned as 'a conspiracy of merchants for their own interests' against those of the consumer, but modern historians have concluded that it proved a vital stimulus to English trade and shipping – a factor as yet unglimpsed in easing the Crown's financial difficulties.

By August the issue of 'rebellion' and 'pardon', so clearly pointed to in the Declaration of Breda, was settled. Members felt they had been generous in the Act of Indemnity and Oblivion. A general pardon was issued, thus ending fears of a prolonged Cavalier revenge, with Parliament 'excepting' the regicides (51 – though many, of course, were dead or in exile) and 29 others. Only thirteen were executed in the end, and some others excluded from ever holding government office. A distasteful air, though, hung over the proceedings: debates in the Convention were vitriolic with Prynne taking the lead in showing the depths of hatred existing in some Parliamentarians for army men; Vane, not a regicide, was put on trial and executed because Charles personally regarded him as too dangerous to live; the most grisly event was the exhumation of the bodies of dead 'enemies' – Oliver Cromwell, Ireton, Bradshaw – and their ritual 'hanging' at Tyburn, decapitation, and the final humiliation of a public display of the heads on a pike on Westminster Bridge.

What happened to the other actors on the stage of the twenty-year-old English Rebellion? On the King's side many of his father's advisers were dead: Bristol, for instance, died in exile in 1653, but Hyde's loyal service to father and son was rewarded in 1660 with the Earldom of Clarendon and he remained a key figure in early Restoration politics. Henrietta Maria, also in exile in Paris in the 1650s, came back with her son, but, finding herself excluded from all influence, returned to France to die there in 1669. Prince Rupert too came back and devoted his considerable energies to naval and commercial matters – he died in 1682. Many 'enemies' were politically agile enough to make their personal peace with Charles, who in any case saw able former foes as necessary to the healing and settlement process. Monck, of course, was honoured and became the Duke of Albemarle, but apart from presiding over the disbanding of the Cromwellian armies he played little part in the future affairs of the nation; he was buried in Westminster Abbey after a state funeral in 1670. Others, too, who had borne arms against Charles I returned, but played only small parts on the Restoration's political stage, Fairfax and Manchester, for instance – both died in 1671. Two of the 'Five

Members' had very different fortunes: Holles, who had long been at odds with army rule, welcomed the Restoration, was given a peerage, and rendered valuable service to Charles as an ambassador before dying a very old man in 1681; Haselrig, though not a regicide, was imprisoned for his staunch republicanism – Monck saved him from Vane's fate, but he died in the Tower in 1661. St John was lucky, backing Monck at the last moment, and he went into retirement, dying abroad in 1673. Lambert was even luckier: his military and political career made him even more dangerous than Vane, but the death sentence at his trial was commuted to life imprisonment in Guernsey, where he died in 1683, says Roots, 'a feeble ghost of the dynamic personality of the '50s'. Of Cromwell's two sons, Henry retired in peace to the family lands in East Anglia, dying in 1671, but Richard lived in retirement until 1712, aged 86, partly in Paris and Geneva, partly as a quiet, silent man living in England after 1680 under a false name, John Clark. Fleetwood, too, lived in obscurity until his death in 1692.

The reward and punishment problem was faced squarely by the Convention over the issue of land. Cavaliers, especially those who had suffered during the Commonwealth, either by exile with the King 'over the water' or by Protectorate 'robbery', expected two things from the King as a reward for their loyalty: office and the return of land. On both counts many were disappointed. There were more 'King's Friends' than posts to distribute, and the legal intricacies of estates which had been seized, sold and perhaps split up seemed to defy solutions which would satisfy all-comers. The land answer proved simpler than anyone had dared contemplate. No act was passed: a clause was simply tacked on to the Indemnity and Oblivion depriving legal title to all possessing Crown and Church lands, for these had been confiscated. Other Royalist lands, not confiscated, but sold to pay punitive taxation, were treated as 'voluntary' sales, and past owners were expected to use the law courts to recover – if they could. Some did; others complained loudly. Modern research has proved that many Royalists, with considerable guile, already possessed their lands – they had paid agents in the 1650s to act as land speculators, buying 'their' property for them, then to lie low until better times (25, p. 276).

The future of the armed forces was also settled (superficially, as it turned out) with greater ease than some anticipated, considering that control of the army was central to the original Civil War disputes, and that the politicised New Model had been for so long the dread of the provinces. Monck would oversee the demobilisation of the 40,000-strong, long service, professional army, with arrears of pay guaranteed by a series of monthly assessments. This was done swiftly – too swiftly perhaps, as discharged soldiers with no inclination to take up a trade became a law and order problem to county society. By the end of 1660 only two regiments remained, a few thousand or so. When these were gone the intention was to rely, as in the past, on the local militia, officered of course by the local gentry. How naive this was soon became apparent, when in the following year a small republican rising caused a change of heart, and the two regiments were retained. A mere three thousand or so (the Coldstream Guards and the Life Guards, with the Grenadiers being added soon) they did not seem at the time to constitute that most dangerous of institutions, a standing army. Opinions on this were to change.

Equally naive was the financial 'settlement'. Apart from the extraordinary grant of monies via the assessment to pay off the army and to settle some outstanding debts, the Convention concluded that £1,200,000 per annum would be the required new ordinary income for the Crown. Crown lands and Customs were estimated to bring in two-thirds, so, as the archaic feudal revenues (wardships and the like) were not revived, Charles was granted the Excise on commodities to make up the difference. This meant, with modification, a return to the old principle of 'live of the King's own', and to be fair to the Convention the decisions seemed to have been arrived at in good faith. How the estimates were arrived at is not known, as no record of the discussions survive. What is known is that the Lord Treasurer, Southampton, was lazy and ineffective – he would certainly have preferred borrowing rather than risk controversy in the Convention by putting forward realistic estimates of the Crown's needs; also MPs had for generations been notoriously ignorant of the intricacies of public finance. The failure to solve one of the most crucial features of the 1640 Crisis – the provision of an adequate government revenue – was already apparent by the end of 1660, when the collection of ordinary revenue was falling short of the estimated need by some £300,000.

No long-term solution either was found to that other bone of contention, religion. In fact the year 1660 has proved on this issue as confusing to historians as it was to contemporaries. The expectations and motives of the leading figures – Charles, Clarendon, Bishop Sheldon, the Puritan Richard Baxter – were inconsistent, even obscure; and the main events in London were probably only a smoke-screen for the more important decision-making in the localities far from the capital (30, p. 161). What seems to have happened is this. Large numbers of Anglicans who had so resented Archbishop Laud's policies found through bitter experience in the 1640s and '50s that the alternative was far worse. To the greater gentry in particular, Puritanism now meant army control, the lack of any stable worship in the parishes, the appearance at times of the wilder excesses of the sects, especially the Quakers; but most of all it had led to their exclusion from real local power by the County Committees and by Cromwell's centralising Protectorate. By 1660 these gentry had learned their lesson. The old link between the traditional landowning 'rulers' of the counties and the clergy of the Church of England was thus re-forged. This alliance of country squire and parson, backed by an assertive body of bishops, created in 1660 a powerful 'lobby' wanting to restore with certain modifications the Church system of the 1630s: hence they were nick-named the Laudians. They did not wait for the government in London to propose solutions. Current research in the county histories has revealed what the Oxford historian, Robert Beddard, has called 'a violently Anglican mood' in the country. A petition from Northamptonshire gentry, for instance, demanded a Church 'under the ancient apostolic government by bishops.' Durham Cathedral library has a 1660 manuscript in which 1,500 people lamented the banishment of their bishop,

> the consequence whereof hath deprived us of the holy sacraments, decent marriages and burials, and caused us to be overrun with errors, schisms and atheism. (30, pp. 161–2)

Within only a month or two of Charles' return, exiled or ejected clergy were back in business. The dean of Peterborough returned to his cathedral in July, revived daily choir services, and began to make appointments to parish livings. He ignored a reprimand from London on his eagerness. Elsewhere there is much evidence (Pepys' *Diary*, for example) to show how 'many ministers began of themselves to read the Common Prayer Book'; and in September 1660 a Dorset jury charged five local ministers with 'irreverent neglect' of the traditional form of service. Before the end of the year nearly 700 ministers, put in by the Long Parliament, had been removed. 'One thing is plain,' Beddard concludes from all this evidence, 'the country was moving in a quite contrary ecclesiastical direction from that advocated by the Court' (30, p. 165).

Events in London, at the Court and in Convocation seemed at the time to be key steps in the making of a settlement. Charles, in keeping with the Breda clause on 'liberty to tender consciences', outwardly strove for toleration: he took non-Anglicans as royal chaplains (Richard Baxter, the Presbyterian, was one), he sponsored discussion between rival church groups, and in October 1660 issued the Worcester House Declaration, proposing a settlement in which restored bishops of the Church of England would work with Presbyterian councils, and in which arguments over worship and ceremony would be settled by committees 'of both persuasions'. A Church synod, later called the Savoy Conference, was promised for 1661 to finalise details. Puritans, especially the Presbyterians who had played such an important role in the Restoration events, could feel well pleased. In the event they were sadly deluded. The real, as opposed to the apparent, attitudes of Charles and Clarendon will probably never be known. Modern historians vary in their assessments of the degree of sincerity of Charles in his actions: 'feigned conciliation', says Robert Bosher (29, p. 54), but others are more cautious, agreeing that the evidence is inconclusive on whether Charles wanted a broadly tolerant, comprehensive Church or not. One thing is certain: Charles and his Privy Council avoided any Convention efforts towards a permanent settlement. Why? First, they wanted to postpone decisions on the highly controversial subject of religion until the royal government was well-established; and, secondly, Charles wanted to keep the making of the final settlement in his own hands. In the end, though, these manoeuvrings in London, hypocritical or not, came to nothing in the face of the Anglican backlash in the county communities. Charles was to lose the battle, yet when the Convention was dissolved at the end of 1660 he thought he had won a tactical victory.

The oddest feature of 1660 was perhaps the Restoration of Charles II unconditionally. The Convention raised none of the central questions about the royal prerogative power, and how King and Parliament might work together in harmony. A simple re-affirmation was made of the statutes passed by the King-in-Parliament up to the end of the summer of 1641. What Charles I had accepted (however unwillingly) was still law, whereas all the Ordinances of the Long Parliament and Protectorate were by implication illegal. The prerogative courts, secular and ecclesiastical, had gone – thus the Privy Council was shorn of its juridical powers; prerogative taxation, too, was gone, and Charles was uncomfortably aware that his return was by invitation from a 'parliament' not of his calling. In practice, though, Charles could choose his ministers, veto legislation, dissolve Parliament; he controlled the army (when raised) and was Head of the Church; he and his councillors framed domestic and foreign policy.

In view of the mischief which many of his powers had caused in the past, Charles II could only marvel at his good fortune. How had this come about? Cynics have argued that the absence of 'conditions' meant that all was still to play for in the political game; ambitious politicians saw openings for themselves, and there was certainly a mad scramble for offices and pensions in 1660. Disillusion with all the paper proposals of the '40s and '50s (the *Newcastle Propositions*, the *Instrument of Government* and the like) which some perceived to have been productive of nothing but argument, was another factor. A key reason must have been the admirably imprecise wording of Breda; everyone was aware that any tightly-phrased set of conditions would produce such acrimony that Charles might go away again. This has long been seen as the prime explanation of the unconditional return. As long ago as the mid-nineteenth century Lord Macaulay wrote:

> Had they (the Convention) held long debates on the principles of government – had they drawn up a new constitution and sent it to Charles – had conferences been opened with projects and counter-projects: the Presbyterians and the Royalists would certainly have quarrelled, the military factions might possibly have been reconciled. (29, p. xiv)

A failure of expectations

The Convention was dissolved late in December 1660. It members departed thinking they had achieved a framework for a settlement. Much had been done which gave them confidence: with Charles II, were restored the institution of monarchy, two Houses of Parliament, the Church of England, much of the country's legal system, and its traditional provincial ruling elite of greater gentry and richer merchants. Roots declares that 'the Restoration settlement was expedient, ad hoc, mundane, practical' (25, p. 259). It was doubtful, though, if it would prove a *lasting* settlement. Impossibly high expectations (of the Savoy Conference, for instance), too many critical unanswered questions (the executive–legislative balance of power), too many decisions based on faulty information (Charles' income, for example) – all point to an unstable future.

Then there was the crass belief that it was possible to restore the past, the hope of some reactionaries that the years 1641–60 could be treated as if they had never existed. Ivan Roots has made possibly the most-quoted judgement on the fatuity of such a hope:

> The Great Rebellion willy-nilly had permanent consequences. Like some kind of many-lived Cheshire Cat it left a persistent grin behind. (25, p. 257)

To prove how real was the failure of expectations, an analysis of the years immediately following 1660 will show that the supposed 'settlement' of four problems – religion, finance, the county community, and the Crown-Parliament relationship – was an illusion. On each some progress had been made, but there were unanswered question-marks, the long-standing residue of the 1640 Crisis. They were perhaps one side of the grin of the Cheshire Cat; the other side was the memory of those terrible years of civil war and near-revolution. Few of the influential members of the community would contemplate any answers to the questions which might involve a return to such troubled times.

──────────── *Study 14* ────────────

A brief stock-taking is required at this point.
1 Re-cap on what you have understood by the word 'settlement' in the Interregnum years.
2 List and define the nature of the five problems of the 1640 Crisis, and draw up a three-column summary of
  (a) What progress had been made 1640 to 1659 (e.g. Triennial Act);
  (b) The decisions of the Convention Parliament 1660 (e.g. non-restoration of feudal dues);
  (c) What questions/illusions remained (e.g. religion, Crown income) which could make for a stormy political scene during the next decade or so.

CHAPTER 11

The Cavalier Parliament
1661 – 79
Gentry and Solvency Issues

The ugly landscape of Restoration politics

What had not been settled at the Restoration was an agreed set of relationships between the different parts of the English polity. The tensions and manoeuvrings in the corridors of power in the 1660s and '70s were symptomatic of a grossly unstable situation; they were so reminiscent of the periods before the years 1642 and 1648 that historians consider that late Stuart England escaped a third civil war only by a whisker (the Cheshire Cat, perhaps?). This time, though, the manoeuvrings were carried on mostly by men bereft of the principles and sense of duty which excited Pym, Strafford, Ireton, Wildman and Cromwell. The historian, James Rees Jones has described the post-Restoration in harshly critical terms:

> Deceit and double-dealing on the part of King, minister and politician, cynicism on the part of the people, produced an appalling debasement of politics. Nothing was taken on trust. Politicians, like revellers in a carnival, were assumed to be wearing masks in order to conceal their true features. (5, pp. 2–3)

Professor Jones is not alone. Another modern writer, Andrew Browning, concludes that,

> Most of the Restoration leaders were singularly inept practitioners of the baser arts of politics, who contrived to do their country the maximum amount of harm, whilst doing themselves remarkably little good. (12, p. 4)

If the evidence is there for such hostile verdicts, then it is not surprising that the story of the Cavalier Parliament is one which lurches from difficulty to crisis and back again; it finally destroyed itself on the rock of suspicion – that the King and his closest advisers were moving towards a more absolutist, pro-Catholic framework of government. That contemporaries thought this there is no doubt. Andrew Marvell, poet, friend of Milton and Restoration MP, wrote anonymously in 1677 that,

> for divers years a design has been carried on to change the lawful

government of England into an absolute tyranny and to convert the established Protestant religion into downright popery. (1, p. 281)

The main landmarks of the Cavalier Parliament period illustrate how disillusioned politicians, ranging from the King himself through his chosen ministers to leading MPs, quarrelled as they drifted from one partisan policy to another. Confusion, distrust and suspicion were such that at the beginning and the end of the period two chief ministers of the Crown (Clarendon and Danby) were hounded by Parliament for being responsible for policies they did not approve or support; and in between the King pursued a secret, devious Catholic ambition (The Treaty of Dover), which, had it become public, would almost certainly have cost Charles his throne.

The eighteen years of the Parliament seem to divide into three main periods – Clarendon's Ministry 1661–7, the loose 'Cabal' group of ministers covering 1667–73, and Danby's years of supremacy from 1673 to 1678. The often savage personal rivalries at Court and in the Council, however, often made nonsense of such neat political packaging. Edward Hyde, Earl of Clarendon, found himself under serious pressure from ambitious seekers after office as early as 1662. Browning's assessment, 'honest, resolute, indefatigable' (12, p. 5), made him an ideal adviser to Charles, but he was ill at ease in the fluid political scene of the 1660s. Charles tired of him, and, harassed by unscrupulous competitors for power, he went into exile rather than face impeachment. He had witnessed the horrors of the '65 Plague and the Great Fire of London in the following year; he had become the scapegoat for the humiliating episode in the Second Dutch War when the Dutch sailed up the River Medway and inflicted a 'singeing of the King of Spain's Beard' in reverse; and he had his name unfairly attached to a collection of repressive religious statutes, the Clarendon Code of 1661–5.

The second period, that of the so-called Cabal, had even less unity of purpose. Charles determined to control policy-making himself, and thus made no move to appoint a new chief minister. Two things made these years perhaps the most politically cynical of the whole Stuart century. First, he gathered together a motley group of ministers, many of them very able, but most opportunist, and Charles played off one's intense dislike of another with ease. The mnemonic CABAL is misleading because several other ministers (Coventry, Downing and Finch) were at least as influential in some areas of policy as Clifford, Arlington, Buckingham, Ashley Cooper and Lauderdale. Secondly, Charles began pursuing policies, some running contrary to those advocated by many of his ministers, while others, developed secretly, were incompatible with his own public statements. As Jones has argued, 'Charles consciously mystified his ministers as well as his opponents and the public' (5, p. 11). Aylmer puts it more bluntly, calling him 'two-faced' (2, p. 185). The landmarks which illustrate the confusing policies of this period were: the

Treaty of Dover of 1670, which bound England and France in a military alliance against the Dutch and contained enigmatic financial and religious clauses; a Declaration of Indulgence in which Charles used his prerogative to ensure a degree of religious toleration; the Stop of the Exchequer which suspended for a year payments to the royal creditors because of the cost of military preparations; and finally the beginning of yet a third war with the Dutch. (Fuller treatment of these events is given later.)

The loose pile of ministers all too neatly termed the Cabal, collapsed in 1673 in the face of Cavalier Parliament hostility to the jumble of expensive and suspicious policies. A real crisis loomed, but Charles (unlike his father) retreated: he withdrew his Declaration of Indulgence, and after only two years of indecisive fighting made peace with the Dutch. For the next five years Charles tempered his personal policies by allowing a new team of advisers, led by Thomas Osborne, later the Earl of Danby, to pursue a more sensible set of political ideas. Danby was keen to build up better support for the King in the House of Commons. Via patronage and not a little bribery he made some progress in a Court-Anglican-Cavalier faction, the 'King's Men', which could hold its own in the jockeying for influence which determined the outcome of policies. Peace, too, allowed a better management of the royal finances, with Danby advocating retrenchment, and improved trade bringing in a much higher customs yield for Charles' ordinary income. Once again, though, Charles could not leave well alone: against a rising tide of parliamentary opposition – the moderates led by Lord Halifax and the radicals by Ashley Cooper, now the Earl of Shaftesbury – Charles insisted on continuing a pro-French foreign policy. A barrier of suspicion hardened into mistrust when menacing issues were raised in the clubs and coffee-houses of London. Was James, Charles' brother and a declared Catholic, acceptable as heir to the throne? Was Charles' government receiving money from Louis XIV of France? And what about the hypocrisy of Danby, so clearly, they thought, the agent of Charles' pro-French policy and yet claiming to support the parliamentary-Anglican/anti-French viewpoint?

The thesis of this chapter and the next is that instability in the daily round of politics gives a distorted picture of the period. Below the surface other tendencies could be detected, some providing glimpses of future 'settlement'. Re-alignments were taking place and old issues were given new twists as priorities changed in the face of fresh developments. As the historian Joan Thirsk has put it, 'a workable system did emerge, but it evolved pragmatically'. An analysis of the issues of 1640 will reveal some aspects still unsolved, but others with partial solutions, which were either arrived at accidentally or even contrary to the ideas of many people who claimed to wield political power.

Control by squirearchy

Charles II, it might be argued, was restored by men of property. Monck and Hyde could have done little without the widespread support of the gentry of provincial England. The price of that support was an end to the centralisation policies which had marked both Charles I's rule in the 1630s and Cromwell's in the 1650s (despite the Major-Generals' attempt at regional government). For a while Charles II and his Restoration governments acquiesced and England returned to what it had been in Tudor times, essentially a confederation of semi-independent counties. Given the lack of political will, the lack of a large army and a large bureaucracy, together with the abolition of the prerogative courts, the old hierarchical social controls were re-asserted. The gentry, especially the greater gentry, whose recovery of their social position had begun in the last days of the Protectorate, continued to thrive: as JPs, Deputy-Lieutenants and officers of the militia they were able to stamp their own attitudes on local county society. They claimed to exercise their duties paternalistically, that is in the general interests of the community, but there was little that was progressive or liberal in their prejudices.

One fear of the greater gentry was an old one: the multi-headed monster of social revolution. For many, Robert Cotton's 1628 warning of revolt by the 'loose and needy multitudes' had all but come true in the 1640s. There were many pamphlets printed in the early 1660s looking back in horror at the two 'revolutionary' decades. The Rev. Newcombe wrote, 'Then we lay at the mercy and impulse of a giddy, hot-headed, bloody multitude'; another, anonymous, writer lamented that in a republic the gentry must be 'reduced to the condition of the vulgar'. Determined never to suffer again, this elite insisted on subjection, obedience and control. The case for this claim was put in the 1680s by the Dean of Worcester when preaching a sermon to the leading citizens of London:

> Civil equality is morally impossible; the poor are necessary for the establishment of superiority and subjection in humane societies. The poor are the hands and feet of the body politic, who hew the wood and draw the water of the rich. (29, p. 177)

The means of social control were varied. JPs had for generations the administration of poor relief in their hands; a further power, through the Act of Settlement of 1662, authorised them to expel and force back to his native parish any vagrant. As landowners the greater gentry imposed their will on their tenants. The Verney family archives, uncovered in some unpublished research by Dr Broad in 1973, reveal a harsh attitude. Sir Ralph Verney wrote, 'No man is bound to suffer his tenants to reap the benefit of his land because they are poor. That were a ready way indeed to make them rich and him poor' (29, pp. 153 and 159). Throughout the Restoration period there is evidence that Verney rents were as high as possible and evictions were common. Game Laws protected by statute (1671) the right of the gentry squires to have plenty of partridges, pheasants, wild duck, thrushes and grouse to trap or shoot; thus poorer yeomen were deprived of good food, even on the land they farmed. Another statute passed by the Cavalier Parliament ensured that new ideas or criticism which might challenge the existing social and political order were easily suppressed – the Licensing Act of 1662 restored the censorship of anything in print. Such censorship had lapsed in 1640, but was not to lapse again for another thirty years.

Crucial, too, to secular control was the pulpit: the alliance of squire and parson was a significant feature of the period. The gentry had learned the lesson which Charles II's father had observed – that 'people are governed by the pulpit more than the sword in time of peace.' An influential divine, Dr Robert South, expressed the inter-dependence of Church and State:

> If there was not a minister in every parish, you would quickly find cause to increase the number of constables. (49, p. 56)

– while in return,

> The Church of England glories in nothing more than that she is the truest friend to kings. (30, p. 167)

The message persistently preached to secure this control was non-resistance to established authority. For the lower orders the 'text' they heard was 'resignation': an Anglican pamphlet, *The Whole Duty of Man*, was widely read and approved by their social superiors;

> To the Poor: be content with whatever entertainment thou findest here on Earth, knowing thou art upon thy journey to a place of infinite happiness, which will make an abundant amends for all the uneasiness and hardship thou canst suffer on the way. (49, p. 13)

Education, especially a little learning for the poor, was viewed with great suspicion, being held responsible for the upheavals of the past years. Endowments for Latin grammar schools fell markedly after 1660, and many village schools run for decades by the local parson died out. There is evidence that literacy declined seriously over the next centuries, and numbers entering advanced education were much reduced. The gentry thought 'an university too low a breeding', said one pamphlet. The historian Lawrence Stone concludes that the numbers entering university dropped after 1640, and did not rise to the same proportion until the mid-*twentieth* century: 'The slowing up of the growth of literacy allowed the parson and the squire to re-establish their predominant role in the village; this helped to ensure domestic peace for about a century.' Another seventeenth century writer phrased it more cynically: 'Ignorance is the Mother of Devotion and Obedience' (29, pp. 173–4).

With such squirearchical control the gentry's fear of social revolution died away. Any future renewal by central government of interference as in the past would be stoutly resisted. But a new spectre worried them. The lesser gentry found themselves without the money reserves to adapt to a rapidly changing economic scene, and they viewed with alarm the emergence of a new social group, the 'monied interest'. A few merchants in Parliament was one thing, but the arrival of a powerful pressure group capable of influencing governments was something they had not counted on.

The beginnings of a financial and commercial revolution

It seems reasonable to suggest that any government ought to collect from the people being governed a fair proportion of the national wealth through a taxation system; equally taxpayers ought to have confidence in their money being used for legitimate purposes of benefit to the community. Of supreme importance, then, would be accountability of one to the other, through officials effectively working an agreed system. The inefficiency of the financial arrangements underpinning Tudor and early Stuart Conciliar Government was an important factor in the collapse of 1640. Yet the efficiency of Pym's Assessment methods of the Civil War when carried over into the Protectorate suggested an unacceptable degree of centralisation to the county communities. If stability were to be achieved, then new ideas and attitudes would have to emerge. In the decades immediately following the Restoration there were two major improvements in government finance, albeit set against a backcloth of chronic problems.

Thoughtful contemporaries, concerned to find some fiscal stability, could see three seemingly intractable problems which rendered the backcloth threadbare, capable only of patching. The first concerned those who occupied the office of Lord Treasurer. This post carried great power and influence, but any occupant conscientiously trying to do his duty would find the work onerous, even crushing. Southampton, who held the office from 1660 to 1667 was a mild, lethargic man, quite incapable of perceiving the nature of the problem, let alone any solutions. Later, two other Lord Treasurers, Clifford and Danby, were very able, but so enmeshed in the tortuous political manoeuvrings of the '70s that neither attempted serious innovation. Only Lawrence Hyde, Earl of Rochester (Clarendon's second son), in the 1680s succeeded in controlling royal expenditure. Capable and dedicated – up at 5 a.m. and at the Treasury an hour before anyone else – he saw clearly the measure of the problem: that any improvement in the King's financial position was followed all too often by a proportionately more rapid rise in the King's expenditure.

The second chronic problem was linked with the first. The men at the

Treasury always felt they were coming from behind. The Convention's arrangements in 1660 to raise £1,200,000 royal ordinary revenue soon fell woefully short of expectation. The average annual income collected over the whole reign was only £900,000 – with the early years worse, and the later ones better than this figure. A new Hearth Tax was granted by Parliament in 1662, with high hopes of making up the deficit: less than half was ever collected. Thus recourse to Parliament for help became regular; in all sixteen sessions of the Cavalier Parliament (only 1672 and 1676 saw no sessions) the government presented demands for 'extraordinary supply' (50, pp. 262–3 and 277).

At times the MPs were not ungenerous. It was obvious that the system of collection did not raise the sums authorised, and this was not the King's fault. Clifford, nicknamed 'the bribe-master general', extracted unprecedented sums from Parliament in the early 1670s. In a determined effort to break the stranglehold of Crown debt he argued that Parliament must accept the 'exceptional' expenditure which had arisen from war, plague and fire in the mid-'60s. Even so such efforts could not contain the steady rise of these debts. Danby left office in 1679 with the Crown in a £2,400,000 debt. Charles II was patently not 'living of his own'.

But could he? The third problem was the inter-relation between the system and the taxpayers' attitudes towards the fairness of taxation and the acceptability of Crown expenditure. In this both Charles and MPs must share the burden of criticism. Sir William Petty in 1662 stated the principle:

> Men should contribute to the public charge according to the share and interest they have in the Public Peace; that is according to their Estates and Riches. (50, p. 139)

In a House of Commons debate on this Sir Thomas Clarges showed how narrowly such a principle could be interpreted:

> No man ought to be taxed but for the spareable part of his revenue.

That only wealth, *minus all necessary expenses*, should be taxed produced much mischief, especially when allied to the age-old aversion of the gentry to a strictly honest valuation of their property. The result was that wealthy landowners with incomes in many thousands of pounds were taxed on 'declared' income of mere hundreds. The gentry saw nothing immoral about this. Their attitude was rather the reverse: they were incensed at what they saw as unwarranted draining of money from the counties to London; and they repeated complaints in the House of Commons that landed wealth was grossly *over*-taxed. How far there was a genuine base for this resentment and how far it was mere crocodile tears can be judged from Professor Chandaman's recent research findings:

1660–88 – £11 million tax paid by 'landed interest'.
        – £18 million tax paid by 'merchant interest'.
        – £19 million tax paid on goods bought (50, p. 190)

Thus parochialism, which had so bedevilled the Royalist cause in the Civil War, was still much in evidence in Restoration England. The inescapable conclusion is that a significant segment of the Crown's financial difficulties stemmed from the reluctance of taxpayers to meet their responsibilities, even when their representatives in Parliament had agreed on a figure.

The other significant segment lies with the Crown itself. Its administration was inefficient and allowed varying degrees of corruption. Office-holders were usually appointed through favour and connection, little notice being taken of administrative or financial ability. Salaries were low, with great reliance placed on separate fees or perquisites. The most notorious of these relied on the antiquated administrative machinery of the Crown's revenue departments: delays in recording paying out money meant that officials could 'borrow' government money and invest it for a short while in some venture of personal profit. Again, the 'Royal State and Dignity' which allowed the King to keep up a Court of considerable grandeur, costing £50,000 per annum, also extended to granting pensions to favoured courtiers which grew in Charles II's reign to an *extra* £180,000 each year. When the cost of Charles' mistresses, or as Chandaman calls it, 'the ramifications of harem finance' (50, p. 270), is added, the political price of Charles' careless generosity can readily be seen. Professors Haley and Chandaman have at different times in the 1960s and '70s investigated documents in the British Museum Library and in Treasury records. In the 1670s two mistresses, the Duchesses of Cleveland and Portsmouth, and their children received permanent grants of £45,000 a year; while Nell Gwynne appears in a manuscript under the heading 'Nelly' as receiving £16,041 15s 6d between March 1676 and March 1679. Haley has judged Nell and Portsmouth to have received in three years the equivalent of one month of the entire royal revenue! (32, pp. 10–11 and 50, p. 271)

The fiscal backcloth of the post-Restoration years has been called thread-bare: the evidence presented so far would seem to support such a conclusion. Two developments, however, offer glimpses of a better organised and more prosperous future – to such a degree that modern historians have labelled it the beginnings of a financial and commercial revolution. A much wider perspective shows that these two 'revolutions' were to be the basis for the great Industrial Revolution of the next century.

The first was administrative reform: unspectacular, largely hidden behind the official doors of the Treasury, the embryo of improvement could easily have been buried under the rubble of the political manoeuvrings and crises of Charles' reign, but it survived. The essence of reform was Treasury authority.

Charles, disillusioned by the financial difficulties of the early '60s, determined to seek something better; on the death of the Lord Treasurer, Southampton, in May 1667 he set up a four-man Treasury Commission of, he said, 'rough and ill-natured men not to be moved with civilities or importunities in payment of money'. The men were Sir Thomas Clifford, Sir William Coventry and Sir John Duncomb, with Sir George Downing in the crucial post as Secretary; they embarked on what Chandaman calls 'the most important financial experiment of the period' (50, p. 215). The key point was a 17 June 1667 'Rule of Specific Sanction', which authorised the Treasury to regulate government departmental expenditure. The Rule still exists today. One important aspect of this Rule was the instruction that before any money warrant was signed by the King, the Treasury Commissioners had to be informed, so that the King could be told 'as to the matter of fact and as to the conditions and present state of the revenue' (30, p. 97–8). This remark, from Downing's carefully recorded minutes, had significant implications, heralding as it did the decline of the authority of the Privy Council in fiscal matters. Downing also insisted on up-to-date information being readily available – treasurers of various spending departments had to submit weekly statements of their receipts and issues of money, and separate registers had to be kept on every aspect of Treasury business.

Another reform with far-reaching consequences was the end of the system of tax-farmers: it had long been the custom to lease out to merchants or courtiers for capital sums the right to collect particular taxes, and such preferential grants to favoured courtiers has been estimated to have lowered Charles' ordinary income by at least £20,000 per annum. In 1671 the Customs Farm was abolished, too, and a new Customs Office built in London, staffed by salaried officials under Treasury control. So successful was this direct collection of revenue that Excise and Hearth taxes were also removed from 'farmers', and the system became permanent.

Downing was responsible for one more financial reform. He had for long been appalled by the hodge-podge way in which the Crown raised loans: interest was high because they always seemed to be needed quickly and lenders were so fearful of the scale of the Crown debts that long-term loans were rare. Downing proposed a system designed to create confidence in the government: his 'credit orders in course' (74, p. 39). This meant that loans were recorded in registers which were open to public inspection, and repayments were made 'in course', that is, in strict rotation by order of receipt; other loans were given a Parliament-guaranteed interest rate of six per cent. This idea made a slow start. As Pepys recorded in his *Diary*, 'Everybody keeping in their money', so suspicious were people of government stability. But the attraction of guaranteed, steady repayment to ordinary citizens gradually broke the monopoly which goldsmith-bankers had had as lenders at high interest rates to the Crown. Downing's idea was to nurture a new financial breed, the friend and ally of governments of the future in times of prosperity and crisis: the small investor had been born.

Many claims have recently been made for the significance of Downing and his Treasury Commission reforms. Professor Charles Wilson of Cambridge University has concluded that 'under Downing the country had taken a major step forward to a modern system of public finance'; further, he argues, that on a larger canvas, 'The Restoration has a better claim than most dates to be regarded as the economic exit from medievalism' – Downing and the year 1667 clearly form a precious portion of this argument (75, pp. 216 and 236). Some reservations must be stressed. Treasury *control* came later. From 1667 it was establishing a code of conduct or 'discipline' in fiscal matters; with a staff of only around twenty the control to be exercised in later years would have been impossible. Also one central feature of the Financial Revolution, a national bank, was not to emerge until the 1690s, and a really professional Civil Service not until the nineteenth century.

The second major Restoration development was the Commercial Revolution, 'a truly astonishing change in the nature of England's export trade,' comments Professor Ralph Davis (38, p. 9). It was a change which largely took place in the three decades following the Restoration. Throughout the Tudor and early Stuart period England's trading prosperity had been dangerously dependent on one commodity – wool (90 per cent of exports), and on one area – north-western Europe. Any effort to participate in a carrying-trade outside this limited area had been blocked by Dutch mercantile hegemony: in ships (better and cheaper), in new ventures (whaling and to the Far East), in credit (long-term on marginal profits) the Dutch had long dominated West European trade. Slowly and imperceptibly changes were taking place. The key position of Antwerp in the entrepôt trade was weakening under the impact of chronic warfare, while England fostered merchants with a broad vision financed by joint-stock companies operating with a pool of capital.

Questions arise, of course, about the engine of this commercial revolution. The accumulation of capital by the landed gentry was an important background factor, for these were the men who invested in the joint-stock enterprises. For them 1660 was a date heralding the end of feudal dues and especially wardship. Land was free from arbitrary death duties and Christopher Hill has commented on the consequences of this: 'long-term planning and investment of capital in estate management were made possible.' Another, more direct, factor was government initiative. The Navigation Acts of 1651 and 1660, as we have seen, promoted an English control of shipping and trade with colonies. The three Dutch wars in mid-century broke the Dutch hold on trade in tobacco, sugar, furs, slaves and codfish. The Acts and wars created an imperial monopoly, allowing merchants to buy English and colonial export goods cheap and sell them dear. The result was a considerable accumulation of merchant capital.

A crucial change, which became the pivot of the commercial revolution, was the growth of a European demand for the products of the tropics – tobacco, sugar, spice, indigo, cotton, rice, coffee, mahogany. As the historian, Gordon Jackson, ruefully remarks, 'It is a pity that the significance of Nell Gwynne's more respectable occupation is so often eclipsed by the glamour of her more lucrative pastime; there had always been royal mistresses, but orange-sellers were the product of a much newer trade!' (30, p. 138).

There is just about enough statistical evidence, both of general trends and particular improvements, to buttress the conclusions being made about the Commercial Revolution, though modern writers have issued warnings: Jackson says, 'the paucity of contemporary evidence permits us to do no more than hint at the likely orders of magnitude in some areas.' Two sweeping trends deserve notice. In a period of slight inflation the customs revenue of the Crown increased ten-fold over the Stuart century, with much of it coming in the later part; its impact on the great crisis of the 1680s will be seen later. The most important development was to be in the re-export trade – goods coming to England from her colonies, then sent to European markets. In value re-exports were a mere £50,000 around 1640; by 1700 they nearly reached £2,000,000. Further statistical support for this trend may be seen in these examples of vessels, companies and commodities (mainly in 30, p. 151 and 38, p. 10):

English shipping (tonnage) 1660 – 200,000
1686 – 340,000

The East India Company: investments in Indian coastal 'factories'
1660s – £100,000 per annum
1680s – £600,000 per annum

Sugar: Imports 1615 – 50,000 lb
late 1660s – 15,000,000 lb
1700 – 37,000,000 lb (including much re-export)

Wool: Exports *c.* 1600 – 90 per cent of English trade
c. 1700 – 50 per cent of English trade

Tobacco: Prices 1620s – *c.* 30 shillings per lb
1630 – 1 penny per lb (vast increase in trade)
1670 – One shilling per lb

e.g. Virginia and Maryland colonies exported:
20,000 lb to England in 1619
9,000,000 lb to England in 1660
15,000,000 lb to England in 1680
22,000,000 lb to England in 1700

A quite different verdict is thus possible on the Restoration age from the politically unprincipled one noted at the beginning of this chapter. Merchants had a clear priority in that they wanted a secure world in which to make their profits. In 1960 Caroline Robbins, assessing whether the Restoration was a blessing or a disaster, decided this was 'a bustling, imperial, materialistic age' (29, p. 151).

Study 15

Charles' money has been the subject of much historical controversy, which shows the great care you are required to exercise in evaluating documents. It all seemed clear when William Shaw produced, over several decades beginning in 1904, his twenty-volume *Calendar of Treasury Books*. The conclusions drawn from this wealth of statistical information was that the House of Commons was niggardly and failed to meet the 'legitimate' requirements of government spending. The effect of this on a proper assessment of Charles is plain: many

Government Income, 1661–79.

	(a) Permanent Ordinary Revenue (£)	(b) Temporary Parliamentary Additions (£)	(c) Non- parliamentary Additions (£)	Total Available for Ordinary Purposes (£)
1661–2	544,911	785,161	123,011	1,453,083
1662–3	809,713	403,347	276,657	1,489,717
1663–4	843,258	284,429	26,986	1,154,673
1664–5	819,447	70,580	2,808	892,835
1665–6	644,544	12,396	50,075	707,015
1666–7	649,347	16,341	–	665,688
1667–8	814,053	16,470	–	830,523
1668–9	873,174	6,406	4,025	883,605
1669–70	953,813	34,148	2,362	990,323
1670–1	840,170	146,339	179,045	1,165,554
1671–2	1,000,432	282,332	619,416	1,902,180
1672–3	1,006,860	336,153	20,382	1,363,395
1673–4	1,027,653	236,864	77,900	1,342,417
1674–5	1,138,010	251,906	40,267	1,430,183
1675–6	1,027,427	293,466	100,070	1,420,963
1676–7	1,042,815	309,744	56,949	1,409,508
1677–8	1,026,020	309,590	24,450	1,360,060
1678–9	1,063,723	241,071	21,100	1,325,894

(a) This represents the whole of the basic ordinary revenue, as settled upon Charles II in 1660–2.

(b) This includes all parliamentary supplies, designed to supplement the ordinary revenue or to pay off debts (arising from whatever cause) which encumbered it.

(c) This includes casual receipts from the Portuguese marriage dowry, the sale of Dunkirk, and all the French subsidies except that provided specifically for the war of 1672–4.

historians were led in the first half of the twentieth century (for example, Sir Arthur Bryant) to depict him as a much-maligned monarch.

In 1975 Professor C.D. Chandaman produced the fruits of his twenty-year intensive study of English public revenue from 1660 to 1688 (50), which has demolished Shaw's thesis. For instance, he argues that Shaw ignored the 'harem finance' problem, because he failed to detect the devious (e.g. Secret Service expenditure) channels by which Charles' mistresses were paid. Chandaman says Shaw also misinterpreted much of the evidence he obtained from the Public Record Office. The trouble was that many medieval exchequer procedures, such as tallies, were still in use at the Restoration, and distortions in the records were easily concealed by involved administrative practices. Chandaman's investigation proved that payments by tally were enormously larger than could be accounted for by entries in the Exchequer Account Books: his conclusion is 'inescapable' – the true distribution of revenue was falsified by future revenue being recorded under present receipts (50, pp. 271, and 281–94).

You are asked to examine the table below, and from information given in this chapter and the previous one to explain the reasoning behind Chandaman's following conclusion:

The permanent ordinary revenue settled at the Restoration clearly proved for more than twenty years incapable of meeting the demands of the legitimate ordinary

	(d) Parliamentary Grants for Extra-ordinary Purposes (£)	(e) Casual Receipts for Extra-ordinary Purposes (£)	Total Available for Extraordinary Purposes (£)	Total Net Income (£)
1661–2	42	–	42	1,453,125
1662–3	65,050	–	65,050	1,554,767
1663–4	65,000	–	65,000	1,219,673
1664–5	1,232,663	68,165	1,300,828	2,193,663
1665–6	1,295,803	102,248	1,398,051	2,105,066
1666–7	864,636	102,248	966,884	1,632,572
1667–8	696,094	8,521	704,615	1,535,138
1668–9	901,157	–	901,157	1,784,762
1669–70	194,775	–	194,775	1,185,098
1670–1	163,037	–	163,037	1,328,591
1671–2	240,941	155,558	396,499	2,298,679
1672–3	316,305	245,516	561,821	1,925,216
1673–4	727,885	197,839	925,724	2,268,141
1674–5	171,941	7,385	179,326	1,609,509
1675–6	18,576	–	18,576	1,439,539
1676–7	93,771	–	93,771	1,503,279
1677–8	621,032	–	621,032	1,981,092
1678–9	401,790	–	401,790	1,727,684

(d) Included here are all the direct taxes (e.g. for war) other than those referred to in note (b).

(e) This comprises casual receipts arising from, and devoted to, war – i.e. the receipts from war prizes in 1665–7 and 1672–4, the French war subsidy of 1672–4, and the Dutch indemnity in 1674.

Source: C.D. Chandaman, *English Public Revenue 1660–88*, O.U.P., 1975, p. 332.

expenditure... But with large re-inforcements obtained from Parliament in 1660–63 and 1670–81 the gap appears to have been closed... To this extent Parliament ultimately fulfilled its financial undertaking to the restored monarchy... the trough of the reign lay in the six years 1664–70 when total ordinary income averaged less than £830,000 per annum... During the second decade the position was entirely different: the ordinary income averaged £1,375,000, providing a very considerable margin, increased by £34,000 on casual receipts, for recovering the 'sinewes of the monarchy'. This was not achieved, very largely because of the wasteful expenditure of the King... Thus Charles' extravagance did not initially create, but subsequently prolonged and greatly intensified the financial difficulties of his reign. (50, pp. 272–73)

CHAPTER 12

The Cavalier Parliament

1661 – 79

Religion and Executive Power

A Religious Divide

The year 1662 may be seen as one of the significant dates of English history: in it the Act of Uniformity was passed through Parliament and sanctioned by the King.

Whereas in the first year of the late Queen Elizabeth there was one uniform order of common service and prayer in the Church of England, compiled by the reverend bishops, and clearly set forth in one book, *The Book of Common Prayer*, and enjoined to be used by Act of Parliament; yet a great number of people in divers parts of this realm following their own sensuality do wilfully and schismatically refuse to come to their parish churches, and the great and scandalous neglect of ministers in using the said order or liturgy, to the great decay and scandal of the reformed religion of the Church of England and the hazard of many souls...

Nothing conduceth more to the settling of the peace of the nation than a universal agreement in the public worship of Almighty God, be it enacted:

– all ministers of any parish church or other place of worship shall be bound to use *The Book of Common Prayer*

– that every person, vicar or minister shall in the church before the Feast of St Bartholomew (24 August 1662), publicly read *The Book of Common Prayer* and publicly before the congregation declare his consent to the use of all things in the said Book

– that all who neglect or refuse shall be deprived of all spiritual promotion

– that every dean of a cathedral, all masters, fellows, tutors of the universities, and every schoolmaster keeping any public or private school, shall subscribe to the declaration,

'I will conform to the liturgy of the church of England, as it is by law established.'

– that no form of common prayers shall be openly used in any church, chapel or college other than what is prescribed. (12, pp. 377–82)

The point of the Act was quite explicit: all positions of power and influence in the Church, schools and universities were now restricted to Anglicans. *The Book of Common Prayer*, so central to the Anglican form of worship, had been revised by Convocation, but it differed little in essence from the original 1559 version, and as such was still unacceptable to Puritans. Thus, far from uniting the people of England in 'a universal agreement', as declared in the preamble, the Act forced a decision of conscience on many committed parsons and teachers. In the 9,000 or so parish livings throughout England and Wales nearly a thousand clergy were 'deprived'. An accurate number cannot be compiled from the records, but the figure of 909, which included 149 ejected from teaching, was worked out in the 1930s and is still the best estimate.

The Act of Uniformity was the most important piece of a legislative series. With three other acts it has been misleadingly dubbed 'the Clarendon Code' (Clarendon was at the very least equivocal about the whole affair; also two further acts of the 1670s may be regarded as part of the proscriptive intent of the Cavalier Parliament). The first one, and preceding Uniformity by a year, was the Corporation Act, which set up special commissioners nominated by the Crown to compel all town officials to reject the Presbyterian Covenant, take the Anglican sacraments and swear oaths of allegiance. The two measures laid the base rules, but it soon became clear that a wide range of Puritan opinion was not going to play the game. Two more persecutory acts followed: the Conventicle Act and the Five Mile Act of 1664–65. The first stopped all religious meetings of more than five adults (outside a family household) if the Prayer Book was not in use; the second halted all preaching and teaching within five miles of a town unless the various oaths and declarations of 1661–62 had been made. The contrast between the freedom of worship of the 1650s and the new draconian laws was startling. The gentry of the Cavalier Parliament had not yet finished. A Second Conventicle Act was pushed through in 1670 imposing penalties on local officials who did not enforce the Clarendon Code with its intended vigour. The Anglican offensive in the political sphere was maintained by the 1673 Test Act, when the spirit of the Corporation Act was extended to central government: all non-Anglicans were to be excluded from holding public office – a measure which within three months forced the resignation of the Lord High Admiral, James, Duke of York, Charles' brother, heir to the throne and by now a known Catholic. A further Test Act of 1678 'disabled papists from sitting in either House of Parliament' (12, p. 391).

Such were the measures: of what significance were they? Was there to be a 'settlement' at last? That it was to be permanent there can be no doubt. Beddard, writing in 1979, speaks of 'the creation of the Anglican establishment as it was to endure into the nineteenth century, the final chapter in the long and painfully idiosyncratic history of the English Reformation' (30, p. 166). Whether it was the best solution is open to question. Robert Bosher in an influential book written in 1957, places emphasis on the Laudian triumph 'of a militant High Anglicanism and the final exclusion of all non-conforming clergy, (29, p. 50). It was certainly a triumph which created a long-lasting rift in English society: that between 'Church' and 'Chapel'. The fundamental effect of the Clarendon Code and its legislative after-thoughts was to make communicant membership of the Erastian Church in England a test of political and social acceptability and respectability. This Church was now more closely defined – its characteristics were episcopal government, a standard liturgy and the maintenance of certain ceremonials. But if it was not Puritan, neither was it Catholic. Bosher concludes,

> The ecclesiastical settlement which thus took effect has been rightly regarded as a major landmark in English Church history, and remains as a permanent achievement of the Laudian party... The limits of its comprehensiveness were finally established by the decision made in 1662. If a century before [i.e. the 1559 Settlement], Anglicans had solemnly affirmed that 'the Church of Rome hath erred', the Laudian triumph resulted in a judgement of equal moment – that the *Ecclesia Anglicana* was of another spirit than Geneva. (29, p.59)

A settlement then it was – of a kind: Erastian, defined, partisan, long-lasting. The persecutory character remained for only a generation (see p. 203 for 1689), but the political exclusion clauses were not removed until the Test and Corporation Acts were repealed in 1828 and the University Test Act was passed in 1871. The memory of what was done is still there: the Puritan-Nonconformist churches held a tercentenary anniversary of the Act of Uniformity in 1962, and commented, 'We recognise the bitterness which marked the controversies following the Great Ejectment.'

All this is, of course, with hindsight. Historians today recognise that there are many points of controversy which blur any final assessment. Bosher acknowledges that 'some mystery still attaches to the ecclesiastical settlement of the Restoration', and he chides various Anglican and Nonconformist writers with telescoping the events of the early 1660s to produce a 'Whig History' version (see p. 220 for the 'Whig' interpretation of history): one that assumes from later events that the restoration of the old church followed automatically, and that the Royalists were united from first to last in their determination to drive the Puritans out. Yet the evidence for this 'determination' presents a complex picture.

The persecution mosaic is there in gaudy colours. Harsh satirical anti-Puritan plays and pamphlets were circulating with titles like *The Lecherous Anabaptist*. The equation 'dissent = sedition' was given popular expression in a contemporary rhyme,

> A presbyterian is such a monstrous thing
> That loves democracy and hates a king.

Another anonymous ballad voiced the view of Cavaliers bent on revenge:

> Pox on Phanatics, rout 'em,
>   they thirst for our blood;
> And let the Popish faction
>   disturb us if they can;
> They ne'er shall breed distraction
>   in a true-hearted man. (51; p. 220)

The treatment of John Bunyan affords the most famous example, suffering as he did intermittent imprisonment over twelve years for unlicensed preaching to his Baptist congregation in Bedford. He wrote in his *Grace Abounding*:

> After I had lain in prison above seven weeks, a bill of indictment was preferred against me: 'That John Bunyan, labourer, hath devilishly and perniciously abstained from coming to Church to hear Divine Service, and is a common upholder of unlawful meetings to the great disturbance and distraction of the good subjects of this kingdom'.

In an exchange with the judge at his trial:

> Justice Keeler said, the Common Prayer Book is lawful for it to be used in Church.
> I said: show me the place in the epistles where the Common Prayer Book is written, or one text of the Scripture that commands me to read it;
> He said he was not so well versed in Scriptures as to dispute and that they could not wait upon me any longer.

Bunyan was sent to prison for another three months with a threat that if he persisted, 'You must stretch your neck for it, I tell you plainly' (51, p. 232).

The Quakers were the most stubbornly unco-operative. George Fox's *Journal* details his refusal to swear an oath of allegiance and how he challenged a judge at Assize Court in 1663:

> Why dost thou not observe the King's declaration from Breda – that no man should be called upon in matters of religion?

Fox was ignored and imprisoned

> ... into a tower where the smoke of other rooms came up so thick that it stood as dew upon the walls, and was so thick that I could hardly see the candle when it burned, so that I was almost smothered. Besides it rained upon my bed – and the place being high and open to the wind. In this manner did I lie all that long winter, that my body was greatly swelled and my limbs much numbed. (51, pp. 235–7)

More than 15,000 Quakers suffered fines, imprisonment or transportation in the generation after 1660.

This is but half the picture. Persecution varied in its intensity: non-conformity not only survived, but thrived in places. The Second Conventicle Act of 1670 showed that the Clarendon Code was simply not being enforced. Too many JPs saw little that spelt sedition in their dissenting neighbours: one member of the greater gentry in Buckinghamshire, Philip, Lord Wharton, allowed his home at Woburn to be used by Nonconformist ministers. The inefficiency of persecution had its humorous side. A dissenter, Vincent Alsop, survived because he varied the time of his services and the authorities found they could not charge him in a court of law because they could not trace his proper Christian name in the records! Despite the law, Quakers, by the end of the century, were holding meetings in every English county. Presbyterianism flourished in the Halifax parish of Yorkshire simply because the Church of England failed to staff the area with sufficient vicars. This was a particular instance of the generally poor financial state of the Church – stipends of the lower clergy were often so low that worthy recruits were few, despite efforts by the bishops to maintain a high standard of appointment. The attractiveness of Anglicanism was further reduced by the revival of the Church law courts dealing as before with moral and matrimonial cases as well as tithes and wills; their procedures were as before long-winded and the fees extortionate. Add the fact that few committed Puritans could stomach the High Anglican liturgy, then, taking the Halifax example again, the existence of nearly two thousand in seven Presbyterian congregations in the area reveals a considerable survival instinct. The exact number of dissenters is impossible to find from the records. The best estimate seems to be that of a 1676 'census' giving adults over sixteen years of age:

Church of England 'conformists'	2,477,000
Nonconformists	109,000
Papists	14,000 (1, p. 253)

The large proportion of 'conformists' covers many dissenters who became occasional conformists – those who attended only a few times a year, or even slept in the back row! – the 'conformable Nonconformists' as they were called.

In conclusion it is worth asking the question: was all this a reversion to the days of Archbishop Laud? Bosher insists on the term 'Laudian triumph', but reservations can be made. The revival of the Church courts came without the Court of High Commission; and other historians have argued that there was a profound difference between the old and the new Anglican leadership. John Kenyon makes the key point that Charles II's archbishop, Sheldon, shut men out: 'Whereas Laud had always endeavoured to coerce the Puritans into conformity and obedience, Sheldon simply rejected them' (6, p. 364). Amid all the controversy surrounding the Restoration Church settlement one crucial fact is all too easily missed: the Clarendon Code did at least give legal recognition to Protestant Nonconformity, harshly circumscribed though this was. This arguably was one of the most important changes of the Restoration.

Executive Power

Charles II, we have noted, was restored with all the Crown's basic preroga-tives intact. Only in two spheres could he feel less of a king than his father and grandfather: he could raise significant amounts of money only through Parliament; and he had accepted that the Acts of 1641 had shorn away some of the Crown's coercive power. Charles could feel well-pleased, though perhaps not over-surprised. Despite the event of 30 January 1649 monarchy was accepted in the seventeenth century by many as the most effective form of government, and kings were expected to govern – that is, to make decisions. So long as a king ruled with some regard for the views of his more influential subjects, so long as his decisions were not arbitrary or clearly influenced by Court favourites, he could expect co-operation in his exercise of executive power.

Whether Charles II could capitalise on his good fortune of 1660 depended much on his character. The whole reign can be seen as a commentary on the personality of the monarch. Contemporaries were much given to character-sketching, and the enigmatic Charles attracted many such portraits. James Welwood, in his *Memoirs*, wrote,

> He loved not business and sought every occasion to avoid it. If he had any one fixed maxim of government it was to play one party against the other. (12, p. 900)

The diarist, John Evelyn, writing at Charles' death, said he was of

> A vigorous and robust constitution: he was a prince of many virtues and a great many imperfections. He would doubtless have been an excellent prince had he been less addicted to women.

Gilbert Burnet, bishop and moralist, chided Charles openly in a letter to him, that the distrust of the people flowed from having 'given yourself up to so many sinful pleasures'. George Savile, Marquis of Halifax, one of Charles' ablest advisers later in the reign, produced verdicts on his monarch which some historians reckon are as close to the truth as is possible:

> He chose rather to be eclipsed than to be troubled; that yieldingness, whatever foundations it might lay to the disadvantage of posterity, was a specific to preserve us in peace for his own time. (52, p. 750)

Over the next centuries verdicts swayed from hostile to favourable. The nineteenth century 'Whig' interpretation damned both personality and

Right: Edward Hyde, first earl of Clarendon, undated
(National Portrait Gallery)

Left: Anthony Ashley Cooper, first earl of Shaftesbury c. 1672
(National Portrait Gallery)

policy. Lord Macaulay wrote in 1848,

> With polite and engaging manners, yet addicted beyond measure to sensual indulgence full of sauntering and frivolous amusements; without faith in human virtue – according to him every person was to be bought. (76, p. 146)

G.M. Trevelyan, in 1904, was as convinced as some contemporaries of royal absolutist plots:

> The secret motive of Charles' actions, lay in his design to erect a Second Stuart Despotism, based on Catholicism. (77, p. 303)

A totally different interpretation was offered in 1931 by the widely-read popular historian, Arthur Bryant, who pictured 'Good King Charles' Golden Days': he wrote,

> To his people the last years of Charles' reign brought a wonderful prosperity; these quiet years when King Charles was leading her [i.e. England] through green pastures. He was now master of as great a power as any king of England had wielded – the sweeter that it was founded, with little help of arms or money, on his people's love. (78, pp. 344–50)

A final verdict on Charles is almost certainly impossible. One thing is certain, though: he practised to deceive. Whatever moral judgements may be expressed about his personal life, some assessment of Charles as king is possible, and modern historians have not shirked the task.

Among the critical is John Kenyon: in 1958 (64, pp. 105 and 152) he stressed 'the vicious animosity that had always been a hidden streak in his character' – it was openly displayed in his campaign against his political opponents later in the reign. On his sexual appetite Kenyon is again derogatory: 'Charles was not a gourmet so much as a gourmand.' Kenneth Haley in 1966 pursued the point: 'Charles' addiction to women was not merely a harmless personal weakness; it had serious political consequences' It was not just the money, as we have seen, (p. 130), but the monarchy's reputation. Haley's final word is respected by many modern historians: 'he was on the whole well enough liked, but he was respected by few, trusted by scarcely anyone, and held in awe by none' (32, pp. 10–11).

The two most recent judgements, without denying these criticisms, have changed the terms of reference: was he an effective ruler? Here Charles emerges in a better light. The Restoration world was a difficult one for anyone in politics. The Cavalier poet, Edmund Waller, in 1660 pinpointed the task: 'born the divided world to reconcile.' Antonia Fraser, in her 1979 biography, is certain of his achievement: 'Cynical and dissimulating, it can be argued that Charles II was not a king for all seasons. But he was the right king for that strange, demanding season in which he lived' (79, p. 469). Barry

Coward, writing in 1980, also sees Charles as the successful politician measured, not morally or with 'Whig' hindsight, but realistically in terms of the age in which he lived. 'Charles' political sense in knowing when a position could no longer be held, regardless of the principle involved, was his greatest strength' (1, p. 248). Halifax, as we have seen, made the same point in one word: 'yieldingness'.

To the exercise of executive power, then, Charles brought this most valuable asset: a willingness to yield to political necessity. His adaptability was finely tuned to the post-1660 scene, for there had been no Restoration political settlement, the balance of contending forces still, as it had been since 1640, in the melting-pot. These forces – the King, the leading ministers on the Privy Council, ambitious members of Parliament, the Commons as a whole representing the views of the county communities – manoeuvred throughout the reign for a better position, a seemingly endless cat-and-mouse game.

Four trends may be detected in this power struggle. First, on the matter of ministerial advice, Charles retained the Privy Council but consulted it less and less. The Council dealt with such a range of matters, including trivial business, that the number grew from 27 in 1660 to 50 in 1675. This was most unwieldy except for formal business of state; real discussions and decision-making took place in smaller groups. Standing Committees were established on special themes (Treasury, Ireland, the Plantations and the Navy), but one, the Committee for Foreign Affairs was not only the most important, but one of its briefs, to supervise communications between minister and JPs 'concerning the temper of the kingdom' obviously went beyond its ostensible business of foreign policy. Behind these smaller offshoots of the Council lay informal meetings, with scant surviving records of what was said between the King and a few chosen advisers. Charles preferred this last informality: as Kenyon concludes, 'The really important decisions were taken in complete privacy.' The hostility of many politicians – at Court, in Parliament and in the counties – to this secrecy led to the use of derogatory terms like 'cabals', 'junta' and in particular, 'cabinet-councils'.

If this element in the constitution was fluid, so too was the position and tasks of the chief minister. The office of prime minister had not yet developed and not every chief minister held the same post. Clarendon was the last Lord Chancellor chief minister, but a trend could be detected with Danby as Lord Treasurer. The growth in Treasury supremacy, we have noted, was one of the significant, unsung, developments of Charles' reign. Danby was also the first minister to use systematically the Crown's control of patronage to gain support for government policies in the House of Commons. Glimpses of future answers to the 1640 problems can be seen in this parliamentary management. Clarendon had made sporadic efforts, but Danby's were altogether different in scope. Documents from his personal papers survive to show sheaf upon sheaf of lists of MPs who might be approached for support. Much stress was placed by Danby on writing personally to particular men, reminders being sent just before a session. Pensions, too, were used: extra revenue from the Excise was allocated and by the mid-1670s £10,000 per annum was being paid out to about 30 MPs. Again, the significance of all this lay in the future, for despite Danby's efforts, no settled structure of politics emerged – the pension 'bribes' rarely had their desired effect, and there was so much hostility to 'influence' that nothing remotely resembling a Court Party could be sustained.

A third development, one linked with the second, was the tacit acceptance by Charles that regular sessions of parliament were necessary (for money, if nothing else), and thus any hankerings he had after Louis XIV's absolutist style of government were pure fantasy. (Whether Charles' successors would make that tacit acceptance was another question.) If royal independence from Parliament, the *sine qua non* of absolutism, was impossible – at least in Charles' circumstances – then some basis of co-operation with it was needed. This must be regarded, without exaggeration, as the central issue of all Stuart constitutional history; but past experience had shown that co-operation was an attitude of mind not easily legislated for – even an acceptable balance of power between executive and legislature was difficult to obtain, as *The Instrument of Government* had shown. Charles struck the right note in letters sent with the *Declaration of Breda* in 1660, in which he declared the interdependence of Crown and Parliament. The length of the Cavalier Parliament (seventeen years) with only two years without a session reflected the new position of the legislature, and during those years Charles vetoed only two bills which passed both Houses. Also Charles continued the Tudor tradition of not depending on professional standing armies (his few regiments did not seem in this category), the basis of so much absolutist authority on the continent.

Despite these promising auguries co-operation proved will-o'-the-wisp. Betty Kemp, in 1957, summed up the problem

> ... of achieving co-operation between a King shorn of some of his prerogatives and increasingly dependent financially on the Commons, and a House of Commons which, though aggressive and privileged, yet depended for its existence on the King. The problem was no nearer solution in 1660, and the next two reigns served only as a second commentary on the 1641 legislation. (55, pp. 1–2)

We are left with surely the most curious of questions: why did Charles, with Anglican and county community support behind him, both of which offered the prospect of co-operative parliaments, choose to antagonise them? There is no doubt that the choice was his: Charles, certainly after the fall of Clarendon in 1667, exercised executive decision-making. Time and again he tried to follow independent lines of policy: through Declarations of Indulgence (1662/72) he endeavoured to tone down the Anglican Church settlement; through treaties with foreign powers (Dover 1670) he pursued his pro-French inclinations: and he cried 'wolf' of imminent dangers abroad on several occasions in order to increase his regiments. The first two cast such doubts on Charles' 'word of a King' (Breda) that papist plans were widely suspected (Marvell's pamphlet, see p. 123). The third seemed to prove this suspicion. Charles was the first monarch for many generations to keep a standing army, albeit a small one, in England in peace-time. The disbanding of the armies in 1660 had been halted the following year when some republican alarms threatened the delicate stability of the Restoration. The army was minute compared with continental practice – mere 'Guards and Garrisons' and a few regiments like the Coldstream Guards and Life Guards, about three thousand – but its capability of expansion by an authoritarian executive so concerned Parliament in 1679 that it resolved

> that the continuing of any standing forces in this nation, other than the militia, is illegal, and a great grievance and vexation to the people. (30, p. 78)

In spite of his ambitions and the fears they promoted, when the great crisis of the reign came in 1678–81 the King acknowledged the forces of opinion ranged against such policies. The thesis that Charles' character affords the real clue to understanding the exercise of power in the post-Restoration period remains a strong one.

―――――――――――― *Study 16* ――――――――――――

Assessments of Charles' reign focus quite properly on his intentions. Before we come to the crisis period after 1678, it is worth asking whether the many hostile assessments delivered by historians are warranted.

1 Argue the case as to whether we should expect Charles' government to have clearly defined 'policies', for instance to resolve the 1640 problems.

2 Work out a list of what Charles, with his advisers, actually had control over; there are plenty of examples throughout the chapter, and it is a useful exercise at this stage to consider how much theoretical power the King had and what were the limitations on the exercise of that power.

Observations on 1:

Most of the 1640 problems remained to be settled, but Charles appeared to have one clear aim: to survive. Solutions, it must be remembered, in the form of quite detailed 'proposals' had dotted the two mid-century decades, many with insufficient support from the politically influential. Perhaps it could be argued that Charles was being realistic in letting things drift a little, with some partial solutions where expedient. There is much to be said for an aura of political mystique in difficult times; Charles, you might agree, cultivated this image. Did he go too far? At some point (around the early 1670s) mystique became deviousness, which quickly in turn aroused suspicion. Turn to pages 34 and 123 to compare Pym's expressed fears over 'a design' in 1640 with that of Marvell's 'design' in 1678. Perhaps for some this was merely an expression of a continuing distrust of the Stuart family. Whether there *was* a design or not is debatable; what is clear is that many people feared there was. This line of argument has already been suggested about 1642 (see p. 57). Was 1679 to be 1642 come again with an implicit vote of 'no confidence' in the King? There are, however, important differences between the two Charles, father and son, which you might take into account in your evaluation of 'clearly defined policies'. Charles II, we have noted, was willing to yield to political necessity: father would not withdraw the Prayer Book, son withdrew (twice) Declarations of Indulgence; father would not dismiss Strafford or Laud, son sacrificed both Clarendon and (as we shall see) Danby; father would not make peace with the Scots, son ended the Third Dutch War in 1674 despite alliance commitments to Louis XIV.

So in 1679 Charles II had survived nearly two decades – at the price, though, of postponing the storm (over executive power and religion) which loomed inevitably throughout the 1670s. In the period 1679–81 Charles faced a crisis of 1640 magnitude.

CHAPTER 13

Dover 1670

Neither Charles II nor, later, his brother James II could in the last resort reconcile their personal feelings about the Catholic faith with their constitutional obligations as Head of the Church and State in England. Their intentions vis-a-vis Catholicism were actually limited, but few believed this and their subjects' perception of their rulers' ambitions was to equate popery with arbitrary government. On three occasions between 1670 and 1688 the Catholic bogey was such as to produce plots or rumours of plots: the Treaty of Dover in 1670; the Popish Plot and Exclusion Crisis of 1678–81; and the final years of James II's reign 1687–8. The first two, in only marginally different circumstances, could have cost Charles his throne, while the third led directly to James' downfall. To set the scene for the great crisis period of late Stuart England we need to go back to 1670 and examine how the curious Treaty of Dover was drawn up, despite a strong undercurrent of anti-Catholic feeling in the country.

'Antichrist: the whore of Babylon'

Future generations have found it difficult to understand the average Englishman's uncompromising hostility to Catholicism, especially as there is much evidence that the same average Englishman was not always hostile (except on rare, crisis occasions) to Catholics, many of whom he knew as his good neighbours. Three analytical points can be made. First, there existed beyond doubt what Lord Chief Justice Scroggs in 1678 referred to as 'the faggot and dagger' element. The Catholic of the past was a conspirator, as witnessed in the plots of Elizabethan and Jacobean times – the most famous of all, the Gunpowder Plot of 1605, was now annually remembered in church services in November. What John Kenyon calls the 'paranoiac fear' (34, p.4) was there again in the rumours surrounding the Irish Rebellion of 1641. Egged on by Jesuits – 'the papacy's elite shock troops,' says Kenyon in an interesting comparison, were 'the Waffen S.S. of seventeenth century Catholicism' – Catholics would seize control. Of course, it was believed that all Protestants would suffer the fate of the 300 who burned at the stake in Mary Tudor's reign, so graphically recounted in Foxe's *Book of Martyrs* of 1563: in the Stuart period alone this book was re-printed five times. Suspicions that monarchs were not wholeheartedly devoted to the Anglican Church gave rise to fears that the Marian persecutions could come again; queen consorts of varying degrees of Catholic bigotry (Henrietta Maria, Catherine of Braganza and the Duke of York's second wife, Mary of Modena) only served to fuel these suspicions. Then again that the Great Fire of London of 1666 was the work of papist plotting was a current rumour, supported by the confession of a deranged Frenchman, Robert Hubert, who was arrested in Kent soon afterwards. Kenyon is impressed by the ease with which people assumed arson by a conspiratorial fifth column: 'the Great Fire took its place in the mythology of ultra-Protestantism; it confirmed the belief of the credulous and fearful that the Church of Rome was an organ of international conspiracy.' (34, p.13). In 1679 the Earl of Essex spoke for many Englishmen when he addressed the Privy Council:

> The apprehension of popery makes me imagine I see my children frying in Smithfield.

Secondly, Catholicism was not just feared: it was considered fundamentally wrong. The hostility, so strongly and emotionally held for generations, needed some intellectual underpinning, albeit that much of this was expressed in colourful language. The basis of the argument has recently been summarised by Dr Robin Clifton (19, ch.5): Catholicism was not acceptable as an alternative form of worship to Protestant practice because it was a 'perversion, a debasement of the original Christian ideals'. The reasoning had several elements. Salvation by 'good works' offended many Protestants, because it savoured of bargaining with God for one's place in heaven, and was the product of man's sinful pride anyway. Catholicism diluted the Christian message – the confessional, for instance, so lightened man's moral burden that it cleared the way for future sinning. The ceremonial aspects of Catholicism too gave rise to much Protestant scoffing: they were designed to appeal to baser or weaker instincts. Milton wrote contemptuously of 'a willingness to be improved by colour'; statues clashed with the Second Commandment of the Bible concerning 'graven images'; and the element of magic was, it was claimed, strong in the belief in transubstantiation. Popular Catholic worship was thus ridiculed for not being a set of doctrines but a set of actions and gestures. Protestants prayed, asking for help, which made sense; Catholics recited in the vain hope that repeating certain words would bring the same help. In sum these prejudices explain why Protestants derided Catholicism as 'the whore of Babylon': seventeenth-century people had a very pessimistic view of human nature, assuming basic weaknesses of character in all – hence the acceptance that because of man's lust for woman, men would inevitably be tempted in the presence of a whore. Catholicism was seen in the same light, for it was a perversion which had prostituted the early Christian message by tempting men through relics, baubles, saint worship, etc. Protestant contemporaries spoke in harsh and mocking condemnation. Andrew Marvell's view of priests as

> jugglers and conjurors, with their exorcisms, whisperings, sprinklings

was much the same as Lord Russell's when he spoke in the House of Commons in 1679:

> I despair such a ridiculous and nonsensical religion. A piece of wafer, broken between a priest's fingers, to be our Saviour! And what becomes of it when eaten, and taken down, you know.

International links with arbitrary government were often made. In the early 1670s Sir Thomas Meres stated in the Commons that

> Our jealousies of popery, or an arbitrary government, are not from a few inconsiderable papists here, but from the ill-example of France.

Later, Sir Henry Capel kept the fear alive:

> From Popery came the notion of a standing army and arbitrary power; formerly the crown of Spain and now France supports the root of popery amongst us. (34, pp.1–2 and 15)

A preacher in the same period spoke on Guy Fawkes Day:

> I do not, I will not, say all our Romanists are inclined to rebellion; but I fear 'twill be hard for 'em to be good Catholics at Rome and good subjects at home. (35, p.176)

Pope Pius V in 1570 had issued his Bull *Regnans in Excelsis* which deposed Elizabeth I and absolved any English Catholics from any loyalty to her; that Bull had never been cancelled. As the 1670s progressed the Pope, the 'Antichrist', was now the key figure in spectacular and costly processions in which huge effigies of him, stuffed with live cats to make him squeal, were burnt.

The paradox was that despite this deep and real hatred of the idea of Catholicism, individual Catholics rarely suffered persecution. Recusancy laws still existed on the statute book: failure to attend an Anglican Church once a week, and take Holy Communion three times a year was penalised by a fine of £20 a month or two-thirds of the income from an estate; it was high treason to convert anyone to allegiance to Rome, a felony to attend a Mass, and a serious offence to possess rosaries, missals etc; Catholic priests were forbidden to enter the country, and any who did faced the death penalty. Yet by Charles II's reign recusancy payments had come to be regarded as nothing more than a sort of income tax. In places the laws were hardly ever enforced. Only in the years following some particular crisis (1588, 1605, 1641 and 1678) was there a widespread strict enforcement. Dr Clifton has quite properly raised a question: do four alarms in four generations constitute a real fear? The evidence points rather to a thin shell of hatred and mortal terror mixed with a fair measure of ridicule, beneath which existed a durable and harmless Catholic community living on good terms with their protestant neighbours. Successive governments had implicitly recognised the irrational phobia as something which could be safely ignored or played down. During the unsettled decades of 1640–60, and despite Pym's claims of papists' designs, there is little evidence of sustained persecution beyond the convenience of raising decimation-style taxes from the Catholic community as well as Royalists. Thus by Charles II's time there existed *de jure* persecution, but *de facto* toleration.

Charles II went a stage further: it was a vital step and focused attention on the close link between religious policies and the powers of the Crown. Instead of tacitly ignoring the statute laws, Charles, explicitly by public declaration, tried to suspend them. He began this in 1662 by announcing his intention to honour 'the liberty and tender consciences' promise of Breda by asking Parliament to allow him to dispense individuals from the penal laws, particularly the recent Act of Uniformity. He retreated before strong Parliamentary opposition. Charles, as we shall see, was to try again in 1672, and James II twice in 1687 and 1688 with Declarations of Indulgence.

Here was one of the central issues of the later Stuart period. Royal leniency to papists had long been a grievance, but with Charles and James it was extended to a dramatic use of the royal prerogative power. Lawyers could point to the fact that monarchs had had this power in religious matters since the Reformation, for the Head of the Church had merely taken over the Pope's power of 'dispensing' or 'suspending' certain laws if it seemed fit or right. The legal argument stated that these powers were not conferred by Parliament; all Parliament had done was to give them statutory recognition. Secretary Williamson of the Privy Council put it thus in 1671:

> In ecclesiasticals it is apprehended that the King has all power; he is supreme, the parliament has no part in it. In civils it is otherwise. (58, year 1671, p.563)

Thus the Catholic factor remained in the late Stuart period, 'the whore of Babylon', a religious and political mesh effectively impairing progress to a lasting settlement. The power of this factor to unsettle was strikingly seen in the decade of the 1670s.

The Treaty of Dover 1670

In May and December 1670 signatures were put at Dover to a treaty between the kings of England and France. In the first month a full, but secret, set of clauses was signed by a very limited number of people: Arlington, Clifford, and de Croissy acting for their respective monarchs. Seven months later a version – which effectively omitted Clause Two – was publicly signed by the full range of Charles' senior advisers, many of whom, of course, were ignorant of the original occasion. Few state documents have created more suspicion among contemporaries, and uncertainty, misunderstanding, even negligent interpretation by historians. In essence the Treaty committed Louis XIV and Charles II to make war on the Dutch, committed certain payments by Louis to Charles, and, in the omitted Clause Two, committed Charles to a declaration of his conversion to Catholicism at some future date.

Professor Kenneth Haley has remarked that 'this is the central problem of the reign', crucially because the rest of the reign was coloured by 'the suspicions which the French Alliance generated' (32, p.15). Historians, though, find themselves in a peculiarly difficult position in attempting an assessment: we know the terms of the Treaty (both versions), but the information on which to study the preliminaries is thin. Barry Coward wrote in 1980, 'Given the secrecy of these negotiations, one is forced to suggest motives for the making of the Dover policy on very little direct evidence' (1, p.264).

The story, as far as we know it, began late in 1668 when Charles told James that he wished to be 'instructed' in the Catholic faith. In the following January both met privately with three others, the Catholics Henry Bennet (the Earl of Arlington), Sir Thomas Clifford and Lord Arundel. What is certain is that at this meeting Charles announced his intention to declare himself a Catholic. He talked of

> how uneasy it was to him not to profess the Faith [i.e. Roman Catholicism] he believed,

adding that he wanted advice

> about the ways and methods fittest to be taken for the settling of the Catholic religion in his three kingdoms. [i.e. England, Scotland and Ireland] (80, p.674)

After discussion it was agreed to seek Louis XIV's help. Charles' motives are obscure, and we have to allow for the known deviousness of his character. Most historians and some contemporaries doubt his probity. John Miller is forthright: 'If Charles was not sincere – and I believe that he was not – what was he trying to achieve by his strange behaviour?' (36, p.61). His mother, Henrietta Maria, had tried in vain to convert him during the years of exile; he was known to be too sceptical and dissembling to have much time for a priest's moral advice; and it would be surprising for a man with Charles II's survival instincts seriously to consider a public declaration, let alone 'settling the Catholic religion' in his notoriously anti-papist kingdom. The only arguments which make sense are that he wanted to impress Louis XIV, whom he much admired, and also to give himself a bargaining lever in obtaining cash for the preparations for England's third war in twenty years with the Dutch, the previous two being inconclusive.

In the event negotiations for the Treaty with the French were carried on in secrecy throughout 1669. Normal diplomatic procedures were avoided, and the chief 'agents' were Minette (Charles' sister, Henrietta Anne, now married to Louis XIV's brother) and later the French ambassador, Colbert de Croissy. The witches' brew of these preliminaries, the ingredients of which historians have found so puzzling, is exemplified by Charles demanding the enormous sum of £800,000 per year from Louis for war with the Dutch; by Charles promising his sister that he would declare his Catholicism *after* the war, but completely contradicting this in his talks with de Croissy by insisting that the declaration should *precede* the war; and by enthusiastic remarks made by Charles to de Croissy about his hopes for a conversion of England to Catholicism which could well involve an element of force.

The most significant clauses of the Secret Treaty of Dover, signed on 22 May and ratified on 4 June 1670, were the second, fifth, sixth, seventh and ninth:

2. The lord king of Great Britain, being convinced of the truth of the Catholic religion, and resolved to declare it and reconcile himself with the Church of Rome as soon as the welfare of his kingdom will permit, has every reason to hope and expect from the affection and loyalty of his subjects that none of them, even of those upon whom God may not yet have conferred his divine grace so abundantly as to incline them by that august example to turn to the true faith, will ever fail in the obedience that all peoples owe to their sovereigns, even of a different religion. Nevertheless, as there are sometimes mischievous and unquiet spirits who seek to disturb the public peace, especially when they can conceal their wicked designs under the plausible excuse of religion, his Majesty of Great Britain... has concluded that the best means to prevent any alteration in it would be to make himself assured in case of need of the assistance of his most Christian Majesty, who, wishing in this case to give to the lord king of Great Britain an unquestionable proof of the reality of his friendship, and to contribute to the success of so glorious a design promises to give for that purpose to the said lord king of Great Britain the sum of two million livres tournois, of which half shall be paid three months after the exchange of the ratifications of the present treaty... and the other half in the same manner three months later. In addition the said most Christian king binds himself to assist his Majesty of Great Britain in case of need with troops to the number of 6,000 foot-soldiers, and even to raise and maintain them at his own expense, so far as the lord king of Great Britain finds need of them

for the execution of his design... The time of the said declaration of Catholicism is left entirely to the choice of the said lord king of Great Britain.

5. ... to humble the pride of the States General of the United Provinces of the Low Countries, and to reduce the power of a nation which has so often rendered itself odious by extreme ingratitude to its own founders and the creators of its republic.

6. ... his most Christian Majesty will undertake all the expense necessary for setting on foot, maintaining and supporting the operations of the armies required for delivering a powerful attack by land on the strongholds and territory of the said States, the said lord king of Great Britain binding himself only to contribute to the army of the said most Christian king, and to maintain there at his own expense, a body of 6,000 infantry,

7. As to what concerns the war at sea, the said lord king of Great Britain shall undertake that burden, and shall fit out at least fifty great ships and ten fire-ships, to which the said most Christian king shall bind himself to add a squadron of thirty good French vessels.... And in order that the said lord king of Great Britain may more easily support the expense of the war, his most Christian Majesty binds himself to pay to the said king each year that the said war shall last the sum of three millions of livres tournois in the aforesaid manner

9. ... after the said lord king of Great Britain shall have made the declaration specified in the second article of this treaty, it will be entirely within the power and discretion of the said most Christian king to determine the time when the said lord kings shall make war with their united forces against the States General,' (12, pp.863–7)

Study 17

A variety of questions present themselves concerning both the preliminaries and the terms of Dover. It could be asked whether the Anglo-French Alliance against the Dutch was in England's best interests; again whether the attraction of money was a factor (compare what Charles asked for with what he received). You are asked to consider in some detail clause 2: what were Charles' reasons for including this controversial clause; and compare the verdicts presented below by some well-known historians of the period with your reading of the clause.

(a) G.M. Trevelyam: 'Louis promised money and soldiers to Charles to enable him to declare his own conversion to Catholicism with a view to re-establishing that religion in England.' (77, p.372)

(b) David Ogg: 'By the secret clauses of the Treaty he undertook to become a Roman Catholic and to foster Roman Catholicism in England.' (*Europe in the 17th century*, 5th edition 1948, p.244) and: 'Louis XIV had undertaken to pay the money not only in order that Charles should become a Catholic, but that he might restore Catholicism in England, by force if necessary.' (52, p.352)

(c) Gerald Aylmer: 'Charles undertook to restore the Roman Catholic religion in England as soon as circumstances were favourable,' (2, p.177)

(d) John Kenyon: 'Charles undertook to declare himself a Roman Catholic on the outbreak of war and return England to the Roman Communion using French troops if necessary.' (64, p.131)

and, in a later edition of the same book: 'Charles merely undertook to announce his own personal conversion; if this provoked a rebellion, then military assistance would be forthcoming from France.' (64, Fontana edition 1970, p.9)

Observations:

In answering any of the questions raised you must bear in mind the paucity and possible bias of the evidence relating to the preliminaries; the source, for example, of Charles' conversations is the Carte Collection of manuscripts in the Bodleian Library in Oxford, but there is also a version by J. Macpherson, printed in London in 1775. The manuscript and the printed document differ in places, such as the use by Macpherson of the word 'reconciled' instead of 'instructed' (see p. 153); you will appreciate that each word implies a very different attitude to Catholicism. Again, we have to depend on de Croissy for much of the detail of the 'conversations' – his dispatches to Louis XIV are in the Public Record Office in a collection called the Bachet Transcripts. Useful as they are, de Croissy was not present at all the talks, so some of it is hearsay, and he might include only what he thought Louis would want to hear; moreover, de Croissy had a reputation for drawing the wrong conclusions: for instance, James' more committed conversion to Catholicism led de Croissy to inform Louis that 'James' devotions have withdrawn him entirely from the pleasure of women', but, as James' most recent biographer, John Miller, has shown, 'James' sexuality was driven underground, into furtive affairs with unattractive women'. Another problem is translation: de Croissy's dispatches use the French word 'force', which may be translated ambiguously into English either as 'force' or 'strength' – the difficulty is obvious if you consider the quite different 'negotiating from strength' and 'negotiating by threat of force' (36, pp.59, 253, 273)

You must also keep the negotiations leading to the Treaty distinct from the terms. People may have fervent *hopes* for something, and say so, but the *reality* (in the final terms) may be quite different. Charles' zeal for his conversion, whatever it might have been in 1669, had waned by the following year and the Dutch War had clear priority by 1672. You will recall also what we have said about Charles' character: he was most proficient at saying one thing and doing another.

The most recent writings by historians (Haley, Coward, Miller and Mitchell) have all stressed those two points in trying to present a more balanced assessment compared with the traditional views, some of whom have been quoted in the question. The 'England's interests' question has always been a minefield for the unwary. Defenders of Charles, such as the Bryant school of thought, have presented a picture of him as a patriotic king: C.H. Hartmann describes Dover as 'a brilliant foreign policy' in which England allied with the French to destroy her real enemy, her commercial rival, Holland. But it was evident to some perceptive eyes in 1670 that the French, not the Dutch, were England's foes of the future. An alarming 'melancholy reflection' had been made three years earlier by the influential English ambassador in Brussels, Sir William Temple:

> If the French shall carry Flanders, the Dutch are sensible that they must fall to be a maritime province of France; what a condition England will be left in by such an accession of maritime forces to such a power as France is already. (30, p.120)

Haley feels that this sort of evidence is most significant: he points out that the commercial companies of London were 'markedly less enthusiastic about the War', and goes on, 'Charles II's foreign policy can only be defended on the basis that Louis' advances in Europe, and particularly the Low Countries, were of no concern to England. This runs counter to one of the main principles of English foreign policy from the sixteenth to the twentieth century' [i.e. that the Antwerp entrepôt area should not be dominated by a potential rival, a great power] (32, pp.18–19).

On the question of money the old argument that Charles became a 'pensioner' of France is no longer acceptable. Detailed figures worked out by Chandaman suggest that *throughout* the reign (England had other subsidies after Dover and the War) Charles received only around £750,000, less than *one* year's ordinary income. The subsidies from the French connection Chandaman dismisses as 'pin-money' (50, p.274), rather than a serious contribution to royal finances. Haley goes further: war with the Dutch 'made a bad financial situation worse', citing the Stop of the Exchequer of 1672 as evidence (see p. 125).

Turning to the muddle over *when* Charles would turn Catholic, and about his *intentions*: compare the negotiations with the Secret Treaty, clauses 2 and 9. Note also Charles' rash, unrealistic views on converting England – based, anyway, on de Croissy's suspect evidence – and compare with what was said precisely in the Treaty. This is where you should be able to detect some curious phraseology in the cited historians. (Kenyon, on advice, changed his account between two different editions of his book.) Mitchell is highly critical of some past writings, and says bluntly, 'neither by this nor by any other treaty did Charles II agree to the forcible re-conversion of England to the Roman Church' (80, p.678).

Why then were such dubious conclusions made? Mitchell thinks the discussions and intentions of the preliminaries have (wrongly) been treated as synonymous with the Treaty. Haley, though, has an interesting reservation. While he says, 'It is a fallacy to suppose Charles promised to restore England to the Catholic faith,' he goes on to suggest that, 'in a century in which the principle of *cuius regio, eius religio* normally operated, few people believed that a situation in which the ruler and ruled belonged to different faiths could be permanent' (32, p.16). In your own examination of the wording of clause 2 you may detect the use (twice) of the word 'design'. The intimate connection between royal policies, centralisation, gentry suspicions and this word has been an important theme of this book between Pym (1640 speech) and Marvell (1678 pamphlet).

You will find two suggestions for Charles' real motives for clause 2 in the two paragraphs preceding the quotations from the Treaty. They are based on Haley, who argues that Charles wanted 'a more personal relationship' with Louis; and on Miller, who thinks Charles would use clauses 2 and 9 as clever bargaining devices – delaying his declaration of Faith in order to increase French subsidies. As Mitchell says, 'Blackmail was not beneath him'.

CHAPTER 14

Exclusion

1678 - 81

Suspicion and succession questions

Charles II did in fact honour his promise in the Treaty of Dover to declare himself a Catholic, but it had nothing to do with the Dutch War of 1672; in the most tactful and delicate of timings with regard to the sensibilities of his subjects, he made the declaration in 1685 on his deathbed! Nevertheless he did provoke considerable suspicion by his March 1672 *Declaration of Indulgence*, two days before declaring war on the Dutch. This gave royal permission to Catholics to worship in their own homes and to Protestants to worship in public if they applied for a licence. Motives, as with Dover, are again obscure. Perhaps Charles was offering this as a measure to half-honour Clause Two of Dover; perhaps he hoped to unite Catholics and Nonconformists into a body to balance the overpowering Anglican control of England; perhaps, as Arlington said, the Indulgence was to conciliate, 'that we might keep all quiet at home whilst we are busy abroad.'

Events proved that the whole Dover–Indulgence independent line of policy was a fool's paradise. The Stop of the Exchequer had revealed faulty financial planning. The war soon turned sour, for Charles had miscalculated Dutch resistance and the stubborn personality of his nephew Dutch William of Orange – there were few choice pickings to be had in this war. With many debts, little glory and heavy Parliamentary criticism he left the French alliance and made a separate peace with Holland at the Treaty of Westminster in 1674. William was to continue to lead the Dutch war effort against Louis for another four years and to survive to fight another day. For Charles an even greater miscalculation was the reaction of his subjects: 'Popery and the French interest' became a cry utterly damning royal policy. The House of Commons duly voted 'that penal statutes cannot be suspended but by act of Parliament,' a clear denial of Charles' prerogative power of dispensation. *The Declaration of Indulgence* was withdrawn in 1673; Charles conceded defeat with the war debts looming. Worse was to follow. In the same year he had to assent to the Test Act, thus barring Catholics from holding Crown office; James resigned from the government. Implications for the future were ominous, as the expressed danger which the Act guarded against was the presence of papists in high places. Fears of popery spread to the county communities, and a determined attempt was made in some districts to enforce the often defunct recusancy laws. Wiltshire saw a marked increase in prosecutions – more convictions occurred in 1673 than in all the years since the Restoration put together.

One man sensed more than most the reality behind all these suspicions: Anthony Ashley Cooper, Earl of Shaftesbury and Lord Chancellor. Although a senior member of Charles' Privy Council, as a Protestant he was not 'privy' to the Secret Treaty of Dover. Over the next few years, however, Shaftesbury became convinced that Charles was promoting Catholicism. Irish priests were noted at Queen Catherine's palace; despite Nell Gwynne, Charles seemed to have a penchant for Catholic mistresses; and both the French alliance and the Indulgence added to the impression. Unlike some Shaftesbury's fears were neither vague nor irrational: he focused on one, that a Protestant people with a Catholic ruler could face a parlous future existence. 1673 became a turning point in Shaftesbury's career. In that year James, heir to the throne, failed openly at Easter to take the Anglican sacraments, and then planned to marry a Catholic as his second wife – Mary Beatrice of Modena, an Italian with French diplomatic backing. As Haley says, 'James was nailing his colours to the mast, and revealing them as a combination of the Roman purple and the white of the Bourbons' (33, p. 331). Shaftesbury's reaction was immediate: he pressed Charles to divorce Catherine of Braganza and remarry with the hope of a Protestant heir. Charles refused and dismissed him from office and the Council.

What Shaftesbury had done was to bring the issue of the succession to the throne to the forefront of politics. Fecund mistresses, barren wives, the succession order of male and female offspring, their marital potential and possible religious commitment: all became matters of serious debate in the corridors of Westminster and St James Palace, in the coffee-houses of London and the drawing rooms of the gentry during the mid-1670s. Around the catch-phrase of the period, 'the unalterable law of the succession', all sorts of possibilities were being canvassed. Five main options had supporters at one time or another over the rest of the decade, each revolving round leading personalities; and it was not entirely domestic – complications from abroad added new suspicions and fears in some, hopes in others (see p. 192).

Charles' brother, James, Duke of York, was heir to the throne because Queen Catherine had borne Charles no children. Rumours of pregnancies in the '60s had only produced one confirmation in 1669; a pet fox jumped onto her bed and she miscarried, 'one of those dynastic accidents', says Haley, 'which modify the course of history.' She never conceived again. Divorce, a solution supported by several leading politicians, was rejected without discussion by Charles.

A barren Queen was unfortunate, for Charles' ability to procreate was not in doubt. His mistresses were legion; Debrett's *Peerage* acknowledges fourteen illegitimate children. A second option was to 'legitimise' by Act of Parliament one of these children. The most famous was Lucy Walter's child, James Scott:

born in 1649, he was raised to the Dukedom of Monmouth and was a well-known, attractive figure at Court. Rumours that Charles had actually married Lucy were the subject of much Court gossip. Later mistresses also produced offspring. Barbara Palmer, Lady Castlemaine, bore five in quick succession in the 1660s. The new French, Catholic arrival in the early '70s, Louise, gave Charles his last acknowledged natural child in 1672 – he became the Duke of Richmond and his mother Duchess of Portsmouth. Louise expressed high hopes of becoming Queen some day; perhaps she saw herself playing the new Anne Boleyn to another Catherine! Yet, argues Charles' biographer, Antonia Fraser, 'If Catherine had died the King would surely have headed for some rich princess.' With Charles' theatrical amours (Mary Davis – 'Moll' of the Duke's Theatre – and Eleanor Gwynne – 'Nell' of the Old Drury Theatre) around from time to time, there was much turmoil at Court. Nell's acid remarks about Portsmouth, that she was 'Squintabella', the 'Weeping Willow', provided passing amusement for gossip-mongers like Pepys, but Nell's claim to be 'the *Protestant* whore' raised much concern on the political scene by her implication. Thus Charles' extra-marital liaisons posed a variety of questions: of cost, of the royal image, of Catholic leanings, of backstairs political influence, and, not the least, of the succession. The last three were in the event irrelevant; what matters, though, is that people of influence thought they were significant.

James was the central figure in the succession question. He was the heir, and for certain conservative gentry there was the not unattractive option of doing nothing, for as Charles' brother, on age grounds alone he would not long survive. But he was becoming thoroughly disliked: aloof, humourless, obstinate, he was not an appealing figure at Court. Vague disapproval turned into open antipathy and fear when James' commitment to Catholicism became evident. His political instincts were very much towards despotism – he had already made it known he was 'a man for arbitrary power'. Shaftesbury's distate for James had also produced a forthright denunciation of him as 'heady, violent and bloody', a man 'who easily believes the rashest and worst of counsels to be the most sincere.' Charles was well aware of his brother's unwelcome traits and beliefs – 'they will never kill me, Jamie, to make you king', he remarked in one of his mordant moments – but he was never to waver from his concern to preserve the principle of hereditary right.

Perhaps the principle could be re-directed by 'Limitation', and several degrees of political side-slip were openly discussed as options. That James would become King, but with some of the royal prerogative powers, especially as Head of the Church, curbed by Act of Parliament, was one possibility. Another more extreme version of this was to allow James the nominal title of King only, with his daughters, Mary or Anne or both, acting as regents with executive powers. These two daughters were the children of Anne Hyde, James' first and Protestant wife; both girls were raised as full members of the Church of England, so this was an attractive option in that after James' death the future of Anglicanism would be assured. Hopes in this direction were complicated in 1677 when Danby and Charles, much to James' disapproval, arranged a diplomatic marriage – of Mary to William III of Orange, the same William who was struggling against Louis XIV. Superficially the future seemed even more secure, yet the Tudor Marian spectre of foreign husbands and their baneful influence emerged once again.

The political alarmists of the day, though, were already preoccupied with a worse apprehension, which gave rise to the most extreme option of all: the exclusion of James from the throne. Anne Hyde had died in 1671, and James' new wife was an open Catholic. Her procreative abilities were of immediate concern: if or when she produced a male child, then he would become second in line to the throne and would certainly be brought up as a Catholic, thus making a long line of Catholic monarchs a fearful prospect. Mary's convent training had led her to expect a nun's life of piety, but at the age of fifteen she was married unwillingly and by proxy to James, a man of forty, whom she had never seen, and sent straight to England. Her biographer, Carola Oman, paints a lurid picture of her arrival at Dover, 'to be wedded and bedded that same night' in the most distasteful of circumstances. She screamed for hours and had to be held down by force before submitting to a consummation of the marriage – and only then because of a letter she was given from the Pope, pointing out her duty to serve the needs of the Catholic religion. The subsequent history of nine out of her ten pregnancies was a personal tragedy: four times she painfully miscarried, three times her babies died in infancy, another survived only to her fifth year; the ninth in 1684 was another miscarriage. Until she conceived again (in 1688) the prospect of a popish dynasty was receding fast.

The ferment of discussion in the mid–'70s indicated that whatever progress was being made in other fields, political stability would remain as elusive as ever until the succession question was resolved. There were in fact too many choices: wait and suffer until James died; divorce Catherine; legitimise Monmouth; limit James' power; exclude James altogether – each had many patrons as well as many equally partisan objectors. It needed a crisis to mobilise opinion and reduce the options to a clear either/or. Three men, in completely different ways, were to precipitate this crisis: Titus Oates, Edward Coleman and Ralph Montagu.

Revelations

Well before Oates appeared on the scene in 1678 most MPs expressed a preference for some kind of limitation of James' power as future King; few supported Shaftesbury's exclusion idea. An occasional meeting to co-ordinate tactics in a particular session of the Cavalier Parliament provoked memories of

1640: independent country gentlemen feared such affairs as suspect of treason. But criticism of Charles' failure to discuss limitations grew; the old 'Country' label could well be applied to this loose alliance of critics, but it was brittle and full of self-doubt.

Revelations of plots in high places in August 1678, December 1678 and April 1679 were to transform the fortunes of this 'Country', and reduce the succession choice to one of either 'Exclusion' or 'Limitation'. The political nation split as in 1640–41. Once again two major parties emerged, and once again the gulf of fear was such as to render civil war a real possibility.

The first exposure was the one that has traditionally held the centre of attention for historians. Titus Oates and Israel Tonge in the late summer of 1678 produced a series of sensational allegations of a Popish Plot, the essence of which was a Jesuit plan to shoot or poison the King, to be followed by a Catholic rebellion in Ireland and England, simultaneous with a French invasion; colouring was added by a reference to firing London again. In questioning before the Privy Council Charles personally showed Oates to be a liar on points of detail, and all sorts of inconsistencies came to light later. Doubts lingered, though. Oates was a confident speaker with a good memory, and he provided a mass of written 'evidence'. Charles had to admit that 'among so many particulars, he did not know but there might be some truth.' No King could ignore threats of assassination, however improbable the informer's story was and however disreputable his background. John Kenyon, in his standard work on the history of the Plot, characterises Tonge as a 'mental casualty of the civil wars with a persecution complex of psychopathic proportions'. He was a clergyman, as was Oates, whose background was even more bizarre. Expulsion from school and Cambridge ('a great dunce who never mastered Latin', his tutor said); expulsion from an Anglican living for drunkenness; flight abroad as a ship's chaplain, but dismissal on return for being a practising homosexual; 'conversion' in 1677 to Catholicism and admission to the Valladolid Jesuit College in Spain, but expulsion after five months for ignorance of Latin; exit from Spain with a bogus 'Doctor of Divinity' degree; the adoption of a false name, but again expulsion from a Catholic seminary in the Netherlands for being bawdy and blasphemous and, as Kenyon puts it, 'no fit company for small boys once the authorities divined his peculiar sexual tastes' (34, pp.45 and 50).

Back in England Oates met Tonge and the monstrous plot with its tissue of manufactured evidence was concocted. Despite the revealed inconsistencies, within two months an atmosphere of anti-Catholic hysteria built up – to the degree that sane members of the gentry in Parliament could resolve:

> there hath been and still is a damnable and hellish plot, contrived on by the popish recusants for the assassinating and murdering the King, and subverting the government, and rooting out and destroying the Protestant religion. (34, p.85)

It seems odd that such a hash of nonsense could be so convincing. There was in fact no Popish Plot: it existed only in the deranged minds of Oates and Tonge. After a careful investigation of the mass of false evidence, surely the whole affair would have drifted into obscurity. This was not to be so. Not only was Oates making his allegations against a powerful anti-Catholic backcloth, but he was lucky. A curious death and further revelations pointed, it seemed to some, to a real plot.

Sir Edmund Berry Godfrey was a JP, and Oates had 'for safety' deposited copies of his 'evidence' with him. Godfrey went missing on 12 October 1678 and his body was found five days later in a ditch; he had been strangled, run through with his own sword, and his personal valuables remained in his clothes. One theory is that, suffering from a period of morbid depression, he hanged himself, but was removed by embarrassed friends. A coroner's jury, though, brought in a verdict of wilful murder by persons unknown. A strong, though unproven suspect was a peer of the realm, the Earl of Pembroke, long recognised, says Kenyon, as a drunken, homicidal maniac who had kicked a man to death in a tavern brawl. Godfrey had played a major role in his trial. The truth or otherwise of this proved irrelevant, as London opinion at all levels seized upon the Oates – Godfrey connection and 'persons unknown' easily became 'Papists'. Catholics had assassinated Godfrey to silence an influential, respected figure in possession of incriminating evidence. The impact of this chain of thought was shown when Godfrey's funeral, a massive public occasion on 31 October, was followed the same evening by the House of Commons' resolution on 'a hellish plot'.

Oates was even more fortunate. In part of his 'evidence' he made a passing reference to Edward Coleman, a known Catholic with fanatical views who in 1670 had been secretary to James, Duke of York, and later to his wife. Coleman had regularly pressed pro-Catholic policies on James, and some of his wilder schemes ('the utter subduing of a persistent heresy', one of his letters said about the Anglican Church) involved correspondence with Jesuits and French agents abroad and some Catholic peers at home. The connection with James, plotting and Rome could easily be made. Yet Oates could not have had knowledge of the details. Kenyon's conclusion is: 'This was an amazingly lucky shot; for if Oates had had an inkling of what Coleman's papers did in fact contain he would surely have given him more prominence.' Coleman was arrested and his mass of letters seized. Sifting them took time, but growing evidence of James and negotiations with Rome emerged. The leap in people's minds was made: James was implicated in Oates' Plot. This was political dynamite, and when a public revelation of part of Coleman's correspondence occurred in April 1679 many MPs who had previously supported Limitation now went over to Shaftesbury and Exclusion.

There was a third strand in the story which had nothing to do with Oates, and several modern historians have argued that the Oates affair has had too much of the limelight. Coward, for instance, concludes that, 'The revelations of Ralph Montagu changed the political scene much more fundamentally than did those of Titus Oates' (1, p.284). Montagu used to be the English ambassador at Versailles, who seems to have had as disreputable a recent past as Oates, albeit at a higher level in society. With a reputation for avarice cloaked in ambition he indulged in murky intrigue, aiming via a liaison with the King's illegitimate daughter to secure a position as Secretary of State on the Privy Council. Danby considered Montagu a rogue and not only blocked the Council appointment but also secured his dismissal as ambassador.

Factional rivalry at Westminster was now to contribute to a new, though parallel plot, one with more politically devastating consequences than Oates' fairy tale. Danby in his years in office had made many enemies who were now to conspire to ruin him. Montagu, at Versailles, had received much correspondence from Danby, in particular secret letters regarding subsidies which Louis XIV had paid to Charles at varying times throughout the early and mid – '70s. As recently as January to March 1678 Danby had written to Montagu of the parlous state Charles' government was in since the end of the last 'gift' of money from Louis. Here was a weapon of considerable political power, something which would destroy Danby and clear the way for putting pressure on Charles over the succession question.

On 19 December 1678, with the Oates investigations growing apace, Montagu, encouraged by Shaftesbury, sprang the trap into which Danby was to fall. From the letters of earlier that year two significant sentences were read out to the House of Commons:

> 'Unless some balm from Heaven be applied to the wound, I do not see but it must bleed very suddenly... in case the condition of peace shall be accepted, the King expects to have six million of *livres* yearly for three years, because it will be two or three years before he can hope to find his Parliament in humour to give him supplies. (52, pp.555 and 577)

The 'peace' was the long-drawn out one (Nyjmegen) being negotiated between the French and the Dutch, both exhausted after six years of costly warfare. Charles, having opted out in 1674, now saw a mediation role for himself – at a price. Hence Danby's letter, the 'balm' being six million *livres* (about £100,000). These letters are now in the manuscripts of the British Museum Library, and include later alterations which Danby made in his own handwriting: he crossed out 'from Heaven' (Louis XIV, of course), and changed Charles' 'I approve' note at the bottom to 'this letter is writ by my order'.

The effect of Montagu's revelations was spectacular: within two days Articles of Impeachment against Danby were drawn up, accusing him of 'the traitorous encroachment of royal power' by secret treaties with foreign princes, by raising a standing army, and also of being 'popishly affected' concealing 'the horrid plot'. The House of Lords wavered and Charles quickly prorogued the session. In January 1679 he dissolved the Cavalier Parliament, after eighteen years.

The Struggle for Exclusion

The parallels were there for those who chose to seek them: 1678, Charles II, Danby, Shaftesbury, Montagu and Marvell's 'popish design' could be made to fit 1640, Charles I, Strafford, Pym, Vane and another 'Popish design'; but the re-run was superficial. One might speculate on what might have happened had there been another Scots' invasion and Irish Rebellion, but certainly the political circumstances and the character and abilities of the leading figures were quite different. What 1640 and 1678 had in common, though, was the dramatic intensity of the crisis. Oates' fictions, the mystery of Godfrey, the implications of the Coleman correspondence, Montagu's revelations – all merged in the early months of 1679 to create a hysterical atmosphere. Three themes ran together in time: the high tide of the Popish Plot investigations; the election of a new House of Commons which became known as the First Exclusion Parliament; and some delicate Privy Council manoeuvrings.

A number of Catholics, in particular Jesuits, were arrested, and trials took place in London and the provinces. These began in November '78 and continued until the summer of the following year. Twenty-two people were executed, including Coleman, amid mounting public fever; law-court procedure suffered severely with hearsay evidence readily accepted by judges, who in turn proved biassed in their summings-up. The worst period for Catholics was June to August when fourteen of the twenty-two were hanged; a reign of terror was feared, but the tide began to ebb from then on. Oates' inconsistencies emerged under cross-questioning, and many began to have doubts – not least because an odd feature of all the trials and speeches from the scaffold was that not one condemned Catholic sought reprieve by confession. John Evelyn in his *Diary* indicates the reservations which moderate men had:

> For my part I do look upon Oates as a vain, insolent man, puffed up with the favour of the Commons; that he was trusted with those great secrets he pretended, or had any solid ground for what he accused divers noblemen of, I have many reasons to induce my contrary belief.

This was written in July 1679 at the trial of Sir George Wakeman, a physician to the Queen. He was acquitted by Chief Justice Scroggs when much of Oates' testimony was torn to shreds by the defence. Yet such doubts as Evelyn had were not shared by the ordinary people of London. Scroggs was seen as a villain, in the pay of the Pope and the Portuguese; he joined James and Portsmouth as the objects of popular fury. A lampoon began,

Right: William III, undated (National Portrait Gallery)

Left: James II c. 1690 (National Portrait Gallery)

His Holiness has three grand friends
  On Great Britain's shore,
That prosecute his (and their own) ends:
  A Duke, a Judge and a Whore. (34, p.177)

Meanwhile MPs were busy electioneering for a new Parliament to be summoned in March 1679. The result was a sweeping change in membership which moved markedly away from 'Cavalier' sentiments. Shaftesbury was jubilant, dividing it into 302 'worthy MPs' set against a mere 158 'courtiers'. Sober analysis, however, shows other factors at work. 'Exclusion' had not been a central issue in the elections. J.R. Jones says that the evidence proves it was 'the inevitable consequence of an excessively long-lived Parliament.' The opening weeks mirrored old Commons' interests – grumbles over a standing army, possible impeachment of Danby and discussions on Limitations. Little was done, except the Habeas Corpus Act, its great latter-day basis for personal liberties being seen by contemporaries as having an only marginal effect on 'limiting' an absolute monarch.

Later that spring though something happened which meant that English politics would never be quite the same again. A significant number of Shaftesbury's 'worthies' were converted to Exclusion and the glimmerings of what proved to be a permanent political divide could be seen. Richard Hampden, son of the Ship Money Trial MP, moved for the introduction of Exclusion. On 15 May 1679 the First Exclusion Bill was read in the Commons. Its terms were brief, in essence disabling and banishing James by name and moving the succession on to the next in line, Mary, 'as if the Duke were dead'. On the second reading, a week later, it was passed by a vote of 207 to 128. Within a few days Charles prorogued this Parliament too (dissolving it in July without its meeting again). This was the first controversial issue in the whole of the reign in which either side had mustered more than 200 votes.

While the Plot trials and the proceedings in Parliament had been occupying the centre of the arena, a third development had some significance. The Privy Council had over the past twenty years become quite unwieldy, increasing steadily in number to around fifty in order it appeared to give voice to all shades of opinion. Charles in April 1679 announced a re-modelling. He

> resolved to lay aside the use he may hitherto have made of any single ministry or private advices on Foreign Committees for the general direction of his affairs, and to constitute such a Privy Council, and by the constant advice of such a Council His Majesty is resolved hereafter to govern his kingdoms, together with the frequent use of his Great Council in Parliament; for the greater dignity of this Privy Council His Majesty resolves their constant number shall be limited to that of thirty. (12, p.101)

The surprising feature was that among the named members of this Council were several men who had been vocal in their criticism of past royal policies, and in particular that Shaftesbury was to be Lord President of the Council. Was Charles making an honest attempt at 1641-style 'bridge appointments' in which the critics would be allowed a full voice in policy-making; or was this another of Charles' devious actions – perhaps an attempt to divide Shaftesbury from his growing support, perhaps, more cynically, as in 1641, to give the shadow not the substance of power? Shaftesbury was probably right in refusing to trust Charles, even though two notable figures were now absent. Danby had gone: he had been lodged in the Tower of London (more for his own safe-keeping than as a prisoner), yet Shaftesbury was well aware of the months wasted in the details of impeachment and attainder, all as it turned out to be of no avail. James too was gone – sent abroad by Charles in March in an endeavour to cool the political situation down. The expectation that Charles really would 'lay aside his private advices' was remote.

It was at this point that Shaftesbury made his worst blunder of the crisis: he chose to underestimate Charles, thinking him irresolute, a man who would give way under continual pressure. Shaftesbury used his position as Lord President throughout the summer of '79 to be more awkward that usual, centring his whole policy on Exclusion. The differences between Charles and Shaftesbury became quite irreconcilable. Haley expresses how the issue between the two men became sharply focused. 'Precisely because Charles was determined to stand by his wife and brother, and because Shaftesbury had committed himself to attacking them, the duel must now go on until one was able to enforce his will upon the other' (33, p.551).

Shaftesbury considered he had a strong case in concentrating everything upon Exclusion. First, James' conversion to Catholicism had produced such terrible fear for the future that traditional constitutional practices of government through King and Parliament were impaired. James, Shaftesbury reasoned, must turn towards absolute methods involving a strong standing army and the support of France – these fitted the known views of James. Secondly, Shaftesbury doubted the sincerity of King's new tactic, that of offering to consider Limitations. Charles had explicitly supported the idea as early as November '78 when he promised MPs that he would sign

> such reasonable bills as should be presented, to make them safe in the reign of any successor, so as they tend not to impeach the right of succession. (5, p.203)

But Shaftesbury was well aware of the snares of Limitation. Time-consuming legislation in the Commons, plus Court obstruction, plus the uncertainty of co-operation from the Lords – these were the ingredients of disaster, recalling 'the labyrinth' (see p.43) which Pym, Vane and Hampden found themselves in during 1641. To Shaftesbury's mind Limitation was a new version of the old corset of statutes within which Pym had tried, in vain, to wrap Charles I. Thirdly, there was the further doubt as to how constitutionally restrictive a statute was: Charles II had already invoked the Crown's prerogative power of dispensing with laws (for example, the Declaration of Indulgence). The merit of Exclusion was simplicity. Shaftesbury hoped for support from the political nation, from those 'of the middling sort', and even from the politically unsophisticated labouring poor for such a direct uncontroversial policy of Exclusion. As we shall see, though, he failed to appreciate Charles' agility in playing the Limitations game, or how controversial the thesis 'Exclusion.. but in favour of whom' could be.

Not all Shaftesbury's supporters accepted his leadership without misgivings. His volatile career had led him to be first Royalist, then Parliamentarian in the Civil War – through Barebone's Parliament and Cromwell's Council of State to eventual critics of the Protectorate and supporter of the Restoration – to the high office and rank of Chancellor of the Exchequer, Lord Chancellor and Earl. Service followed by opposition to Charles I was now being repeated under his son. Friend and political foe alike knew him as 'the Dorsetshire eel', such was his talent for wriggling out of any commitment. There was no shortage of hostile comment, so controversial was his image, but it must be said that his reputation has suffered because three of these verdicts come from men with a gift for words which left lasting 'portraits'. Bishop Gilbert Burnet had no liking for James, as Duke or King, but he also resented Shaftesbury:

> He had no sort of virtue, for he was both a lewd and corrupt man, and had no regard either to truth or justice.

John Dryden, poet of genius, savaged many politicians in his *Absalom and Achitopel*, a long poem on Monmouth and Shaftesbury and their contemporaries. Shaftesbury was 'the false Achitopel':

> For close designs and crooked counsels fit;
> Sagacious, bold and turbulent of wit;
> Restless, unfixed in principles and place,
> In power unpleased, impatient of disgrace;
> A fiery soul, which, working out its way,
> Fretted the pigmy body to decay...
> In friendship false, implacable in hate,
> Resolved to ruin or rule the State.
> Now manifest of crimes contrived long since,
> He stood at bold defiance with his Prince. (12, p.919)

The King himself had a reputation for wit, especially the brief aside: Shaftesbury was a remarkably small man, and Charles' devastating pun was, 'Little sincerity.'

There was much more scurrilous abuse of the man, and there is some irony in the fact that Shaftesbury and Charles have both been called devious and unprincipled. Yet if Charles had unswerving devotion to that abstraction, hereditary right, equally Shaftesbury adhered to the name of liberty. John Locke, his friend and later the great philosopher, wrote in his *'Epitaph for Shaftesbury,'*

'Libertatis civilis, ecclesiasticae,
Propugnator strenuus, indefessus.
(a vigorous and tenacious champion of civil and religious liberty.)

Shaftesbury was no Leveller, though, having more in common as a believer in Parliamentary government and religious liberty with Oliver Cromwell. He would have said that his basic principle was that 'sovereignty lies with the people' – meaning the political nation, those who carried the greatest weight in society's affairs. This conclusion bears close resemblance to Aylmer's judgement on Charles I's execution (which we have noted, p.93): that he was 'accountable'. Shaftesbury would have agreed.

This, then, was the man who in the summer of 1679 expected, through pressure, to compel Charles, however grudgingly, to accept the exclusion of his brother from the throne. With the dissolution of the First Exclusion Parliament formally in July, another parliament was summoned for October. Shaftesbury found that, far from submitting, Charles could play the political game as deviously as himself. With a fresh parliament elected and hearing that many members were openly committed to Exclusion, Charles used his prerogative power to prorogue the session even before it met. Unlike his father in 1640 he was not faced with a Scots army and such serious money problems. His use of this power was the crucial weapon in Charles' survival of the crisis. J.R. Jones calls it 'the ace in the royal pack', for it was not used just once. Seven times in little more than a year Charles successively employed the tactic of prorogation.

It was a hectic time: difficult for students of the period to make sense of, considering the rapidly shifting sands of political opinion, made worse by a sudden illness of the King and James' return from Brussels to be on hand 'to claim' his throne. Charles recovered from what seemed to be a kind of malaria by taking 'Jesuit's powder', an early form of quinine. James retired once again into unofficial exile. Monmouth, too, had made sure he was on hand, and his popularity with the mobs rose, with bonfires being lit on his behalf. On the King's recovery Monmouth reluctantly departed to the continent – to the hospitality of William of Orange. George Savile, Marquis of Halifax, one of Charles' key supporters for Limitation on the Privy Council also left London, for his country estates, disillusioned by Charles' tactic of prorogation. The re-modelled Privy Council, which looked so promising six months before, was disintegrating. Shaftesbury had been for some time nothing more than a figure-head President: in October Charles dismissed him, and returned to his old 'inner ring' procedures of obtaining advice. New names, openly against Exclusion, appeared on the scene: the Earl of Sunderland, Sidney Godolphin,

Lawrence Hyde. They were a curious blend of recklessness, talent and arrogance. Meanwhile Charles was seeking other advice and help: from Louis XIV in the form of subsidies 'in the interest of preserving the Stuart Monarchy'. French State archives, *Affaires Etrangères*, have many documents over these months, but the French ambassador found the whirligig of English politics so difficult to follow that the negotiations lapsed. He wrote later to Louis:

> It would be very difficult to explain to Your Majesty what is the real design of the King of England and his ministers.

If the French were bemused, Shaftesbury, too, was on difficult terrain. Disconcerted by the repeated prorogations, he had to find means of maintaining the tension and keeping his Exclusion supporters steadfast, without the valuable platform of Parliament at his disposal. To this end he used any way possible. Exclusionists, despite Privy Council efforts to stifle them, produced most of the news-sheets, some of them sensational and crude, feeding on the gullibility of readers. The most famous appeared in October 1679: *An Appeal from the Country to the City for the Preservation of His Majesty's person, liberty, property and religion*. It sketched lurid pictures in words:

> Whenever Popery prevails: imagine you see the whole town aflame, occasioned this second time by the same Popish malice; behold troops of Papists ravishing your wives and daughters, dashing your little children's brains out against the walls; cast your eyes towards Smithfield, imagine your father and mother tied to a stake in the midst of flames – a frequent spectacle the last time Popery reigned amongst us (i.e. Mary Tudor)...
> Without a miracle, our apparent ruin is at hand; if ever a Popish successor comes amongst you, let his promises of keeping your religion and laws be never so plausible; if you think to bind and fetter him the laws that will be no better than the wise men of Gotham hedging in the cuckoo, for when he governs by an army, what will all your laws signify? You will not then have parliaments to appeal to. (6, pp.466–9)

Sheltering amid the tub-thumping agitation of this pamphlet was a more sober, calculated appeal to 'reason' – 'the last time', for instance, and the logic that any army would render 'binding and fettering' (i.e. Limitation) as nought. How far Shaftesbury himself influenced, even paid for, such publications is impossible to say. Haley investigated the problem, but apart from finding in the Carte Manuscripts in Oxford that a friend of Shaftesbury was arrested for distributing 'the damned libels now in print against the government', he concludes with a reminder of the problem facing all historians: that 'the scent is now too cold' (33, p.553).

What is certain is that Shaftesbury benefited from such writings. Further benefit came from a most lavish 'Pope-burning' procession on 17 November, the anniversary of Elizabeth's succession. This had not yet been transformed into Guy Fawkes' Night, but tens of thousands thronged the Cheapside of Fleet Street route in London. He was also lucky in that over the next years other plots than Oates were 'discovered'. Pepys noted in his *Diary* that

> there is hardly a day passes without some new plot discovered or an old one laughed at.

Other 'discoveries' included the celebrated one which maintained coffee-house gossip through the spring of 1680: that a sealed Black Box had been opened to reveal a former Bishop of Durham's story of how he had 'married' Charles to Monmouth's mother, Lucy Walter. It was too convenient to be anything other than a piece of Shaftesbury–Monmouth fabrication. In the summer of 1680 the great self-confidence of the Exclusionists was well shown when Shaftesbury and a dozen others prepared to indict James, Duke of York, for recusancy and the Duchess of Portsmouth with being a common prostitute and a public nuisance. It was a piece of impudence which was only stopped by a judge in the courtroom who lectured Shaftesbury on not interfering in matters of state! Lurid pamphlets, Pope-burnings, Black Boxes and court-room sensations did their job for the Exclusionists. The issue was not going to die for want of neglect while Parliament was not in session.

Whigs and Tories

Amid all this the English political party system was being conceived. Its parents were those two unlikely political dreamers, Exclusion and Limitation, whose attractions were such as to lure to each side a significant number of previously independent-minded men. The conception took place in the strangest of beds: amid the gaudy, even tawdry, surroundings of anti-papist hysteria, nine members of the aristocracy met on 7 December 1679 to petition the King to allow Parliament to sit. These nine had the support of seven others, but there were some notable absentees, including the Earl of Bedford and Lord Wharton, who remarked significantly that 'his heart was with them, but neither hand nor foot.' Many in the House of Lords were highly suspicious of the ambitions of the House of Commons, even in recess, and of their fellow-peer, Shaftesbury, in particular. Charles received the petition coldly, and when two days later an organised effort was made to gain signatures for the petition throughout London, he reacted with speed, issuing a declaration which forbade 'tumultuous petitions' raised by 'evil-disposed persons' tending to promote rebellion. It was ignored. The collection of names went on, and early in 1680 a monster petition of a hundred metres long and with 50,000 names was presented from the inhabitants of Westminster and Southwark, followed soon by a 30,000 strong Wiltshire petition brought by Tom Thynne, the wealthy owner of Longleat. Charles merely snubbed these petitioners, saying he 'remembered '40 and '41', and that he regretted that men 'of fortune and estate' should be concerned 'in anything that looked so like a rebellion.' The signatures, he thought, were those of 'a rout' (i.e. a rabble). By April, though, Charles' own supporters made a counter-move. Some of the inhabitants of Westminster published a signed address 'abhorring' the earlier petitions. The number of names, though, was much fewer.

It seems that during this long Parliamentary recess English political opinion was being polarised. Supporters of Exclusion were nicknamed 'Petitioners'; they were very confident of country-wide support. Those supporting Limitation were called 'Abhorrers', less in number and in confidence, but committed to the view that anything more extreme than a restriction of James' powers as King would bring trouble, possibly civil war. Over these early months of 1680 the growing commitment to 'party' led the Marquis of Halifax to comment, with pardonable exaggeration, that 'half the world' was absolutely confident that the King would 'quit the Duke of York', and the other half absolutely confident he would not.

There was considerable political tension, then, when Charles finally agreed to allow the Commons and Lords to meet, on 21 October 1680; it had been over twelve months since the election, and this soon acquired the name the Second Exclusion Parliament. A foreign policy problem was imminent over the possible loss of Tangier (part of the Queen's dowry) to Moorish besiegers, and Charles wanted money for an expedition. The Commons though, brushed aside the King's concern for this tiny western Mediterranean outpost, and began drafting a Second Exclusion Bill. Emotions ran high. Charles was bad-tempered on learning that Monmouth had returned 'with a wonderful acclamation by the rabble'. Acute observers noted that he had removed the baton sinister (acknowledging his bastardy) from the coat of arms on his coach. A senior member of the Privy Council, Sunderland, wrote a panicky letter to William of Orange to come over and thwart Monmouth and preserve his and his wife's interests.

The Exclusion Bill went through the Commons in nine days. The manuscript – held today in the House of Lords – had as its main clause:

'Whereas James, Duke of York, is notoriously known to have been perverted from the Protestant to the Popish religion and great encouragement hath been given to the Popish party to enter into the most devilish and horrid plots; if the said Duke should succeed to the imperial throne of this realm, nothing is more manifest than that a total change of religion within these kingdoms would ensue.

It is enacted that James, Duke of York, shall be and is by the authority of this present Parliament excluded and made forever incapable to inherit or enjoy the imperial Crown. (12, p.113)

A few spokesmen for the Crown tried to argue that this would reduce England to an elective monarchy, but the enormous attendance (about 400) crushed such reasoning. It was noticed significantly that the Bill omitted the May 1679 Exclusion Bill clause that the Crown should descend as though James were naturally dead. Thus, Mary, William, Monmouth and Charles' re-marriage remained as future options. It was clear that Shaftesbury was sticking to Exclusion without any 'in favour of...' complications – for the moment. The Bill passed without a division-vote, so large was the majority for it.

The Bill was debated in the House of Lords on 15 November. The Commons and Lords had rarely been comfortable partners in past seventeenth-century constitutional wrangles, the Lords often expressing concern at the 'insults and insolencies' of their junior partner. So, despite the manoeuvrings of Shaftesbury as a member of the Lords, the passage of the Bill was not a foregone conclusion. The debate is famous: it was decisive on Exclusion, and crucial to an understanding of delicate political atmosphere and alignments which had emerged during the crisis; yet the only record we have is in fragmentary notes. It was well-attended, with nearly one hundred (two-thirds of the possible membership) there. Charles arrived early in the ten-hour debate, sat on the throne for a while, but then moved to the side of the large fireplace where his tall and obvious presence dominated the proceedings. Later still (the debate went on by candlelight until well after 10 p.m.), according to Burnet, he moved around 'like a common solicitor' canvassing members on behalf of his interests; he had both dinner and supper brought to a side room of the Lords.

Lord Ailesbury sought a new solution: perhaps James would turn Protes-tant, as Henri Quatre had turned Catholic a century before: if 'Paris was worth a Mass' then London was surely worth a pulpit. Few members thought this realistic in view of James' known stubbornness. Ailesbury's other argument made more sense:

> If the right heir should be thrown out, may we not be subject to invasions abroad or wars at home? More insecurity from wars than to suffer him to reign. (79, p.393)

Then Halifax spoke: he did so many times to counter Shaftesbury's proposals. Halifax said Limitation was the only solution, for civil war loomed with Exclusion; time and again he referred to the fear that James, now in 'exile' in Scotland, could 'with the Fleet' organise an armed rising. His powerful oratory matched that of Shaftesbury's. At one point swords were drawn, recalling the 1641 Grand Remonstrance debate. When the vote was taken the Exclusion Bill was defeated by 63 to 30. Monmouth was one of the thirty, and Charles remarked loudly on 'the kiss of Judas'. Haley's expert evaluation of this vital vote is that Charles' 'presence, towering by the fire and detering any waverers, was probably more effective in procuring the Bill's rejection than all the fifteen speeches that were made by Halifax' (33, pp.601–2). Yet contemporaries gave considerable credit to the Marquis. Dryden's poem put it thus:

> ... piercing wit and pregnant thought
> Endued by nature, and by learning, taught
> To move assemblies... (79, p.394)

Charles (and James) had survived; Exclusion was dead, for the time being. But the immediate danger to the Crown was not over. There was none of the rioting, feared but expected, in London, yet rumour was strong. Shaftesbury and his supporters met regularly at the Green Ribbon Club, which had in the recent past subsidised the great pope-burning processions; now there was talk of using the power of the mob, especially a group from the East End of London known as 'the brisk boys from Wapping'.

Charles thought it expedient to dissolve Parliament in January 1681, and to summon a new one – to Oxford. Fresh elections took place. In the City of London there was much verbal kite-flying: one MP at a City dinner proclaimed,

> Hang Tangier! We resolve to raise no money to pay the whores at Whitehall and arbitrary government. And, as the King has called us to Oxford we know that next will be at York, but for all that we will give him no money. (79, p.401)

The voters were as deeply divided as ever, though the original labels, Petitioners and Abhorrers, were now out of date. Over the past months of vitriolic exchanges of opinion between the two groups in scurrilous pamphlets and abusive speech-making each had coined a damning expression for the other. The Exclusionist-Petitioners were referred to as 'Whiggamores' or Whigs, after some rebellious Scots' Covenanters; and the Limitationist-Abhorrers were called 'Tories' after a group of Irish Catholic brigands. The labels stuck.

Both the elections for the 1679–80 and 1681 Parliaments had been fought over the issues of Exclusion, and it was clear that two rival camps had developed to which these labels were being applied. The traditional 'independent country gentlemen' of politics still existed, but in declining numbers. Either side of them two political parties had been conceived and born; though still in their infancy, they exhibited characteristics which made them proper 'parties' in the modern sense, differing as they did from other political groupings of the immediate past, best called 'factions' or 'interests'. First, they pursued publicly stated objectives, in that they were known to be committed to supporting or attacking specific policies. Secondly, they were organised with only a little emphasis on family or local connections; in this respect the leadership imposed a remarkable level of discipline on its supporters. For instance, as the 1681 Oxford Parliament met, the Whigs used a new device, sending 'instructions' to their MPs to insist on Exclusion; if they did not, there was an implied threat that the Whig leadership, organisation and printing press would not be available to them in future elections. The last especially was crucial to party cohesion. Whig pamphlets were known to be powerful determinants of public opinion: they were written for different levels of literacy, and widely distributed through the coffee-houses and taverns of the country. The Tories, too, were better organised for the 1681 election – in order to get the measure of Whig propaganda, they had to imitate their techniques. A Tory press came into being as combative as anything the Whigs had; the charge that the Whigs were rebels was endlessly repeated.

Each party had several interwoven strands of support. The Whigs attracted part of the independent country group of the Cavalier Parliament because of a principle in common, the defence of the integrity and independence of Parliament against arbitrary government; they saw themselves as heirs of Pym, Holles and Haselrig. Also most of the town corporations, including London, lined up behind the Whigs; in the borough communities many officers of a corporation were elected and these towns put much value on their independence from Crown pressure – though they were well aware that their charters, granting them important legal and fiscal privileges, were mainly medieval royal grants, which could be taken away. The Nonconformists were another group who saw the Whigs as allies, hoping, by the political path, to establish toleration by statute. Labelling can be dangerous, and though the generality that most dissenters were Whigs was true, especially at election times, the reverse was not the case (few of the Whig peers, for example, were dissenters). London support was important in the Exclusion crisis, but the City was not quite the same as in Pym's day. Despite rumours of the 'brisk boys' the Whigs made no serious attempt to use violence; also the clergy were conspicuously Anglican, with little evidence of the old Puritan pulpit invective.

The Tories had their support firmly among the Anglican clergy and the county gentry, especially from Crown-nominated JPs. The Party had not been created by the Court, despite Whig jibes that Tories were Crown lackeys; Danby had gathered together a small group of courtier 'friends' of the King in the mid-1670s, but this had disintegrated in 1678. J.R. Jones' researches have shown clearly that 'Toryism, when it developed as a reaction to the introduction of Exclusion in May 1679, represented a fresh start' (30, p.60). Alarm at the uncompromising and extremist policies of Shaftesbury was the basic fodder on which Toryism fed. Yet many of its supporters still had a distrust of the King (not a few thought, as did Shaftesbury, that Charles would weaken and give in to Exclusion). Thus the Tories attracted those country members of Parliament who retained their suspicions of the Court, but were more fearful of Shaftesbury. They were far from being well-wishers of despotic rule, regarding themselves, not as heirs of Laud and Strafford, but of Hyde, Falkland and the constitutional royalists of the early '40s. Tory leadership in the 1680s came from men like Sidney Godolphin and Lawrence Hyde, Clarendon's son, and they developed a powerful response to Whig pressure with the election rallying-cry, 'Forty-One is here again.'

The hostility of each party to the other was monumental. There was no question of accepting the other as a legitimate 'opposition' group with an alternative set of policies. Each saw itself alone as representing the true interests of the nation; the other was a perversion of the truth, a deviation from the norm of 'good governance'. The Whigs characterised a Tory as

> A monster with an English face, a French heart and an Irish conscience. A creature of a large forehead and no brains. They are a sort of wild boars that would root out the constitution.'

The Tory's view of the Whig was:

> His principles are like chaos, a gallimofry [ie. hotch-potch] of negatives. His language is 'Overturn, Overturn'. His prayer is a rhapsody of holy hickops, sanctified barkings, sighs, sobs, gasps and groans. (52, pp.610–11)

Opponents stigmatised the Tories as being mothered by 'the Scarlet Woman', while the Whigs were descended from the first great critic, the Devil.

The Oxford Parliament, 1681

Elections to the Oxford Parliament were fiercely contested in many constituencies; the general pattern of the results was still Exclusionist.

At the weekend of 18–19 March Oxford saw the arrival of MPs and their attendants, some of whom were well-armed. The two parties had by now acquired some of the outward trappings of differentiation: in expletives (the Whigs' 'So Help Me God!' was matched by the Tory's 'God Dammee!'); in drinks (Whig coffee *versus* Tory ale); and in colours (blue for Monmouth set against scarlet and red ribbons for Charles and James respectively). Shaftesbury came on horseback on Saturday night 'with holsters and pistols before him, attended with a great many horsemen, well armed, and coaches', so ran the local news-sheet. The younger university students had been sent home, and several colleges were taken over for lodgings. Shaftesbury went to Balliol, while the King and his Court, who arrived after a day at the races at Burford, entered Christ Church and Merton Colleges. On Monday the King spoke to the assembled Lords and Commons in the University's Geometry School. It was observed as a 'subtle and crafty speech':

I need not tell you how much I love Parliaments. I want to remove all reasonable fears that may arise from the possibility of a Popish successor's coming to the Crown, and will harken to any such expedient by which the religion might be preserved. (74, p.403)

Word circulated that perhaps a form of regency was being offered. Shaftesbury and the Whigs hesitated: seeing no urgency they postponed a fresh Exclusion debate until the Saturday. In the meantime Charles and Shaftesbury had several confrontations, the one on Thursday 24 March proving critical. Shaftesbury presented a note to Charles while awaiting the Lords' sitting: it was a six-line suggestion that Monmouth should have the Crown. Charles turned to Shaftesbury and said,

Here is an expedient indeed, if one would trample over all the laws of God and man

Shaftesbury offered:

Give me leave to make it as lawful as we can (33, p.634; 52, p.618).

There are several versions of this conversation, including one prepared for publication within twenty-four hours. What is clear is that Shaftesbury had committed himself to Monmouth's cause, and 'make it lawful' meant legitimising him by statute. Not all his Whig supporters were that keen, Mary being preferred to Monmouth. Charles was as aware of the disagreements as anyone. He replied to Shaftesbury that he would not yield:

By the Grace of God I will stick to that that is law.

Within a few days canvassing revealed that the House of Lords would still not go with Shaftesbury. Without warning, on Monday 28 March, while the Commons were considering a third Exclusion bill, Charles sent for them. In one sentence he dissolved the Oxford Parliament:

All the world may see to what a point we are come, that we are not like to have a good end when the divisions at the beginning are such. (79, p.405)

What Shaftesbury did not know was that the Treasury was benefiting from an excellent boom in trade, and that during the week-long session of the Parliament Charles had been promised about £350,000 over three years by Louis XIV. It was not much, but with the increase in customs, it gave Charles the confidence to dispense with Parliament. Between the Oxford Parliament and his death in 1685 no further Parliament was summoned.

Charles' firmness on principle but lack of scruple in political behaviour, Whig division, Louis' last minute 'pin-money', but above all, customs profitability had destroyed Exclusion.

Study 18

It had been a long crisis, nearly three years of Plot and Exclusion. You will find it worth asking whether the Crown's survival was the result of Charles' abilities or of Shaftesbury's over-confidence. Modern historians are by no means agreed, while some suggest that the character-assessment problem be merged with several other factors.

1 Survey the story of the crisis from 1678 to 1681, picking out the occasions when Charles' or Shaftesbury's decisions or actions could be found at fault or skilful.

2 Present an analysis of other factors which seem to you to be relevant to the outcome of the crisis.

Observations:

1 One interesting puzzle is why Charles dissolved the First Exclusion Parliament in May–July 1679. It is possible to argue that he was foolish. John Kenyon thinks his motives are not clear, while J.R. Jones says, 'Exclusion was rushed forward with insufficient preparation', which should have left Charles in a fairly strong position – with the Lords on bad terms with the Commons, Danby the scapegoat gone, James in exile, and the Plot losing a little of its momentum. Perhaps, on this reasoning, the dissolution was a rash act, comparable with Charles I's irate dismissal of the Short Parliament in 1640. Another historian, K.D.H. Haley, says, 'My interpretation of the vote [ie on Exclusion] differs from that of Dr. Jones; it is difficult to believe that delay [in dissolution] (which would mean maintaining the anti-Popish excitement consistently) was either desirable or necessary.' Haley makes out a strong case, pointing to the number present (more than 200 – noting that 204 voted on Strafford's Attainder in 1641) and the vote ('a majority of 79 was exceptional. This was a large number of members prepared to go to the length of declaring themselves publicly against the King's brother.') (33, pp.521–2)

Over the whole crisis period Jones shows himself to be a great admirer of Charles:

'He emerged as a politician in his own right, quite unrecognizable compared with the usually indolent, but intermittently active figure of the past years. Charles originated all the unscrupulous, subtle and cleverly disguised moves that led to the decisive royal victory, during the Exclusion Crisis, over the first Whigs.' (5, pp.11 and 204)

Haley has reservations:

'Unquestionably Charles showed considerable skill in outwitting the Whigs; but even here his astuteness has probably been over-estimated. His success was not the result of a consistent plan, but rather a matter of clinging to certain assets which he possessed, and after several tactical defeats, seizing his chances when they came.' (32, p.20)

What do you think?

2 If Charles retained his nerve, he also had 'certain assets'. Undoubtedly the monarchy was in a much stronger position than in Charles I's reign. You should note that Scotland and Ireland are conspicuous by their absence from the Exclusion story. Why was this significant? The Lords too was an obvious royal asset: you may agree with Haley that, 'the King's majority in the Upper House was impregnable', and see this as the key to success – so long as the Whigs stuck to constitutional methods. Or you might think, with Barry Coward, that 'Charles' greatest asset was his financial strength', with the work of the Treasury Commissioners being the vital element, not the more sensational French subsidies. You will have to balance your argument carefully.

Money was critical, of course, in allowing Charles to play that superb game of prorogations. Playing for time, especially set against the Plot hysteria, was a valuable ploy. Here you will need to look at Shaftesbury's tactics, problems and mistakes. He became very confident after the first Exclusion vote (justified?), and he had an organised, though infant, political machine behind him. But he made at least three errors which you will have to explain with chapter and verse: the proven artificality of the Plot meant that Shaftesbury's agitation and pressure were difficult to sustain; the emphasis on Exclusion was blurred by his wavering over Mary or Monmouth, which split the Whigs; his worst miscalculation was assuming Charles would yield to pressure.

A final observation: in the last analysis Englishmen had memories. The grin of the Cheshire Cat was still there. Having worked through the constitutional stages, you must ask the question: why did the Whigs not resort to force (as the Parliamentarians had done late in 1642)? Some pointers: fear of civil war was greater than the fear of popery – Christopher Hill's pungent comment that 'the ghost of the Interregnum was walking again' (56, p.233) – would Shaftesbury be another version of Warwick the Kingmaker when at Oxford he declared for Monmouth? – overmighty subjects and evil counsellers were powerful seventeenth-century images. The evidence for this fear was there in March 1681. When Charles dissolved the Oxford Parliament there was always the possibility that the Commons might refuse to go, and that in the tennis court of a nearby Oxford college they might swear on oath and seize power, as was to happen at Versailles 108 years later. They did not; they dispersed quietly to their country estates, many stopping off for a while to take in the horse-racing at Burford.

CHAPTER 15

James II – A Real Plot or Incompetence?

Prelude: Charles' declining years

Despite the Tory cry during the Exclusion Crisis that 'Forty-One is here again', a comparison of the two crises shows marked differences. 'Forty-One' produced a welter of statutes designed to restrict Charles I's power; 'Exclusion' produced only Habeas Corpus. Charles II and his heir emerged with their prerogatives largely intact. There was one important new element in the situation. What the crisis did produce was parties: Charles had not 'won' on his own; he had 'won' with the support of the Tory Party.

Charles' political instincts told him to recognise this fact, and King and Tory, master and dog, got on well in his declining years. He tossed a massive bone of power to his newly acquired political spaniels. In the years 1681–5 the Crown purged both county and borough governments of all identifiable Whigs, thus securing a total monopoly of key local offices in the county militia and in the Commission of the Peace (JPs); in the boroughs, too, the Corporation Act was rigidly enforced. If there proved to be any difficulty in the formerly Whig-dominated towns Charles used his prerogative to issue *Quo Warranto* writs requiring that the old, mostly medieval charters be put up for inspection; lawyers then easily found technical points of error, enabling them to declare a charter invalid. The attack on the City of London was a long-drawn out legal affair (December 1681 to June 1683), but the eventual Crown victory was a lesson to other towns, which crumbled quickly. Fifty-one new charters were issued in Charles' last four years, and James speeded up the operation, issuing 47 more in his first four months as King. Royal consent was now required for offices like mayors and sheriffs; as sheriffs enrolled local juries the outcome was a virtual Tory stranglehold on the legal system of England and Wales. 'Virtual' because it could never be total: many 'new Tories' were not in office from conviction. A significant number of Nonconformists, for instance, faced with the rigidity of the Corporation Act, traded their religious scruples – 'it is madness,' said one, 'to lose an office for a bit of bread and a cup of wine' (36, p. 112)

The Whigs were defeated. They had lost the Exclusion contest, and without a Parliament they had no platform, an isolation made worse by their removal from central and local offices of power. Whig leadership disintegrated. Shaftesbury, still pursuing the mirage of Monmouth, was arrested, then prosecuted, and was lucky to have a Whig jury in London before *Quo Warranto* took effect. Disillusioned and ill he went into exile to Holland, where he died in 1683. Other leading Whigs were persecuted, some charged and executed for the treason of plotting. Today it is thought doubtful if one such conspiracy, the Rye House Plot, existed at all, such was the fabricated and circumstantial evidence presented at the trials.

The King and the gentry: this was the alliance of the early 1680s that offered much for future settlement and stability – something James could surely build on. It was doubly powerful with the addition of the Anglican Church; Charles not only gave Tories his political support, he recognised Tory–Anglican sympathies too. He abandoned his occasional forays into toleration, his wooing of Dissenter and Catholic as a counterweight to Church of England power; he buried his previous fears of being an Anglican puppet, and, recognising that he could not beat them, joined them. He was rewarded by receiving effusive loyal 'addresses' from Tory county communities, and the pulpit once more preached the political doctrine of loyalty and obedience to the King. The surprising thing was that when Charles ignored the Triennial Act in 1684 there was no expression of grievance. It seemed, John Miller concludes, that the Tories 'were quite content that the King should bend the law, provided he did it in their interests.'

Charles enjoyed his last years. Sir John Reresby's *Memoirs* portray him at the races and elsewhere:

> He let himself down from majesty to the very degree of country gentleman. He mixed himself amongst the crowd; he went a-hawking in mornings, to cock matches in afternoons, to plays in evenings (36, p. 113)

He was, he recognised, the leader of a party, of the intolerant, High Church Tory gentry. It was not an active leadership: he left those in control of local administration largely to their own devices; it became the heyday of JP independence, and one of the 1640 Crisis problems – hostility out in the provinces to centralisation – seemed solved. Yet Charles' idleness did not appeal to James, who favoured the use of Tory support to foster royal power. James' error was in not realising that dogs, even docile King Charles spaniels, sometimes turn on their masters.

James' lost opportunity

Charles II died of a stroke in February, 1685. James became King without any of the disturbances which might have been expected from the fears of yesteryear. He could only wonder at his good fortune. The last thing which could have been expected from the horrible days of the Exclusion Crisis was that he could succeed his brother with Crown prerogative powers intact. Also the signs were that England was following continental trends towards absolutism – this suited James' temperament, though how far he could push the trend was a dark question of the future. To date the salient factors which had held up this development were lack of money and lack of an army. One at least, what his grandfather had called 'the canker of want', was, in the sunset of Charles' reign, slowly disappearing. Financial solvency came not from France, but from the hard work of Rochester as First Commissioner of the Treasury. The effective control he had over government departmental expenditure, built up from the 1667 reorganisation, now bore fruit. Direct collection of customs and excise was proving far more efficient than the old 'farming' methods; and Rochester achieved what others had failed to do – he persuaded Charles to cut his extravagent expenditure. The real bonus came with the trade boom of the 1680s. The original £1,200,000 revenues agreed to in 1660 as Crown Ordinary income had rarely raised £800,000 until the '80s; now they rose well beyond the original sum to nearly £1,400,000. Critical to those calculations was the increase in customs yield, as the following figures show:

1672–3	£425,000
1675–8	£430,000
1681–4	£570,000

The boom carried over into James' reign, so that in his first three years:

1685–7	£590,000 (50, p. 32)

The first days of James reign augured well for the future. He reassured the Tories at an early meeting of the Privy Council:

> I shall make it my endeavour to preserve this government, both in Church and State, as it is by law established; and as I shall never depart from the rights and prerogatives of the Crown, so shall I never invade any man's property (36, p. 120)

He confirmed all his brother's officers of state in their positions, promoting only a few of his own trusted advisers, like John Churchill. Rochester seemed likely to be James' senior minister, which meant continuation of financial skill on the Privy Council, despite his known arrogance and growing addiction to port. James was more akin to Louis XIV than his brother in that he worked hard at state affairs for many hours each day, and he endeavoured to set high standards of personal conduct at Court and in his Council. But he could not control his amours: a variety of women, whose twin reputation of being both Protestant and plain caused much sly humour at Court, came and went by the backstairs of his private apartments.

If James had had the wit to appreciate the excellent political situation he found himself in, if he had learned the lessons of 1681–4, and not offended the susceptibilities of the Tory gentry of provincial England, then the history of his reign would have been entirely different. But James threw away his initial favourable position: first, by pursuing a personal political control and a centralising policy which went far beyond the limited absolutism which the gentry would tolerate; and, secondly, by openly encouraging Catholicism, a policy-line which, misunderstood as it was by contemporaries, generated so much fear that foreign intervention in 1688 precipitated a crisis of 1640 proportions. The explanation of these developments is rooted partly in some unattractive points in James' character, and partly in the activities of two other rulers, William of Orange and Louis XIV.

The few promising points of James' personality already noted were marred by several other unpleasant features. One, that of blind panic in a crisis, did not emerge until 1688, but some were unmistakable from the start. He was not very intelligent; he was quite unable to assess whether a policy was workable; and he had a mulish will. Clarendon, back in the '60s, had remarked on James' 'obstinancy in his will, which he defended by aversion from debate'; Burnet agreed, saying James 'was obstinate against all other advices'. A remark of James, early in his reign, in refusing a minor change of diplomatic office: 'Let the reasons be what they will; I am resolved not to do it', summed up his negative approach to reasoned debate (36, p. 123).

James and Catholicism: a basic misunderstanding

James' views on religion were, of course, subjected to much scrutiny, yet so incompetent was his failure to explain and put across these views to his subjects that most of them drew wrong conclusions about his intentions: 'to subvert and extirpate the Protestant religion' was a commonly expressed fear. He repeatedly used the word 'establish' – for instance, to the French ambassador he spoke of his aim 'to establish the Catholic religion in England so that those who professed it could live as Catholics in complete security.' This did not mean that he intended extending his personal conversion into a vigorous campaign to stamp out Protestantism and allow only Catholic-style worship – though that is what many feared. He told his brother in 1680 that though he wished 'all men alike' in his religion, yet he thought 'it unlawful to force any man, much less a kingdom, to embrace it.' What he wanted, it seemed, was for Catholic and Protestant to be on equal terms, both in worship and in holding office. He also believed that religious persecution in itself was wrong – 'an unchristian thing and absolutely against his conscience', he told a Nonconformist in 1669 – only if religious opponents were a political menace were they to be suppressed.

Yet James was quite naive about the position. He expressed firm hopes of many willing converts from the Church of England; 'he flatters himself,' remarked the French ambassador, with more realism. An investigation would have shown that there were simply not enough Catholics in the country to help this ambition – 20,000 would be a generous estimate. Their leadership was of poor quality. Among the few Jesuits at Court was Father Petre who pressed a violent catholicising policy on James – hardly practical in the circumstances. He could find even fewer laymen of ability: no lawyers, no financiers, and in the diplomatic field he could only appoint Protestants to represent England at Louis XIV's court. Catholic peers thought James' ideas a dangerous threat to their estates!

James and his few able enthusiastic supporters did make a real effort, though. They considered they had a strong intellectual case. Pamphlets designed to appeal to the mind rather than the emotions were circulated. One, *A Papist Misrepresented*, argued,

> Without the guidance of an infallible Church the Scriptures could not afford a sure revelation of God's will. Protestants could only offer private reason, which, when put to the test, proves in thousands and thousands [of cases] to be nothing better than Passion, Prejudice, Interest, Imagination, Guessing and Fancy.

James himself declared with some accuracy,

> The laws enacted since 1558 [i.e. the Elizabethan Anglican Settlement of 1559] had *not* produced unity or internal peace.

Most of James' subjects regarded the argument as specious. Across the Channel Catholic France in the same period had had more years of internal strife than England, and Louis XIV's years of persecution of the Huguenots had culminated in the 1685 Revocation of the Edict of Nantes, denying the French Protestants their 87 year-old right to independent worship. Jones is convinced that the Revocation 'doomed to failure the whole Catholic endeavour' in England.

James' actions alienated more people than did his arguments. His immediate aim was crystal clear: to get rid of the penal recusancy laws and the Test Act. Ninety Catholic officers were commissioned in the Army in 1685, and in answer to the protests that this was a flagrant breach of that Act, James and the judiciary 'arranged' a test case in the law-courts. The outcome of the 1686 *Godden v. Hales* Case was an eleven out of twelve judges' verdict for James' power of 'dispensing'. They ruled that

> the laws of England are the King's law, and therefore it is an inseparable prerogative of the Kings of England to dispense with penal laws in particular cases and upon particular necessary reasons; of those reasons and those necessities the King himself is the sole judge.(12, p. 83)

Memories of the Ship Money Case of 1637 were stirred. The Crown case was fairly strong since this had always been an inherent prerogative power; but it was also obvious that the judiciary was subservient to the Crown. In recent years both later Stuart monarchs had sought compliant judges whose hold on their offices was very much at the Crown mercy. Charles removed eleven between 1675 and 1683, and James another twelve in his brief reign. Judges received instructions from the Privy Council before going on circuit, and it was manifest that they were being used as semi-political agents, preaching loyalty to the Crown as well as administering justice in the Assize Courts. The University of Aberdeen historian, Jennifer Carter, makes a crucial point about the judges: 'They were still royal servants rather than independent judges' (30, p. 88).

James made immediate use of the *Godden v. Hales* decision. He demanded pledges of support for his Catholic policies from a wide range of individuals – ministers and gentry alike. Many refused and were dismissed. His chief minister, Rochester, was the most celebrated victim, but the purges also extended to the county communities with over 250 JPs being discharged. At the same time he put pressure on the universities, where, by law, only those who took oaths of allegiance and supremacy could study, sit degree examinations and hold the research and teaching post of 'Fellow' of a college. Magdalen College, Oxford, was a most sensational illustration of this pressure, when, in 1687, the Fellows defied James' command to elect a Catholic sympathiser as their President. On a personal visit to Oxford James raged against the College: 'Know I am your King. I will be obeyed, and I command you to be gone.' Most of the Fellows were expelled and Catholics admitted in their place.

James' three-year propaganda and appointments campaign showed his determination, but also marked the limits to what he could do. By 1688, for instance, less than a quarter of JPs and Deputy-Lieutenants were admitted Catholics. There were far too few of them to fill all the positions of power, and James had to turn to opportunists and time-servers. The whole process alienated the Tory-Anglican gentry to such a degree that by 1687 James had squandered all the support for the Crown so carefully nurtured in the 1681–5 period. To these people James was seen as a revolutionary, engaged in a major upset of the established social order and political power base.

In 1687 James accepted Tory–Anglican hostility as a regrettable political fact, and appealed to the Dissenters for support. First, he allowed individual Nonconformists to buy certificates granting them freedom from persecution if they practised their faith; then he issued, in April 1687, a *Declaration of Indulgence*, which suspended all penal laws and the Test and Corporation Act.

For Liberty of Conscience:
We so earnestly desire to establish our government on such a foundation as may make our subjects happy; by granting to them the free exercise of their religion for the time to come. None of our subjects may for the future be under any discouragement or disability by reason of some oaths or tests that have been usually administered on such occasions. (12, pp. 395–7)

It was made plain that in return for this royal generosity Nonconformists would support his plans to influence Parliament to repeal the Acts. It was a tempting offer; but could James be trusted? Many regarded him as disingenuous as his father and brother had been. In 1669 he had confided that he had 'no bitterness against nonconformists', yet by 1685 he was announcing to his bishops that he would 'never give any sort of countenance to Dissenters, knowing that it must be faction and not religion, if men could not be content to meet five, besides their own family, which the law dispenses with'. Halifax, in his *Letter to a Dissenter*, voiced in the summer of 1687 many people's distrust:

> Dissenter: to be hugged now, only that you may be better squeezed at another time (35, p. 227)

There was considerable doubt, then, whether James could rely on Dissenter aid for his schemes. The crunch would come in the political field when James tried to put his policies into statute form.

The Army and Parliament

James' efforts to secure control in both Church and State had so far revealed much determination yet limited effect. Partial victory with the judges and JPs, and the many thankful letters and loyal 'addresses' he had received from some Dissenters gave James naive expectations that he was succeeding. To buttress this feeling in two other key areas, the army and Parliament, there were promising levels of royal authority. John Kenyon has argued forcefully that the control of military power was 'the central problem of the seventeenth century constitution' (6, p. 3). This is not just a historian's verdict: the Parliamentarian, Edmund Ludlow, writing in 1659 of the Civil War days, said, 'The great quarrel between the King and us was the militia.' In 1660 the militia remained, though as an amateur force largely under the direct control of the gentry; it was mainly a police force. Charles, we have noted, had a standing army, a few garrisons and a few regiments. James despised the militia, especially when it showed itself an incompetent and untrustworthy instrument in Monmouth's Rebellion of 1685. Monmouth in a belated attempt to force Exclusion on the country raised his famous insurrection in the West Country with 4,000 men. James quickly used his emergency powers to increase the standing army (this was most definitely Hannibal *ad portas*!) to 14,000, and he was lucky that Monmouth proved militarily hesitant. Total disaster ensued for the rebels at Sedgemoor in Somerset in July. James not only retained this successful army but gradually increased it, his much larger revenue being an important factor in this policy. By 1688 he was in a very strong military position, and the chances of an internal rebellion against his policies being successful were slim indeed.

The irony of all this was that James had been supported in the beginning by the active co-operation of the Tories in Parliament. Few Whigs made an effort in the elections which followed Charles' death, and it was an overwhelmingly Tory House of Commons which assembled in May 1685. It seemed not to concern itself with any investigation of the Crown income – a simple vote renewed Charles' life revenues, which, as we have seen, were now adequate if not lavish. Monmouth's Rebellion frightened MPs and further supply was granted to James. But he soon lost this initial favour, Members voiced their hostility to the retention of the standing army: 'Trust to mercenary force alone,' said one, 'is to give up all our liberties at once.' James became angry, and more so when the Lords denounced the illegal appointment of Catholic army officers. Prorogation occurred in November 1685, and dissolution followed later.

He now began a campaign to produce a 'packed' (i.e. compliant) Parliament, one whose election of members had been extensively influenced by royal pressure. The full extent of this campaign has only recently become clear. J.R. Jones from his researches concludes that

> James initiated the most extensive process of canvassing and questioning that has ever been attempted in English history, bringing pressure to bear directly on virtually every individual within or on the fringes of the political nation. (5, p. 241)

The campaign began in mid-1687 when eleven out of the fifty Lords-Lieutenant were changed. Then, in October, Privy Council orders were sent out to the counties to canvass several thousand JPs, Deputy Lieutenants and even minor parochial officers on three questions:

1 if elected would they vote for the repeal of the Test Act and penal laws?
2 if not standing for election, would they vote for candidates favouring repeal?
3 would they accept liberty of conscience?

Historians have not always agreed over the classification of the results. Simply put: 26 per cent said 'Yes'; 27 per cent said 'No'; 47 per cent were evasions or ambiguous answers. James might have been much encouraged by the 26 per cent affirmative answers, but many of these were men put into office by the previous purge – men who must have regarded the 'Questions' as preaching to the converted. Nevertheless James conducted another sweeping purge. The same thing happened in the boroughs, where manipulation and intimidation were easier. By August 1688 James was preparing to issue writs for new elections. Other matters, though, intervened: 1688 was a crisis year of equal importance with 1640. The Parliament James was so carefully preparing for never met; even the elections never took place.

Would the campaign have worked? One historian, John Miller, is convinced that in the counties James 'had little hope of securing the election of his candidates.' In the boroughs his verdict is that 'all depended on the attitude of the dissenters' (36, p. 179–80). The French ambassador observed that the campaign was going badly, and Sunderland was very pessimistic. Another historian, James Jones, however, says, 'the effect [of the campaign] was considerable', and that 'a working majority must have seemed within reach' (5, p. 243). Forecasting people's voting behaviour has always had, then as today, a tinge of crystal-ball gazing about it. In this case historians will never know.

CHAPTER 16

1688 – A Second Crisis Year and a Second Foreign Intervention

The events which took place in England between June and December 1688 are well-documented, but afford different interpretations, depending on one's perspective – contemporary or with hindsight, national or international. The traditional label has been 'The Revolution of 1688', even 'The Glorious Revolution'. Englishmen, horrified at James' policies, rebelled and invited William of Orange to rescue them from a papist and absolute tyranny; William, like the U.S. Cavalry in Indian country, swept in to preserve English religious and constitutional liberties. More recent views doubt whether there was 'a revolution' at all, and research has suggested that the determinant factor, far from being an 'English' rebellion, was the continental aspirations of William of Orange and Louis XIV.

The Events

In the spring of that year James re-issued, from the previous year, the Declaration of Indulgence, with the requirement that it be read from the pulpits. The unease of the clergy was given spectacular form when seven bishops, led by Sancroft, Archbishop of Canterbury, distributed a petition; they refused to read the Declaration,

> Not from any want of tenderness to Dissenters, in relation to whom they are willing to come to such a temper as shall be thought fit, but because that Declaration is founded upon such a dispensing power as hath often been declared illegal in Parliament. (12, p. 84)

Nonconformists seized on the Anglican-preferred olive branch in the phrase 'willing to come to such a temper'. James' hopes began to evaporate: set against a background of tension generated by the twin policies of preparing a packed Parliament and maintaining a standing army, the petition of the bishops brought Anglican and Dissenter, gentry and merchant, Tory and Whig, together.

James was astonished: 'This is a standard of rebellion,' he declared, and,

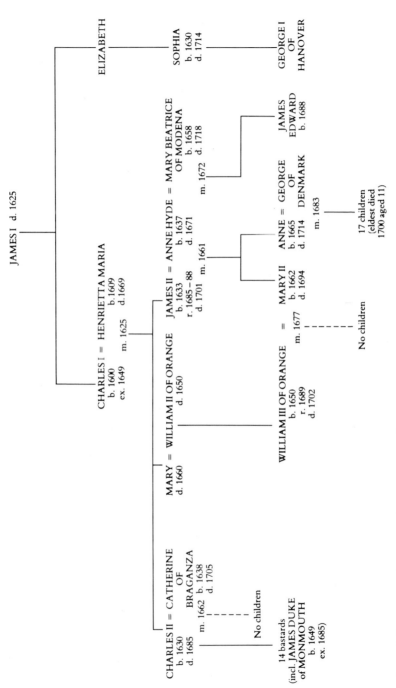

The English Succession Question in the Late Seventeenth Century

after dithering for a while, had the bishops arrested and committed to the Tower. While preparations were afoot for the trial on charges of seditious libel – the offence against the State of inciting public disorder – rumours of the King's plan to remodel the Army by increasing the existing 12 per cent of its Catholic officers only served to increase the tension.

This turned to alarm on 10 June when Queen Mary Beatrice gave birth to a son. Her pregnancy had been known since December, when a letter to James' daughter and heiress presumptive, Mary, in Holland spoke of 'the Great Belly of which people have different sorts of jealousies,'; but the Queen's history of miscarriages and a serious illness at Easter meant that only idle speculation about a popish future took place. Confusion over the date of her expected confinement, and a late rush to prepare a room at St James Palace next door to a convent led to a rash of rumours. Princess Anne had already written to her sister fearing 'there may be foul play intended', a clear expectation that a spurious male child could alter the order of succession. Anne was in the West Country on 10 June and she was furious: 'I shall never now be satisfied whether the child be true or false,' she said. But the chance of a substitution – the 'warming-pan legend' it was called – in one of the best documented royal births in history is unlikely. Professor Kenyon has been over the evidence and it is possible to place most people in the crowd of Ladies of the Bedchamber, Privy Councillors and others who were in the small room. His graphic account tells that,

> For nearly an hour on a June morning more than thirty people were cooped up in a small bedroom, with a fire burning, and several found the atmosphere overpowering... When the prince was born the midwives carried him through a door by the head of the bed; some of the company enquired, "What is it?" The King should have been notified by pre-arranged signals from a midwife of the child's sex. After a few moments he followed the ladies into the next room and emerged about five minutes later to announce to the throng that a Prince was born. (81, p. 420)

If the child lived a succession of Catholic kings seemed guaranteed. James' political ineptitude was quickly illustrated: he announced he would ask the Pope to be godfather.

Three weeks later, in Westminster Hall, the seven bishops stood trial. From the government's point of view it was badly mismanaged; noisy crowds hissed at prosecution witnesses, and it became obvious that once again a courtroom was being used as a public platform for voicing a variety of discontents. The jury returned a verdict of 'Not Guilty', and the last day of June 1688 witnessed cheering and bonfires. It was an ominous sign which James failed to understand – a capital city which had taken the lead in 1640 in petitioning for the removal of bishops had now been persuaded to make heroes of them.

That same day seven other men met and drafted a letter of invitation to

William, Prince of Orange:

> The people are so generally dissatisfied with the present conduct of the government in relation to their religion, liberties and properties (all of which have been greatly invaded), and they are in such expectation of the prospects being daily worse, that your Highness may be assured there are nineteen parts of twenty of the people throughout the kingdom who are desirous of a change, and who, we believe, would willingly contribute to it; and there is no doubt but that some of the most considerable of them would venture themselves with your Highness at your first landing. (53, p. 201)

These men, 'the immortal seven' as they became known, were aristocrats of both Tory and Whig opinion, and included Bishop Compton of London and the Earls of Danby and Shrewsbury.

William did come – in the words of his September 1688 Declaration to

> preserve and maintain the established Laws, Liberties and Customs, and above all, the Religion and Worship of God. (53, p. 205)

Events moved quickly in November and December. On 5 November William (protected, later argument had it, by a 'Protestant Wind', an easterly, which kept James' 'Catholic' fleet in the Thames estuary, yet blew William safely down the English Channel) landed at Torbay; the date too was held of course to have special significance in a Catholic-Protestant combat! By the 12th gentry declarations 'for' William were emerging, and some of James' army began deserting on the 16th. James, however, with a degree of confidence moved the bulk of his 40,000-strong army to Salisbury, intent on containing William's 12,000 soldiers in the West Country. On the 23rd the plan was abandoned: James, nervy and worn-out by many sleepless nights, became prey to rumours – that William was already on the march, and that his soldiers would desert in 'Monmouth' country – so he ordered a withdrawal to London. On the same day one of his senior commanders, John Churchill, went over to William; within forty-eight hours his daughter, Anne, also joined the 'rebels'. In James' eyes these were two pieces of gross ingratitude; he never recovered his nerve after this. An eye-witness recalled that by the end of November no one in London was willing to trust his neighbour:

> I can never forget the confusion the Court was in; the King knew not whom to trust, and the fright was so great. (36, p. 202)

By early December the King's fear for the safety of his wife and son was at such a pitch that on the 8th he sent them to France. He set out himself two days later. A tragi-comedy intervened: he was stopped on the north Kent coast, brought back, then, loosely guarded on William's order, he escaped again to be received with much pomp at Louis' XIV's Court at Versailles. With remarkable speed affairs in England returned to normal. Elections for a Convention Parliament were held, and William and Mary, after some haggling over the title of 'King' or 'Prince Consort' for William, were declared joint monarchs in February 1689.

Interpretations

A revolution, at least of a kind, appeared to have taken place. James had departed, and seen through the tunnel-vision of English domestic politics, there was a trio of catalysts for the event: a portentous pregnancy, seven bloody-minded bishops, and another seven aristocratic *agents provocateurs*. It certainly seemed so to many Englishmen at the time, who soon began covering the year 1688 with a layer of myth. It was not merely a 'Glorious Revolution', but a justification of Whig principles. Anthony Ashley Cooper, Earl of Shaftesbury had not lost the Exclusion Crisis after all: 1688 was his posthumous victory.

A closer consideration of certain people's motives and behaviour at the time (not, that is, how they represented themselves *after* the event), linked to the wider perspective of continental affairs, shows the traditional story to be only a half-truth, and that distortions convenient to English pride were allowed to mask some of the realities.

First, it is arguable that there was no English rebellion. This would have entailed a large-scale movement actively opposing, threatening and, in the last resort, fighting James. There is no evidence of such a movement. Cautious gentry were most unlikely to challenge a King whose financial position was good, and who had a numerically formidable army and navy. The option of civil war had already been tried back in the '40s and found wanting. 'The immortal seven' was a label of hagiography given later; at the time they were not a particularly representative group, and careful examination of the famous Letter reveals a mixture of vagueness and unsubstantiated claims. William would want to know the answer to 'desirous of *what* change'? Shadowy, implied restrictions on James would be all he could make of the opening sentence. 'Nineteen parts of twenty' was an outrageous assertion by the Seven, inviting William's sceptical response, 'How could you know that?' William already knew from his spies and correspondence that some influential people would *not* be among those referred to in the last sentence; the Earl of Nottingham stated that the Letter of 30 June was

> high treason, in violation of the laws (which are the rules of our conduct) and the allegiance which I owed to the sovereign. (35, p. 237)

Even when William landed there was much hesitancy among the gentry: one lamented, 'If this thing do miscarry, we are all undone.' With this line of reasoning it is possible to conclude that a serious rebellion was unlikely; but should James get into difficulties, and need the co-operation of the political nation to deal with, say, a foreign invasion, then support would be unlikely unless he made immediate, substantial concessions and radiated the necessary trust that he would keep his word.

Secondly, it is arguable that James' character was one decisive factor in explaining the events of 1688. His flight, an exit made without a real defence of his throne, was as surprising to the gentry of England as it was to William and even Louis XIV. He left without handing over authority to anyone; he ordered the army to be disbanded without pay; he even threw the Great Seal, the symbol of legal authority in the realm, into the Thames, and destroyed the writs he had prepared for the summoning of Parliament in November. Some historians have interpreted all these as a deliberate creation of anarchy, and they have endorsed the later Whig claim that by a total abdication the so-called 'Revolution of 1688' could be justified. Bishop Burnet at the time wrote, 'It was thought necessary to stick to the point of the King's deserting his people.' Much later, the mid-nineteenth-century 'Whig' historian Lord Macaulay, wrote,

> The tyrant [James II] pleased himself with the thought that he might avenge himself on a people who had been impatient of his despotism, by inflicting on them at parting all the evils of anarchy. (82, p. 502)

Modern historians regard this argument as a too-convenient reading of history backwards. James, for all his faults, does not seem to have been an evil man. A better explanation is that he simply lost his nerve. He was not a coward (there are examples of personal courage in his early life, especially during the mid–'60s), but in a crisis, when events and problems tumble one upon another rapidly, he revealed a fatal incapacity to think quickly. He hesitated; and when he acted – as when he made some concessions – it was too late. Nobody believed him. Most of his contemporaries regarded him as too rigid to make a genuine compromise, shown a little later in his exhortation to his baby son, written as *The King's Advice*, echoed his grandfather's belief in Divine Right: 'Kings are accountable to none but to God alone for their actions.'

The historian, J.R. Western, writing in 1972, has produced a more convincing explanation of James' flight than Macaulay: he attributes it to 'the collapse of his limited mental powers in the face of a situation too unusual for them to cope with'. There were three stages in James' demoralisation. He had no appreciation that others could hold valid opinions different from his own: he was thus unnerved by the Tory gentry when they broke with him over the religious issue; such general disloyalty was beyond his comprehension. Then, the two particular desertions on 23–25 November distorted his mind even further. He told the Catholic earl, Ailesbury,

My daughter [Anne] hath deserted me, my Army also, and him [Churchill] that I raised from nothing the same, on whom I heaped all favours.

Finally, fear for his own safety and that of his son drove him to flight. Again he told Ailesbury,

If I do not retire, I shall certainly be sent to the Tower, and no King ever went out of that place.

He would not wait to be deposed and then murdered, as had happened to Richard II in 1399. (35, pp. 266 and 287–88)

Yet a third component is necessary to a proper understanding of 1688: a re-appraisal of the motives and actions of William of Orange. Now thirty-eight, and in poor health, he had already showed himself sincere, highly intelligent, competent in financial affairs, and above all a courageous and determined soldier who saw in the ambitions of Louis XIV the greatest threat to Dutch independence and to the stability of Europe. He had been Louis' implacable enemy since the French invasion of the United Provinces in 1672. His marriage to James' daughter, Mary, in 1677 had been for political reasons, but it proved a personal success: she was beautiful, intelligent, and idolised William; he, in turn, adored her. Since that date he had manoeuvred in vain to get English support against Louis. 1688 afforded a fresh opportunity. But William's timely intervention, in response to the famous Letter, to save the English from a Popish despotism is a caricature of the truth. There is documentary evidence which suggests he intended to intervene as early as April, though he couched his remarks in diplomatic language. He told a visitor from England, Edward Russell, (who was to be one of the 'immortal seven') that 'if he was invited by some men of the best interest, to come and rescue the nation, he believed he could be ready by September'. It would have been inappropriate, to say the least, to have suggested his real motives. As late as October, when he was well-advanced in his preparations to intervene in England, William issued a manifesto which stressed his sole aim was 'to have a free and lawful Parliament assembled as soon as possible'. All this would suggest that a concern for England's constitutional liberties was uppermost in his mind. In truth, though, William was a man who kept his private views much to himself; all the signs were that he disliked the pomp of the English Royal Court, disliked even more the capital city (on his several visits to London he was often ill), and had expressed poor opinions of English politicians, whose self-importance he thought conflicted with his own authoritarian views on government. He seemed to have no desire to reign in England, and as late as 24 December he spoke publicly of kingship, 'which I have no ambition for'.

Yet sometime in the autumn of 1688 he accepted in his mind that reluctantly he would have to intervene to take the crown of England in order to secure his objectives. These are to be explained by reference to William's appreciation of the desperate position in which the Dutch saw themselves on the continent. Louis XIV had for a generation been extending French dominion, and his powerful armies and use of French money and pressure to gain client states around western Europe registered nothing but mortal terror in William's Hollanders. War and uneasy truce had been their lot with Louis since 1672. William came to the conclusion that only the revolutionary reversal of England's role – from being variably an ally or benevolent neutral with France to active military participation against France – could save Europe from French hegemony.

Motives apart, William played a waiting game in 1688; he was, says Jones, 'flexible, adaptable, observant.' No one was more aware than William that an intervention which failed would be catastrophic for his people. He needed two things: assertions from the 'immortal seven' were of only passing interest – what he wanted, and received in September, were, first, clear assurances that James' army was so disaffected that William could rely on desertions to undermine any serious resistance to himself; and secondly, some guarantee that Louis XIV could not turn on Holland the moment William left for England. The second proved the crucial factor in 1688: James' fate, it could be argued, was determined not in England, but by decisions made in The Hague and Paris.

William's decision to come was a compound of appalling risks, and modern historians and military experts are agreed it was 'preposterously rash'. The Dutch army was small compared with James'; he had to leave some covering troops on the Dutch borders; the late autumn weather in the English Channel was notoriously poor. William had practical knowledge of the costs of military operations in the seventeenth century, and manuscripts today at Nottingham University reveal something of the enormous sums involved (54, p. 244). Fully operational, William's army cost £10,000 *per day*; £384,000 was provided for an anticipated 30-day campaign on land, but when sea transport, the whole battle-fleet and army pay before and after the fighting is added, the total has been put at a staggering £1,500,000. The final factor was a nightmare question: what if the balance of military forces proved more or less even, and William found himself slipping even unwittingly into the quick-sands of another English Civil War? So, with a cold appraisal that the prize was worth the above risks, and with the September 'assurances' of desertions, William settled down to wait for a lapse in French military concentration on Dutch affairs.

By luck this came in September also. Working the chain of this argument backwards it will be seen that events in England in 1688 were in the last analysis determined by what Louis did – or rather, did *not* do about England. Conrad Russell has written illuminatingly on this, calling on the services of Conan Doyle to prove a point:

'I would like,' said Sherlock Holmes, 'to draw your attention to the curious incident of the dog in the night-time.'

'But the dog did nothing in the night-time,' said Watson.

'That was the curious incident,' said Holmes.

The 'dog in the night-time' in 1688 was Louis XIV. Offers of help for James, made in the summer, were declined, and later it was reasoned by Louis' advisers, quite sensibly, that William would never risk a naval and land campaign so late in the year – even if he did, the resulting civil war would be so prolonged that Louis would be around much later to pick up the pieces and decide matters in his own interest. So Louis did nothing – about England. Instead, he turned to the middle-Rhine, where two issues had preoccupied him for a time. With the looming appointment of a new Archbishop of Cologne, he was much engaged in diplomatic activity to ensure it was someone friendly to France; and in Germany as a whole he was worried that his old enemy, the Habsburg ruler of Austria and Holy Roman Emperor, Leopold, was re-asserting his authority, and in particular was driving Louis' old allies, the Turks, back into the Balkans. To make a show of power and take the pressure off the Turks, Louis made a crucial decision to invade and devastate the Palatinate, a German state of the strategically important middle-Rhine area – well away from the Dutch border. More than ever these events convinced William that Louis' aggression was but a prelude to a renewed and major extension of French power. He had to gain control of English foreign policy, in order to draw England into an active role in an anti-French alliance. Such an ambition, based on William's international perspective, was totally different from what most Englishmen expected as a result of William's arrival. Also, given this perspective, it is fair to argue that William, knowing the risks, would not make a suicidal attempt on England: he had to be sure of Louis. Conveniently, Louis' Palatinate Affair allowed William a few months in which to make his bid.

The change of ruler in 1688 resulted from a combination of factors: an English king losing his nerve, English politicians defecting and soldiers deserting, a Dutchman uncharacteristically acting rashly though not suicidally, and a Frenchman equally uncharacteristically allowing his attention to wander. Without Louis' move, William would not have come; without William there would have been no 'Revolution of 1688' – 'Glorious' or otherwise.

Study 19

1. Traditional assessments of the year 1688 have used the words 'inevitable', 'Glorious' and 'Revolution'. All were penned well *after* the event. You are asked to consider how 'inevitable' was James' downfall, whether there was a tinge of glory about the year's events, and did these events constitute a 'revolution' given the proper meaning of the word?

2. 1640 and 1688 are manifestly the two crisis years of the century. A difficult but rewarding exercise is to compare and contrast the nature of the two crises.

Observations (on 2).

An analytical approach will require you to compare the personalities of Charles I and James II and the extent of their respective authority. Did they receive (or take) good advice? Was there an element of conspiracy in each set of circumstances (both kings spoke of 'rebels')? Was a rigidity of religious commitment at all central to each crisis (Charles II died as King in his bed – neither his father nor his brother did)? You will find evidence that both kings mishandled a promising situation: Charles' conciliar-style government had been growing in confidence up to 1637; James had superior prospects with his improved financial position and impressive (by past standards) standing army. A common circumstance seems to be that, far from trying to *increase* their constitutional power ('progress' according to the old Whig interpretation of history – see p. 220), most members of the political nation were fearful of *losing* their liberties to encroaching royal power of continental proportions.

The lack of co-operation from the county communities is an interesting factor: the passive resistence which both monarchs faced (and Cromwell, too) in their policy of centralisation has been a thread running *seriatim* through this book, offering a partial explanation of the elusiveness of settlement. Was this passive resistance a masterly inactivity or mere sullen resentment? Taxpayers' strikes and desertions from the army were significant factors in 1640 and 1688 respectively.

Finally there is the military-foreign intervention element: did it take failure in foreign policy (not domestic – at least in the active sense of 'rebellion') to destroy Charles' and James' authority? Scots and Dutch interventions may be seen as the determinant forces in each crisis – but you will have to argue this carefully. There was no English rebellion, except in the passive sense that with Hannibal *ad portas* (the Tweed and Torbay) the subjects of each monarch refused their support. The traditional allegiance of subject to sovereign had melted into nothing. You may think we have come full circle with the arguments of the Ship Money Trial of 1637 being as relevant to the 1688 Crisis as to the 1640 one.

CHAPTER 17

Settlement... of Sorts and Piecemeal

1689 – 1701

The pursuit of settlement – by statute

Once again Englishmen tried to catch that will o' the wisp, the stable settlement of an acceptable framework of government. The need was well recognised. In the interregnum following James' flight, Lord Falkland warned,

> Before you fill the throne, I would have you resolve what power you will give the King [i.e. William] and what not.

An influential Whig, William Sacheverell, pleaded also for a comprehensive act of Parliament:

> Since God hath put this opportunity into our hands, all the world will laugh at us if we make half a settlement. (37, p.66)

These were timely warnings, and a bevy of proposals emerged urging 'a new Magna Carta'. Yet again, as in 1660 and 1641–2, what emerged was very far from what idealists with their vision of all-embracing solutions to England's problems anticipated. Not a few were to regard the events of 1688–89 as jumping out of the frying pan of James' rule into the fire of foreign control in the name of Dutch William and his increasingly obvious intention of committing England to a full part in the continental struggle against Louis XIV. With hindsight the supreme irony was that England, within a generation and a half, would achieve not only a pragmatic settlement of all the 1640 Crisis problems, but also emerge as a major military, naval and colonial power, and acquire a political stability and advancing prosperity which were to be the envy of her continental rivals.

The groundwork of this achievement lay in the years 1689–1701, and might properly be called 'The Revolution of the 1690s'. Its main features were five-fold. There was a remarkably expedient settlement of the hereditary right question, quickly followed by a much-regretted but realistic passage through Parliament of a diluted Bill of Rights. Then came some statutes, widely separated in time (1689 to 1701) and theme (toleration, army discipline, frequency of elections and further control of the succession to the throne). These constitutional measures were accompanied by a far-reaching change in foreign alignments and commitments. The fifth feature was a substantial shift in the balance of political power, resulting partly from the statutes, but arguably more from the personality and ambitions of King William III and from some radical financial developments.

John Evelyn, while pondering the events leading to the exit of James II, recorded in his *Diary* on 2 December 1688: 'It looks like a Revolution'. But over the next few weeks it became plain that influential people were anxious to preserve as much order and tradition as could be rescued from the confusion. Some peers, MPs from Charles II's old parliaments and common councillors who happened to be in London sent out instructions for a 'Convention' Parliament to be elected; it met on 22 January, and early speeches revealed how keen members were to cover up England's constitutional nakedness. Very few advocated a new set of clothes – the ageing Cromwellian regicide, Edmund Ludlow, returning from Switzerland with high hopes of pleading the cause of a new republican Commonwealth, found himself faced with arrest and was forced to flee again. The search in debate for a neat phrase which would maintain continuity found a majority in favour of James 'abdicating' and therefore the throne was 'vacant'; with most also believing James' 'son' to be a warming-pan pretence, it became elegantly convenient for Tories as well as Whigs to plump for Mary as Queen and William as Prince Consort. Such niceties had to be modified, though, when William refused to be his 'wife's gentleman usher'. All concerned made a virtue out of necessity, and, as a constitutional novelty, offered the crown to William and Mary as joint monarchs on 13 January 1689. In the Coronation Oath they swore to govern according to 'the statutes in Parliament agreed upon, and the laws and customs of the same'.

The retreat from utopian principles to severe practical realities continued during the immediate debate for a new 'Magna Carta' of English liberties. Members of the Convention were warned by lawyers that a comprehensive scheme of reform would take many months, even years; all feared that amid the expected wrangling a Jacobite counter-coup would occur, led by the by no means negligible supporters of the restoration of James II and the hereditary line. So an early programme of sweeping constitutional changes was watered down into a quickly-framed Declaration, which was passed as an Act later in the year:

The Bill of Rights –
An Act for declaring the rights and liberties of the subject and settling the succession of the crown.

Whereas the late King, James, by the assistance of evil councillors, did endeavour to subvert and extirpate the Protestant religion and the laws and liberties of this kingdom... and having abdicated the government and the throne being thereby vacant:

The Lords and Commons now assembled in a full and free representative of this nation, do declare that,

- the pretended power of suspending of laws without consent of Parliament is illegal
- the levying of money by pretence of prerogative without grant of Parliament is illegal
- the keeping a standing army in time of peace, unless it be with the consent of Parliament, is illegal
- elections of members of Parliament ought to be free
- Parliaments ought to be held frequently

An oath be taken [by office-holders, MPs and clergymen]:

I do sincerely promise and swear that I will be faithful and bear true allegiance to their Majesties King William and Queen Mary.

All who shall profess the popish religion or marry a papist shall be forever incapable to inherit, possess or enjoy the Crown and Government of this realm. (7, p.26)

Most of these were a statement of existing rights which it was felt James had infringed, and the several 'oughts' were more an indication of vague hopes that William would play a responsible political game than a set of conditions to which he must agree. There was no restriction on his power to appoint ministers and frame policy. Manifestly William was expected to rule as well as reign with his wife.

The religious issue could not be avoided. One half of the problem, the safeguarding of the Church of England 'as by law established' had been covered in the Bill of Rights and the Coronation Oath; but the other half, the Nonconformists' plea for reward for loyalty against James' temptations, had to be faced:

May 1689 – an Act for exempting their Majesties' Protestant subjects, dissenting from the Church of England, from the penalties of certain laws, [including] An Act for the Uniformity of common prayer and service in Church [1559]

Neither of these laws shall be construed to extend to any person dissenting from the Church of England that shall take the oaths [of loyalty and allegiance].

Provided that – any assembly of persons dissenting in any place of worship with doors locked shall not receive any benefit from this law

Provided that – no assembly of worship shall be permitted until such meeting be certified to the bishop of the diocese. (7, pp.42–6)

Not included in the half a dozen 'certain laws' were the Test and Corporation Acts. Puritan dissenters could therefore worship freely only with the permission of the Anglican hierarchy and only with open doors, and they remained 'second-class' citizens, unable to hold local or national office. It was a grudging reward, and the abbreviated title – The Toleration Act – a misnomer.

In 1689, too, a Mutiny Act was passed (to be renewed annually), which enlarged on the Bill of Rights' strictures regarding a standing army:

> ... it is judged necessary by their Majesties and this present Parliament that during this time of danger: [in the Army] raised for the safety of the Kingdom for the common defence of the Protestant religion, an exact Discipline be observed. (7, p.34)

Future generations, looking back with satisfaction on the progress England made in the eighteenth and nineteenth centuries in social and political stability, prosperity and military reputation, have attempted to exalt 'the men of 1688/89' as high-principled revolutionaries who swept away, 'gloriously' and 'bloodlessly', a Stuart despotism; they then became 'the Founding Fathers' of constitutional government, analagous to the great Jefferson–Washington group who made the American Constitution a century later. Comfortable as such reflections are, they hardly fit the facts, and might properly be seen as a fairy story of the 'Whig Interpretation of History' tradition. John Kenyon has helped dispose of this interpretation: he caustically observed that 'the Revolution Settlement [of 1689] is chiefly remarkable for what it did *not* settle', and he labels the Bill of Rights 'a singularly defective document' (3, pp.261–2). Barry Coward is equally derogatory about the Toleration Act: 'It is difficult to imagine a less satisfactory outcome' (1, p.319). The efforts of the men of 1688–9 then were essentially stop-gap measures, not final solutions to long-standing issues. Over the next decade or so more statutes were thought necessary to clarify matters.

For instance, in 1694 the Triennial Act was passed:

> Whereas by ancient laws frequent parliaments ought to be held, it is hereby enacted that a Parliament shall be holden once in three years at least... and no Parliament shall have any continuance longer than for three years. (7, p.49)

It seemed clear enough, but as is often the case, what is *not* mentioned is as significant. In this Act there was no restriction on the royal power of prorogation; also, given favourable circumstances, every one knew that 'laws' could be evaded (the issue of recusancy and Charles II's failure to summon Parliament in 1684 were two examples).

Yet another clarification was required in 1701 when the Act of Settlement was passed. Mary had died in 1694, William and she had no children, and Anne, the heir, had suffered the tragic experience of seventeen pregnancies all resulting in miscarriages or early deaths. The succession had to be guarded, and the opportunity was taken to fill in some of the gaps left by the Bill of Rights. Its full title indicated high expectations:

An Act for the further limitation of the Crown and the better securing the rights and liberties of the subjects.

- — be it enacted that the most excellent Princess Sophia, electress and duchess dowager of Hanover, daughter of Elizabeth, late Queen of Bohemia, daughter of King James I of happy memory, be next in succession [after William and Anne] in the protestant line.
- — provided that all persons who shall profess the popish religion or shall marry a papist shall be subject to incapacity.
- — whosoever shall come to the possession of this Crown shall join in communion with the Church of England, as by law established.
- ★ — [monarchs] shall not go out of England, Scotland or Ireland without the consent of Parliament
- ★ — all matters relating to the well-governing of this kingdom which are properly cognisable in the Privy Council shall be transacted there.
- ★ — no person who has office or place of profit under the King shall be capable of serving as a member of the House of Commons.
- — judges' commissions be made *quamdiu se bene gesserint* [i.e. during good behaviour, not royal grace]
- — no pardon under the great seal [i.e. the King] be pleadable to an impeachment by the Commons in Parliament. (7, p.56)

The intentions were bluntly expressed: 57 senior, but Roman Catholic, heirs were passed over in favour of a Protestant foreigner (Sophia and her son George, etc.), who would be restricted in movements and who must govern openly through the Privy Council. There would be no more secretive 'committees' or 'cabals' or 'cabinets'; Crown influence over judges and through pardons was to be abolished. So real supervision by the elected representatives could now be exercised over the executive through Councillors' vulnerability to impeachment and through the exclusion of office-holders. Perhaps, at last, the dreams of Pym and Haselrig, and certainly Shaftesbury, were coming true. Yet practice fell far short of intention. The Act was only to be implemented when Anne died (not until 1714), and many of its clauses were subsequently repealed or ignored (including those marked with an asterisk) as being unworkable or mere prejudice. The evaluation of most modern historians is that, allowing for the Act's immediate victory for Parliament over the King's government, and also for settling the Protestant succession, the long-term effects were limited; in Coward's phrase, the Act 'failed to live up to its full title' (1, p.345).

A working relationship – the key to the future

Many times during the seventeenth century comprehensive statutes had been mooted and some passed through Parliament. Most were found wanting as solutions to England's real problems, which centred around the exercise and control of power. The settlement that emerged was more the result of the fourth and fifth features of 'The Revolution of the 1690s' (page 201) than the precision of statute law.

It is arguable that the most significant aspect of this Revolution was the immediate reversal of England's foreign policy, and that everything else stemmed from this. William certainly intended it, but most Englishmen, though vaguely anticipating a re-alignment, never expected nor wanted the full military commitment and prolonged war which William's plans in the end entailed. Reality was abrupt and harsh. William as King, and therefore Commander-in-Chief of England's armed forces, pointed out the unpalatable truth: if Englishmen wished to preserve the Protestant succession, then they had to fight for it and pay for it. Reluctantly, over a period of several years, a significant portion of the tax-paying nation came to recognise that war was imperative to preserve their country from a French invasion and the restoration of James II as a French puppet. William's task remained very difficult, though, for there existed a tiresome remnant of independent country gentlemen whose county horizons and uninformed prejudices on national and particularly foreign policy matters mirrored those of their predecessors, so much the bane of Pym and Cromwell.

William's vision of a Grand Alliance – a coalition of kings, emperors and princes to curb the ambitions of Louis XIV – emerged in full light in 1689. The Dutch declared war on France in February, and Emperor Leopold of Austria joined in the signing of the Alliance in May; England, Spain and many German states of the Holy Roman Empire added signatures within months. The detailed events and long-term military and diplomatic effects of this war, which with a four-year 'truce' in the late 1690s ran on until 1713, are outside the confines of the argument of this book (although it is intended to include them in a future book in this series), but certain of its features may be summarised. Its early part has been variously named – the Nine Years' War, the War of the League of Augsburg, the War of the Grand Alliance – but the most accurate in an English context are either the War of the English Succession or King William's War. There was an immediate campaign in Ireland where William was forced to deal with James II and his French and Irish Catholic supporters, and at sea control of the Channel and later the Mediterranean was hotly disputed. After serious reverses two decisive victories – at the Battle of the Boyne in Ireland and off Cape La Hogue in the Channel – gave England vital security. Thereafter the war became one of appalling attrition: siege-style warfare went on year after year in Flanders with both sides collapsing in exhaustion at the Truce of Ryswick in 1697. The renewal of war in 1701, as the War of the Spanish Succession, still had Anglo-Dutch hostility to French power as its mainspring. By then James II was dead (1700) and William died in 1702, but the English Protestant succession issue remained when Louis merged his ambitions for the Spanish throne with support for the Jacobites and the 'Pretender', the now adolescent boy born to Mary of Modena in that small, warm bedroom in June 1688. The charactor of the struggle changed – it extended beyond the sea and Flanders to Spain, Italy and the Danube, and in ripples to colonial possessions in America and elsewhere; it also saw the forging of the superb team of John Churchill, now first Duke of Marlborough, Prince Eugene and Antoine Heinsius, whose military and diplomatic talents kept England, Austria and the United Provinces together to defeat the French at Blenheim, Ramillies and Turin in 1704–06.

These victories brought a massive increase in national confidence ('John Bull' and 'Rule Britannia' were eighteenth-century creations), but the cost was enormous. Two examples will give its measure. The dramatic expansion of the Army after 1688 would have struck horror into early Stuart minds. James II's standing army was viewed with great suspicion for its size as well as its 'catholicity'; yet it rose by 1711 to 70,000, its number of regiments quadrupled since James' day, thus laying the foundation of Marlborough's invincible force. The cost of the earlier Nine Years' War was £50 million, more than £5 million per year, and over three times the total government annual expenditure of James' reign. Taxation sharply increased, and regular government borrowing became imperative.

Modern historians are agreed on the severity of the effects of such prolonged war. Yet, says James Jones, the searching test of government and administration was passed. He goes on to conclude:

> The Nine Years War, far more than the political events of 1688–89, constituted the really significant revolution of the late seventeenth century... this War permanently transformed England, equipping it with the military, diplomatic and fiscal machinery and generating the self-confidence, that were to enable it to expand and develop so spectacularly in the next century.(5, p.258)

William's containment of French power followed by Marlborough's later victories would not have been possible without some dramatic changes in English government. Money had to be found in vast quantities and old attitudes hostile to central government discarded. In essence a working relationship between the King and the gentry was established. It was not fashioned through any single act, perhaps not even consciously, but three factors may be seen as the bases on which the relationship was built.

First there was the special nature of King William's personality. So single-minded was he in his European ambitions that in effect he split his attention into two almost mutually exclusive spheres. The conduct of the war and foreign affairs he kept jealously in his own hands, and he concerned himself with the details of English government only in so far as the war necessitated an even flow of money. Despite his known authoritarian temper, he nevertheless proved less determined than his predecessors to preserve royal prerogative power. The historian, Angus McInnes, writing in 1982, concludes that William

> cheerfully signed away the royal position in order to get the necessary war supplies. He was the arch-saboteur, the quintessential fifth-columnist. He was, more than the feeblest native-born monarch, the betrayer of English absolutism. (57, p.392)

What was happening was that a certain line of reasoning was being gradually and unconsciously adopted by influential sections of English society, which ran something as follows. If William wanted *his* war (and the gentry could at least see the defence of the English succession as the point of it), then, through Parliament, the gentry would insist on the voice in affairs that had so long eluded them. There was nothing gracious about this 'bargain': there was much acrimony and hesitation on both sides. McInnes is perhaps being provocative – whatever William signed away, it was not done 'cheerfully'! And the gentry gradually became aware that the price of their voice in affairs was, paradoxically, strong government demanding at times an escalation in military expenditure. They did not acquiesce without expressing considerable misgivings in Parliament well into the eighteenth century. Yet in perspective this working relationship transformed the 'Royal Government' of the Tudors and early Stuarts into the 'Mixed Government' of the eighteenth century Hanoverians. In terms of division of power what might be described as a 7:3 split in favour of the Crown before 1640 became under William nearer to a 5:5 balance. More than anything else this was the 'final' settlement of the 1640 Crisis.

The achievement of this fresh balance was only partly determined by the various statutes already noted. The impact of war created a second factor: Parliament changed almost unwittingly from being an occasional institution into a permanent one. It is startling to record the difference *before* 1689 – when parliaments were summoned irregularly and sessions were often measured in weeks – and *after* 1689 – when war demands made five months' duration common and sessions became annual without exception down to the present day. Speaker Onslow of the Commons noted,

> If Parliament sits annually, which they may always secure to themselves now if they will and should never depart from it, it is almost impossible that any exorbitancy of power [of the Crown] should subsist long enough to do mischief.

Such regularity established a routine which had crucial effects. Legislation could be properly prepared and debated, and the monarch saw that, instead of prorogation and dissolution, it was more effective to cajole and manoeuvre

MPs and to seek out able, responsible ministers who could work with Parliament.

In turn, MPs found the party system indispensable. It had its critics, as when Lord Halifax scathingly remarked,

> Party is little less than an inquisition, where men are under such a discipline in carrying on the common cause as to leave no liberty of private opinion.

There were many in succeeding generations who would agree with this sentiment – even today. In the 1690s a 'rage of parties' developed with annual sessions and three-year elections which kept disputes at fever pitch. Vendettas and ugly antagonism were endemic in the localities at election time; and in the House of Commons the first party 'whips' were employed to prevent their own MPs leaving (usually for dinner!) before a vote, and bitter hostility existed between those in office and those out. Yet party division had one supreme virtue: it replaced the violence of civil war, actual or feared, by the stylised conflict of party warfare waged in words across the divide of the House of Commons. The confrontation of Stuart politics was replaced in the eighteenth century by Hanoverian manoeuvre.

The watershed of this change in Parliament's status came in the 1690s. No better illustration of this can be found than on the right of inquiry. The Parliaments of Elizabeth I's time could not demand government papers, question Crown servants, or examine accounts: Hanoverian Parliaments did all these.

The third factor was money. The thread of government finance has run through the whole story from Ship Money, a taxpayers' strike and the Bedford–Pym proposals of the early years, through Civil War finance, Cromwellian decimations and army costs to the vagaries of Restoration revenue and expenditure. The essence of the difficulty was that the old system of the King 'living of his own' with an occasional Parliamentary top-dressing had become anachronistic, even in Elizabeth's time. Inflation, dishonesty and ramshackle administration had rendered the system of taxation in need of serious overhaul. The sensible Bedford scheme (see p. 44), shelved in 1641, but implemented in principle by Pym under war conditions in 1643, was again shelved in 1660 when its main object – the collection of an Assessment based on the true needs of government from year to year – suffered from association with the unpopular Ship Money and the equally hated upstart collectors, the County Committees. The problem of the later Stuarts may be thus stated: how to reconcile executive power, efficiently provided with adequate revenue, with the consent of the representatives of the tax-paying nation. Subsumed in this problem were four of the five 1640 Crisis issues (as opposed to the peculiarly religious one). Regular sessions would allow regular supply (as well as an orderly airing of grievances); ministers of the Crown should in some way be accountable for policies involving expenditure; armies were expensive (as a contemporary noted, an army 'is a beast that hath a great belly, and must be fed'), and some political control of them was required – which meant by the early eighteenth century a parliamentary influence on the determination of foreign policy; and finally the county communities must recognise that efficient government required higher taxes as well as accountability. Here, then, was the basis of a compromise: the Crown had to accept greater Parliamentary control, and Parliament had to insist that the gentry tax-payers met their full obligations. The Revolution of the 1690s saw the shaping of this compromise – at least in outline, though not without much resistance and alarm.

The base of a radical financial change, arguably the most significant development of the entire seventeenth century, had already been laid: Bedford and Pym provided the theory, and the Treasury improvements of 1667 had established a vital degree of control. The war years of the 1690s completed it in two main ways, through the Bank of England and through the Civil List.

The rapid growth of commerce already noted in chapter 11 had revealed serious deficiencies in the financial world. Liquid credit facilities – i.e. ready cash for merchant enterprises – was desperately needed, and loans from goldsmiths had only partly relieved the problem. By the 1680s cheques were in common use, drawn on 'the running cashes' held by these goldsmiths; and the whole problem of speedy buying and selling of stocks and shares was eased by the growth at the end of the century of Exchange Alley (between Cornhill and Lombard Street in London) with coffee-houses like Garraways and Sam's Coffee-house, where much commercial business was conducted. But even such borrowing and investment facilities were quite inadequate for both burgeoning commerce *and* the needs of war. Public spending multiplied three-fold from £2 million in 1688 to nearly £6 million in 1702 – some larger-scale borrowing system was urgently needed. Many schemes were suggested, and in April 1694 one of them, for a Bank of England, was launched by some leading merchants in consultation with the government's Treasury Commission and Charles Montagu in particular. Subscribers would be guaranteed 8 per cent from a Parliamentary allocation, and they would be incorporated as 'The Governors and Company of the Bank of England.' Henceforth more money could be 'borrowed' by the Bank on security of parliamentary taxation. These borrowings became in effect a National Debt underwritten by Parliament, and of course it still exists today.

The Civil List idea was as a complement to the Bank. William in 1689 had merely taken over 'the Revenue of James II'. Parliament, says Burnet, was 'full of jealousy and ill-humour', highly suspicious of the new King, and constantly evaded William's plea for a proper settlement. Slowly, stubbornly, but inevitably, William gave ground on his financial prerogatives in return for military revenues. He accepted the idea of a Commission for Accounts, and year after year he had to depend on parliamentary supply. By 1697 he had all but lost control of the old independent Crown income. A settlement was arranged in that year by the Civil List Act:

> An Act for granting his Majesty a further subsidy of tunnage and poundage towards raising the yearly sum of £700,000 for service of his Majesty's Household. (7, p.50)

The practical effect was obvious when linked with the Bank of England scheme. Future monarchs would have a small (but politically influential) sum called the Civil List, but Parliament would be responsible for army costs and the servicing of the government's borrowing debts incurred at the Bank. The notion of 'Live of the King's Own' as far as government revenue and expenditure was concerned was at last dead. 'William,' says E.A. Reitan, the American historian and authority on the Civil list, 'accepted half a loaf, but he was glad to get it' (83, p.571).

Neither the Bank of England nor the Civil List emerged without long and often savage wrangling. Old attitudes died hard. The Bank was despised by the Tories as 'fit only for republics', and the independent country gentlemen in the House of Commons saw the Civil List as the engine of corruption – for it allowed the King, they said, an unacceptable level of influence in Parliament through bribery. The Revolution was there to stay, though, and remains so today. In Professor Chandaman's words, the 'Financial Revolution', begun in 1667 and rounded off by the Bank and the Civil List,

> involved a decisive shift in financial balance of power. By drawing part of the public revenue and borrowing under the aegis of direct parliament responsibility and guarantee, it provided for the first time an unshakeable foundation for credit – immune from the risks of default or the mortality of kings. (50, pp.279–81)

Study 20

1. A straightforward but important task must be a final stock-taking. Refer to the thesis of this book set out in the Introduction (p. vii) and to the five 1640 issues (summarised on p. 35, and part-added to in 1641 by the military factor). How many have been 'settled'?

Observations:

Consider whether the germ of any final solution was present in the 1641–42 events (bridge-appointments? – Bedford's financial scheme?); whether any solution was a 'victory' for Crown or Parliament, or if in essence a compromise was needed. It might seem obvious that on the broad question of power the Crown's prerogatives were reduced (see the 7:3, 5:5 line of reasoning), but can you explain the paradox that the Crown, although checked by Parliament, was also an executive more powerful in some spheres than in the past? (The clue is 'in some spheres' and in the idea of a balance of power; a list of William's prerogatives would still include the calling and dissolution of Parliament, the appointment of ministers, the vetoing of legislation, and the making of war and peace – but in each case you must now develop the argument.)

You may feel irked that there was no tidy, once-and-for-all settlement of the five issues. Patently mankind does not manage its affairs – in government as in other areas of life – in neat compartments for future students' study! Each of your five 'settlements' will entail some or much qualification; the most difficult will be how far harmony or at least balance of power was established in Crown–Parliament relationships, especially over ministers. Only vague glimmerings of an answer could be seen in the later Stuart period (Danby, Rochester, the Civil List Act). What proved to be a workable solution came some decades later with Walpole: a 'prime' minister would emerge who could rely on the confidence of both King and Parliament. This confidence came from persuading the King that he must follow sensible policies acceptable to Parliament, and Parliament that the needs of government were real and that the King harboured no despotic designs. The triumphs and traumas in the working of this 'Mixed Constitution' belong to another book.

2 The last sub-section of this book is headed 'A Working Relationship'. You might construct an essay on this theme:

> To what extent did the establishment of a working relationship between executive and legislature offer a better chance of future stability than the passage of statutes?

Observations

Begin with the general point of the co-operation which existed, with strains, between Crown and the gentry throughout Tudor and early Stuart times until the mid-1630s; show how confrontation developed, and why efforts to restore the working relationship failed in the next decades. How far was it restored after 1660? What happened in the 1690s? Conrad Russell provides an illuminating marital metaphor on this: he argues Parliament was never seeking sovereignty, or a separation from the Crown; what was wanted was 'not divorce, but a restitution of conjugal rights' (4, p.346). As part of your argument you must consider the strengths and defects of written enactments (Nineteen Propositions through to the Bill of Rights). An eighteenth-century wit, commenting on the problem of creating a constitution, said, 'You may as well build a tree.' It should provide you with a useful organic metaphor. Also you might ponder whether 'the working relationship' was a revolution at all – or merely the re-packaging of the system, so that the strengths were preserved (England was still a monarchy), with its more obvious and worrying defects cured or disguised? At this point you ought to develop further your understanding of the word 'Revolution' from your consideration of it in the last chapter. Lawrence Stone has a useful discussion (though you will have to accept that much of it is couched in American sociological jargon) in his *The Causes of the English Revolution*, Routledge and Kegan Paul, 1972, pp. 3–22.

3 One of the purposes of this book has been to ensure that you study history with due regard for the evidence on which judgements are made – hence the proliferation of documents, some at length, some in very brief extracts. An important requirement in the study of Advanced History today is not only that you must show awareness of such evidence, but also that you can show a real understanding. (Students and teachers will find the Cambridge Board's 'Advanced Level History Proposals for 1985', published in January 1982, of considerable interest). In examinations lengthy extracts may be set, with particular questions attached, requiring explanation of content; comparison of content between documents; assessments of reliability and usefulness of documents, sometimes by external reference to other evidence; the testing of assertions against given sources. Also 'gobbets' may be set – these are brief extracts followed by the brief instruction 'Comment'. Any quotations in this book may be taken, but you might try the following, heeding the advice given below.

> 'These papers I hope are sufficient to establish the throne of our great Restorer, our present King William, to make good his title in the consent of the people.'
>
> (John Locke, *Two Treatises of Civil Government*)

> 'All the life and power of religion consist in the inward of the mind: and faith is not faith without believing. The civil magistrate's power consists only in outward force, and it is impossible for the understanding to be compelled to the belief of anything by such a force. Even if the vigour of the law could change men's opinion it would not help to the salvation of their souls.'
>
> (John Locke, *Letters on Toleration*)

You are advised to treat these (and all other gobbets) in the following manner. In about 300–400 words:

(a) consider the document in its historical context – what led to the event of writing, what followed, when was it written and was this significant? Do not write a detailed narrative, and use only about 100 words on this part.

(b) consider the extract as part of the whole – who wrote it, was there any likely bias? (Locke was a friend of Shaftesbury: what would you expect from this?). What is the nature of the document – treaty, diary, newspaper, statute law, etc.? Why was it written?

PART F

(c) consider the extract in detail – any special phrases or points to be clarified or significance brought out? (e.g., 'William the Restorer' and 'consent')
(d) consider its usefulness as evidence for the historian – for what in particular? Its accuracy? The soundness of the author's judgement? Do you need the support of other sources before accepting it as a reliable historical document? (You can only raise possible queries here – the checking for authenticity is an expert, long, often expensive procedure).
You will need to do a little background reading on Locke; and also to refer to other documents in Chapters 5 and 6 which might throw light on the two extracts (e.g. the *Declaration of Indulgence* and Halifax's *Letter to a Dissenter*).

Special Study

A Biographical Approach

'Read no history: nothing but biography, for that is life without theory.'
(Benjamin Disraeli, *Contarini Fleming*, 1832)

This book has been concerned to develop a theme; many personalities, some of great significance, have graced its pages. You may properly think, though, with Disraeli's dictum in mind, that some of the people emerge as less than rounded characters. Below are some guidelines for further work to correct this imbalance; you might also assess whether the present author has been fair in the necessarily brief character impressions given throughout the book. You ought to undertake such work at appropriate intervals in your course of study.

Biography is an essential component of historical study, and has attractions peculiar to itself. Unlike 'History' it has a beginning, a middle and an end – perhaps this accounts for its popular appeal, a point confirmed by booksellers and librarians. Both biographer and reader can become 'involved' with the character, seeing events through his or her eyes. Distortions have to be guarded against: some sympathy, yes, but too much identification can produce hagiography not biography – when the defence lawyer/biographer gets enveloped in hero-worship and thus loses the qualities of a judge/historian. Biographers too have been charged with viewing history through a cracked lens: voyeurs prying into long-forgotten private lives, pandering to the sensational and scandalous at the expense of... well, you will have to bear in mind these attractions and demerits in your own character-sketching from the sources below. Remember, a person's character is rarely frozen at a particular point – later developments occur, and with some people it is interesting to consider, as in Shakespearian tragedy, whether there is a flaw in the personality which only emerges under the impact of critical events.

You ought to consider in your reading the nature of the sources which a particular biographer has used. Diaries and autobiographies have a self-evident bias, but beware too the hostile writings of contemporary opponents – such as the lampoon on Charles II: 'A pretty, witty King...' Dryden's superb poetry leaves a damning, more long-lasting impression of the politicians of the post-Restoration era than does, say, the more prosaic writings of Halifax which are less quoted but possible more generous and accurate. One of the interesting books in your references below is Richard Ollard's *The Image of the King* (on Charles I and Charles II). You might pause for thought on the responsibility of the theatrical profession as well as academic historians in this matter of image-creation. Swashbuckling Hollywood-style romances might be good entertainment, but in the compression into a couple of hours the subtleties of character (and even proper chronology) get lost; whereas in the ten hours of a television series such as *Elizabeth R* someone like Glenda Jackson is given time for a considered treatment. Sir Alec Guinness' portrayal of Charles I in the Columbia film, *Cromwell*, was one of the better features of an unsatisfactory film. He remarked to the author of this book that 'in trying to find an empathy with someone dead 320 years... I mostly studied portraits of Charles I – trying to absorb something from them.'

For the ten major figures in this study section, begin with a reading of the brief sketches in

    C.P. Hill, *Who's Who in History* Vol III 1603–1714, Blackwell, 1965

All the standard works you have been using (Aylmer, Coward etc.) also have concise verdicts. Then pursue the references given to the more specialised works (chosen in part for their accessibility). Some of the people have been over-written about (Cromwell and Charles II), whereas other have not attracted a modern biographer (Pym and Hyde).

1.   Thomas Wentworth, the Earl of Strafford.
        C.V. Wedgwood, *Strafford*, Cape, 1935
        C.V. Wedgwood, *Thomas Wentworth, the First Earl of Strafford*, Cape, 1961; read pp. 67–72 for the 'apostasy myth'; 84–86, 95–98 and 302–03 for his reputation; and 395–97 for an assessment.
        also: J. Kenyon, *The Stuarts*, Batsford, pp. 93–95 and P. Zagorin, *Court and Country*, Routledge and Kegan Paul, 1971 pp. 68–70

The two Wedgwood books are crucial: her assessment in 1935 was that Strafford was 'a great good man whose death was one of the tragedies of English History.' But after new research had criticised this view, she re-wrote the whole book, showing less sympathy for her 'fallen idol'.

2.   William Laud, Archbishop of Canterbury.
        H. Trevor-Roper. *Archbishop Laud*, Macmillan, 1940. Read pp. 32–39 and 433–36 on his character, ch. 5 on his work as Archbishop, and ch. 9 on the Puritans, especially pp. 317–25. Also read the new introduction to the new edition, published in 1961.

C. Hill, *Society and Puritanism in Pre-Revolutionary England*, Secker and Warburg, 1964, ch. 8 on the Bawdy Courts.

C. Hill's article on Laud in *Encyclopaedia Britannica* (1974 edition).

Trevor-Roper's book is the standard work: the two editions have interesting differences, though he lacked Veronica Wedgwood's rare courage in re-writing the whole book. In the new introduction he criticises his earlier writing, admitting an unacceptable degree of over-simplification; also that he now had more sympathy with Laud as a person, and less with his ideals.

3. John Pym
    There is no recent biography.

    D.H. Pennington's article in *Encyclopaedia Britannica* (1974 edition) is the best start.

    J.H. Hexter, *The Reign of King Pym*, 1940, is not strictly a biography – more an analysis of political structure; but use the index which has some good character references.

    E. Wingfield-Stratford, *King Charles and King Pym*, Hollis, 1940, is a racy account; pp. 8–15 and 66–95 are useful.

4. King Charles I
    A shadowy figure who has eluded his biographers until very recently; Pauline Gregg has received favourable reviews for her book.

    P. Gregg, *Charles I* (Dent) 1981 – look up the character references in its very good index.

    C.V. Wedgwood in the Historical Association pamphlet on Charles, 1949.

    Richard Ollard, *The Image of a King*, Hodder and Stoughton 1979.

5. Oliver Cromwell
    Has attracted many biographers.

    Start with C. Hill, *God's Englishman*, Weidenfeld and Nicholson, 1970, p. 265 for a survey of the 'many' Cromwells.

    Then: J. Wroughton, *Seventeenth Century Britain: Documents and Debates*, Macmillan, 1980, pp. 36–46 for a brief selection of the varied historical opinions on Cromwell.

    A. Fraser, *Cromwell, Our Chief of Men*, Weidenfeld and Nicholson, 1973, Part IV.

    C.V. Wedgwood, *Oliver Cromwell*, Duckworth, revised edition 1973 (John Kenyon, in his review of these two books, called Wedgwood's 'a brief sten-gun burst of 122 pages as against Fraser's artillery bombardment of 706 pages.')

    I. Roots (ed.) *Cromwell: a Profile*, Macmillan, 1973: read the first and last sections.

M. Ashley, *The Greatness of Oliver Cromwell*, Hodder and Stoughton, 1957, chs. 2 and 24.

6. Edward Hyde, the Earl of Clarendon
The servant of two Stuart kings, and a key figure at significant points between 1641 and 1667.
His reputation is of being 'uncounsellable' but be careful of the hostile writings of his opponents. There is no modern full-scale biography. His own *History of the Rebellion* gives the classic account from the contemporary viewpoint despite its manifest partiality. The standard edition is the six volume one of W.D. Macray (1888), but more easily accessible is
Selections from Clarendon, ed. G. Huehns, O.U.P., 1955, in the Worlds Classics series.
Begin with the *Encyclopaedia Britannica* article in the 1974 edition.
Then trace the different stages of his career by using the index in:
J. Kenyon, *The Stuarts*, Batsford 1958.
Kenyon is very critical – Hyde was 'frozen in the attitude of 1641' and then became the 'universal whipping-boy' of 1660s.
D. Ogg, *England in the Reign of Charles II*, O.U.P., 1955, pp. 149, 189 and 314.
C.V. Wedgwood, *The King's War*, Collins, 1958, pp. 24–27 and 81–83.
See also Gilbert Burnet's contemporary view in:
English Historical Documents vol. VIII, ed. A. Browning, Eyre and Spottiswoode, 1953, pp. 912–13.

7. King Charles II
Start with Haley's fine portrayal of the fashions in assessments of Charles in
K.D.H. Haley, *Charles II*, Historical Association pamphlet, 1966.
See also Ollard's book under Charles I
There were many contemporary verdicts, but note Browning's comment about 'character-sketching throwing light no less on the authors than on the individual portrayed.'
English Historical Documents Vol VIII, especially p. 900.
M. Ashley, *Charles II*, Weidenfeld and Nicholson, 1971, ch. 19.
A Fraser, *Charles II*, Weidenfeld and Nicholson, 1979 – called by Christopher Hill in his review, 'Lively, based on careful study of the sources... a very good read.' Use the very good index on his character on p. 506.

8. Anthony Ashley Cooper, the First Earl of Shaftesbury
The 'Dorsetshire eel', rivals Strafford, in the present author's opinion, as the most interesting 'flawed' character in your period of study.

K.D.H. Haley, *The First Earl of Shaftesbury*, O.U.P, 1968, pp. 323–26, 462–67 and ch. 31 (the standard biography).

Encyclopaedia Britannica (1974 edition) for A. Browning's article on Shaftesbury.

J.H. Plumb's article in *History Today*, April 1953.

English Historical Documents vol. VIII, especially Burnet's and Dryden's famous verdicts pp. 918–19.

9. King James II

A very good recent biography has replaced past 'standard' works (like F.C. Turner's *James II*, Eyre and Spottiswoode, 1948):

J. Miller, *James II*, Wayland, Hove 1978; read the preface, chs. 9, 13 and 16.

English Historical Documents, vol. VIII, for Burnet on James, p. 901.

10. King William III (of Orange)

The standard biography is S.B. Baxter, *William III*, Longman, 1966 – use the index for character references.

English Historical Documents, vol. VIII, for Burnet's assessment, written about 1687 on p. 904.

D. Ogg, *William III*, Collins Brief Lives, 1956.

A Note on Sources

Finding and using sources

The historian has three functions: research, evaluation and communication. In seeking out the facts, in asking questions of them, interpreting them, explaining them, and in writing for different kinds of readers his raw material is the primary source, the original document. It is interesting and instructive to see how different historians may argue, even disagree, in their interpretation, though students may find it an easy option to rely entirely on this secondary source of historians' writings. You ought to regard it as essential to divide your attention equally between the 'authorities' and the 'documents'. An up-to-date text will no doubt give you a sensible grounding in the essential facts, explanations and analyses; you will also need to be acquainted with some of the recent, relevant research in the universities (the county histories of the past decade or so, for instance, have given new insight into the Civil War period). Yet the strengths and weaknesses of the documentary sources will require a sound understanding. Such evidence is the historian's stock-in-trade, and on its availability and evaluation he bases his claim to reconstruct the truth about the past.

Some brief examples will warn you to raise questions about all the evidence you meet in this book and elsewhere. First, the account of the 1640s here laid out has focused heavily on the King *versus* Parliament struggle: yet the records of the Privy Council where crucial decisions were made (e.g. the 5 May 1640 meeting) are woefully inadequate; the remarks of ambassadors at Court (again an important place where policy was decided, and on which the Venetian and French envoys wrote at length) are good for rumour, but gossip is notoriously unreliable; and it has been calculated that on any one day only a quarter of the House of Commons' speeches have been preserved, much in note form, from memory, written hours or days later. Secondly, there is the bias of document survival. Damp, fire and rats have destroyed as many records as the human 'attic-clearers'; this means that Parliamentary records are in better shape than provincial ones, and this can dangerously distort an assessment. Thirdly, there is an obvious problem of accuracy in reportage which can occur today let alone in the past, as the following story illustrates. In 1970 Charles Haughey, then the Irish Finance Minister, (later prime minister) could not make his budget speech to the Dáil in Dublin; the next day the *Irish Times* recorded that he was 'in hospital with concussion after hitting his head on a beam'; the London *Financial Times* said that he 'had been thrown from a horse'; the *Daily Telegraph* announced that he had 'been knocked unconscious by a piece of guttering which fell from the roof of his house'. The truth of Sir Henry Vane's scribbled notes of 5 May 1640 is still a matter of doubt!

You are recommended to read A. Marwick, *The Nature of History*, Methuen 1970 (second edition 1982), chapters 1, 5 and 7.

Where do you find these sources? The major depositories of seventeenth-century documents are the local county record offices, the Public Record office (the PRO at Chancery Lane and Kew in London), the British Library (of the British Museum) and the Bodleian Library in Oxford. They are very extensive, as three examples will show. The PRO has the state papers (called CSPD – Calendar of State Papers Domestic) for the 1640s; SP16 for Charles I's Secretaries of State records consists of 541 volumes; SP23 for the committees concerned with 'delinquents' and sequestrations is in 266 volumes. In the North Library of the British Museum are the Thomason Tracts – George Thomason was a London bookseller from 1641 to 1660 who collected some 20,000 newspapers and pamphlets of the period, which has been estimated to be 95 per cent of the total published, and form superb source of opinion (but remember Charles Haughey). At Oxford the Bodleian contains many valuable collections – the Tanner manuscripts have all the letters of William Lenthall, Speaker of the Long Parliament. Like the others the Library is massive: it has 4.3 million volumes, which occupy 70 miles of shelving, and its 36 reading rooms are much used by students of all subjects; its staff can find on request any book or set of manuscripts within an hour or so.

The Whig Interpretation of History

Periods of history involving civil war, radical and revolutionary change are divisive. Not only at the time but generations later, people regard the events with strong, conflicting emotions. Unfortunately this can lead to over-simple or distorted claims and counter-claims. After the event it is all too easy to accept the victors as 'right' and the vanquished as 'wrong'; also from a distance it is comfortable to assume the 'winner' as inevitably contributing to the improvements and thus progress towards the present day.

Many people in the eighteenth century regarded the outcome of the whole struggle in the seventeenth century with great satisfaction: they perceived that the early efforts of Pym and Cromwell and their Parliamentary supporters were finally rewarded in 1688 with a victory of the representatives of the people against royal despotism, with the Whig Party claiming to have been the divine instrument in the success. This view of the struggle was given further support in Victorian and early twentieth-century England by such historians as Lord Macaulay (the 1840s), S.R. Gardiner (the 1880s) and G.M. Trevelyan (the 1910s), all of whom traced Britain's splendid prosperity and stable Parliamentary institutions (much envied by continental countries plagued with revolution) to the glorious Parliamentary triumph of the seventeenth century.

This glowing generalisation was challenged in the 1930s by several historians, notably Herbert Butterfield and Lewis Namier. It was attacked as a sentimental 'reading of history backwards'. There was much admiration for Gardiner's immensely detailed scholarship, but his interpretation of the Civil War period owed more to his comfortable, stable Victorian political world of Gladstone and Disraeli and their two-party musical chairs than to the realities of the seventeenth-century political scene. Butterfield wrote a book in 1931, *The Whig Interpretation of History*, which castigated this view, and pleaded for the study of a period on its own terms, not with present achievements and disasters in mind. Already, in 1930, Sellars and Yeatman had produced their famous lampoon, *1066 and All That*, which ingeniously merged schoolboy howlers with the pillorying of the 'Whig' interpretation: Royalists were 'wrong but wromantic' and the Roundheads 'right but repulsive'.

For a brief, but entertaining, 'Whig' construction of seventeenth-century history read J.P. Kenyon, *Stuart England* Penguin, 1978, pages 7 to 11.

For an analysis of the whole period and how it has been written up by partisan and academic historians from the seventeenth to the twentieth centuries read R.C. Richardson, *Debate on the English Revolution*, Methuen, 1977.

Select Bibliography

A. Recommended further reading and document collections

Chapters and pages are suggested to help in making a start on the more detailed works. There is some overlap with the biography section on p. 214 and with the specific reading references in the study sections of the book.

1. B. Coward, *The Stuart Age*, Longman, 1981: the best 'textbook' currently available.
2. G.E. Aylmer, *The Struggle for the Constitution*, Blandford, 1963 (4th ed., 1975): an excellent commentary on the whole period.
3. J.P. Kenyon, *Stuart England*, Penguin, 1978: a very readable, often provocative account, recommended from 1660 onwards.
4. C. Russell, *Crisis of Parliaments*, O.U.P., 1971: a fine standard text; read the last hundred pages.
5. J.R. Jones, *Country and Court*, Arnold, 1978: a standard post–1660 text. Read especially chapters 2 and 4 on the workings of politics.
6. J.P. Kenyon, *The Stuart Constitution*, C.U.P., 1966: with 7 the most easily accessible collection of documents on the period. It also has pungent introductory commentaries.
7. E.N. Williams, *The Eighteenth Century Constitution*, C.U.P., 1960.
8. J. Morrill, *Revolt of the Provinces*, Allen and Unwin, 1976, (2nd ed., Longman, 1978): highly recommended for its documents and commentary on recent county history research; read pages 24–31, 42–51, 97–111.
9. J. Wroughton, *Seventeenth Century Britain*, Macmillan, 1980: some useful, brief sources for the student.
10. R. Lockyer and J. Mason (ed.), *Case Studies*, Longman, 1980: five of the seven 'investigations' through documents refer to this book.
11. J. Fassnidge, *Documents in History: the Civil War*, Longman, 1983: read especially 'Finance' and 'Words of War'.
12. A. Browning, *English Historical Documents*, Vol. VIII, Eyre and Spottiswoode, 1953: a vast collection of post-1660 documents with valuable introductions.
13. T. Barnard, *The English Republic*, Longman, 1982: like 14 a highly recommended analysis, with appended documents.
14. J. Miller, *The Glorious Revolution*, Longman, 1983–4.
15. K. Wrightson, *English Society 1580–1680*, Hutchinson, 1982: read especially chapters 1, 2 and 6 on the gentry.
16. P. Gregg, *King Charles I*, Dent, 1981: a very good narrative. Read pages 266–367.
17. C. Russell, *Parliament and English Politics*, O.U.P., 1979: read chapter 1.
18. C.V. Wedgwood, *Thomas Wentworth, First Earl of Strafford*, Cape, 1961: read pages 337–377 on the trial.
19. C. Russell (ed.), *Origins of the English Civil War*, Macmillan, 1973: read chapters 3 and 5 on finance and popery.

20. H.G. Alexander, *Religion in England*, Hodder, 1968: a very readable account; pages 57–122 give excellent background.
21. G.E. Aylmer, *The King's Servants*, Routledge, 1961 (revised 1974): a very detailed standard work. Read pages 7–68 on central government.
22. H. Shaw, *The Levellers*, Longman, 1968: read chapters 4 and 5 on Putney Debates.
23. D. Underdown, *Pride's Purge*, O.U.P., 1971: a very detailed work. Start with chapter 8 on the 1648 'revolution'.
24. J. Morrill (ed.), *Reactions to the Civil War*, Macmillan, 1982: read chapters 1 and 5, which are excellent on the impact of the war on ordinary people.
25. I. Roots, *The Great Rebellion*, Batsford, 1966: highly recommended; a fine, stylish account. Start on pages 181–220 and 257–80.
26. A. Fraser, *Cromwell, Our Chief of Men*, Weidenfeld and Nicolson, 1973: begin with pages 455–706 for a flowing narrative of the Protectorate.
27. C. Hill, *God's Englishman*, Weidenfeld and Nicolson, 1970: read chapters 6, 7 and 10 for a commentary *after* you have studied the narrative of the Protectorate.
28. G.E. Aylmer (ed.), *The Interregnum*, Macmillan, 1972: read chapter 7 on the Protectorate.
29. J. Thirsk, *The Restoration*, Longman, 1976: read pages 1–36 and 153–78.
30. J.R. Jones (ed.), *The Restoration Monarchy*, Macmillan, 1974: read chapters 2, 4 and 7 on parties, finance and the church.
31. G. Holmes, *Religion and Party*, Historical Association, 1975: a fine, brief commentary on a difficult subject.
32. K.D.H. Haley, *Charles II*, Historical Association, 1966: the best short introduction to the problems of assessing Charles.
33. K.D.H. Haley, *The First Earl of Shaftesbury*, O.U.P., 1968: the massive standard biography; read pages 734–46 for an assessment.
34. J.P. Kenyon, *The Popish Plot*, Heinemann, 1972: begin with chapter 1 on the fear of Catholicism.
35. J.R. Western, *Monarchy and Revolution*, Blandford, 1972: read chapters 8 and 9 for a challenging analysis on 1688.
36. J. Miller, *James II*, Wayland, 1977: read chapters 9 and 13.
37. J.H. Plumb, *The Growth of Political Stability*, Macmillan, 1967: read chapter 3 on elections.
38. R. Davis, *A Commercial Revolution*, Historical Association, 1969: the best brief summary by the authority on the subject of trade.
39. D.C. Coleman, *The Economy of England*, O.U.P., 1977: read chapter 8 on trade.

B. More specialist works referred to in the text

40. J. Tanner, *Constitutional Conflicts of the Seventeenth Century*, C.U.P., 1928.
41. J.G. Barnes, *Somerset 1625–40*, O.U.P. 1961.
42. P. Zagorin, *Court and Country*, Routledge, 1969.
43. S.R. Gardiner, *Constitutional Documents of the Puritan Revolution*, O.U.P. 1889 (3rd ed. 1906).
44. R. Ashton, *The English Civil War*, Weidenfeld and Nicolson, 1978.
45. C.V. Wedgwood, *The Trial of Charles I*, Collins, 1964.
46. D. Underdown, *Somerset in the Civil War and Interregnum*, David and Charles, 1973.
47. B. Manning (ed.) *Politics, Religion and the English Civil War*, Arnold, 1973.
48. A. Everitt, *The Community of Kent*, Leicester U.P., 1973.
49. C. Hill, *Some Intellectual Consequences of the English Revolution*, Weidenfeld and Nicolson, 1980.
50. C.D. Chandaman, *English Public Revenue 1660–88*, O.U.P., 1975.

51. W.M. Lamont and S. Oldfield, *Politics, Religion and Literature*, Dent, 1975.
52. D. Ogg, *England in the Reign of Charles II*, O.U.P. (2nd ed.), 1955.
53. M. Ashley, *The Glorious Revolution of 1688*, Hodder, 1966.
54. J. Carswell, *The Descent on England*, Barrie and Rockcliff, 1969.
55. B. Kemp, *King and Commons*, Macmillan, 1957.
56. C. Hill, *Century of Revolution*, Nelson, 1961 (slightly revised, Van Nostrand Reinhold, 1981).
57. A. McInnes, 'Was there an English Revolution?' in *History*, 221, October, 1982.
58. CSPD: Calendar of State Papers Domestic, Public Record Office, London.
59. The Bodleian Library, Oxford.
60. L. Hutchinson, *The Memoirs of Colonel Hutchinson*, Everyman, 1908.
61. J.B. Owen, *The Eighteenth Century*, Nelson, 1974.
62. C.V. Wedgwood, *The King's Peace*, Collins, 1955, Reprint Society, 1956.
63. D.L. Keir, 'The Ship Money Case', in *Law Quarterly Review*, 50, 1936.
64. J.P. Kenyon, *The Stuarts*, Batsford, 1958.
65. J. Bowle, *Charles I*, Weidenfeld and Nicholson 1975.
66. S.R. Gardiner, *History of England from James I to outbreak of Civil War*, Vol. IX, Longman 1884.
67. J. Thirsk and J.P. Cooper, *Seventeenth Century Economic Documents*, O.U.P. 1972.
68. A. Fletcher, *The Outbreak of the English Civil War*, Arnold, 1981.
69. D. Brunton and D.H. Pennington, *Members of the Long Parliament*, Allen and Unwin, 1954.
70. P.R. Newman, 'Catholic Royalist Activists' in *Recusant History*, 14, 1977.
71. B. Bond and I. Roy (ed.), *War and Society*, Croom Helm, 1975.
72. H. Trevor-Roper, *Religion, Reformation and Social Change*, Macmillan, 1967.
73. C. Hill, *Puritanism and Revolution*, Macmillan, 1965.
74. P.G.M. Dickson, *The Financial Revolution in England*, Macmillan, 1967.
75. C. Wilson, *England's Apprenticeship*, Longman, 1965.
76. T.B. Macaulay, *History of England* , Vol. 1 (the fifth edition, 1911).
77. G.M. Trevelyan, *England Under the Stuarts*, Methuen, 1904 (21st edition, 1949).
78. A. Bryant, *Charles II*, Collins, 1931, (revised edition, 1955).
79. A. Fraser, *Charles II*, Collins, 1979.
80. A.A. Mitchell, 'Treaty of Dover' in *History Today*, October, 1967.
81. J.P. Kenyon, 'Birth of the Old Pretender' in *History Today*, June, 1963.
82. A.A. Mitchell, '1688 Revolution' in *History Today*, July, 1965.
83. E.A. Reitan, 'Revenue to Civil List' in *The Historical Journal*, 1970.
84. P. Christiansen, 'Reappraisal of Causes of the English Civil War' in *Journal of British Studies*, XV,2, 1976.

Index

The Five Central Issues

General Index